Cricket in Wales Volume 3

Front Foot to Front Line

Welsh Cricket and the Great War

Andrew Hignell

CAERDYDD
CARDIFF

Llyfrgelloedd
www.caerdydd.gov.uk
Cardiff Libraries
www.cardiff.gov.uk/libraries

St David's Press
Cardiff

Published in Wales by St. David's Press, an imprint of

Ashley Drake Publishing Ltd
PO Box 733
Cardiff
CF14 7ZY

www.st-davids-press.wales

First Impression – 2017

ISBN 978-1-902719-429

British Library Cataloguing-in-Publication Data.
A CIP catalogue for this book is available from the British Library.

Typeset by Replika Press Pvt Ltd, India
Printed by Akcent Media, Czech Republic

CONTENTS

To all those who gave their lives for King and Country

FOREWORD

In 2009, prior to the start of the Ashes Series against Australia and in my role then as Managing Director of the England and Wales team, I took the squad to Flanders where we witnessed at first-hand the battlefields of the First World War. We also attended the daily ceremony at the Menin Gate, where we laid a wreath in memory of all those who had fallen, besides laying a memorial stone cricket ball at the grave of Colin Blythe, the Kent and England cricketer.

It was a very moving experience for me, and the rest of the party, but despite having been to Flanders, watched films and television programmes about life in the trenches during the Great War, and read books about the appalling conditions that Allied troops faced during the battles with enemy forces on the Western Front and elsewhere, I just cannot imagine the mental anguish, torture and physical depravity that the soldiers faced as they did their bit for 'King and Country'.

I've been in involved in professional sport since my late teens, firstly as a young cricketer for Glamorgan CCC, then as club captain and a senior player, and now as an administrator. I was also fortunate enough to play at the top level, winning three Test caps for England, besides subsequently being Managing Director of the national team and overseeing three successive Ashes series wins against Australia. Therefore, I'm fully aware of the pressures that all of the players, coaches and support staff are under during these high-profile games, but even so, what was going through the minds of those men before they went over the top of the trenches in the Great War was on a completely different scale.

Sport prepares you for many of the challenges you will face in life, but certainly not for war. The friendship and camaraderie of the changing room helps to bond and unite a team and, with this in mind, I can fully understand why so many sports teams joined up *en masse* and answered Lord Kitchener's rallying cry of 'Your Country Needs You'. But, just as these men played together on the cricket fields of Wales, many died together on the battlefields of Europe.

After reading this excellent book, several things were uppermost in my mind. First, the cruelty and brutality of warfare, the harshness of life in the trenches and the terrible poison gas, as well the psychological trauma and shell-shock which so many endured for the rest of their lives. Secondly, the scale of bloodshed and the way so many generations in so many places were affected by the loss of loved ones. Set against this backdrop, it seems almost trite to complain about losing a cricket match or to moan about an umpire's decision. But by playing sport again, and cricket in particular, it helped communities to resume their regular activities following the end of the War and the return of the troops to their towns and villages. I avoid saying getting back to normal, because for so many, there was never to be a normal again after what they had endured and witnessed between 1914 and 1918, but at least, by donning their whites and putting bat to ball, they were doing what they had enjoyed before those long and grim years of warfare.

My final, and most important thought after reading this book, is that we must never forget what these people did, either at the crease or in the trenches. In many ways, they are a lost generation and we can only wonder what this group of men might have done if they had they not fought – and in so many cases died – in the First World War. As a tribute to their deeds, whether on the 'Front Foot' or on the 'Front Line', this book is a most fitting one.

Hugh Morris
Chief Executive – Glamorgan CCC
August 2017

ACKNOWLEDGEMENTS

This book would not have been possible without the generous support and assistance of a number of people and organisations, including the Archivists at the Regimental Museum of the Royal Welsh in Brecon, the late Roderick Suddaby of the Imperial War Museum in London, Phil Jones of the Royal British Legion and the Archivists at Llandaff Cathedral School; Christ College, Brecon; Rydal School and Monmouth School. Others to have significantly assisted are Richard Meads, Roger Gibbons, Bryn Jones, Gwyn Prescott, the Mercer family, John Jenkins, Ryland Wallace, Katrina Coopey and Lynne Forester, J.L. Nicholls, David Bevan, Jeff McInery, Bill Gaskell, Campbell Read, the late Bob Harragan, Tim and Roger Mathais, Jeff Bird, Gareth Watkins, Clive Franklin, Edwina Smart, Paul Robathan, Jane James, the Firing Line Museum at Cardiff Castle and the staff of the History Department at Royal Holloway, University of London.

Radyr CC in 1916, containing several servicemen who were convalescing in nearby nursing homes and military hospitals to the north of Cardiff.

INTRODUCTION

This book is a commemoration of the contribution made by members of the sporting community of Wales during the First World War. It has a focus on the activities by the nation's professional and amateur cricketers whilst they were on military service, besides highlighting the involvement of others involved at the grassroots of Welsh club cricket.

The First World War saw the sporting community of Wales engage in many deeds whilst on active service for King and Country, and the research for this book stems from projects associated with a series of exhibits and displays in the CC4 Museum of Welsh Cricket at the headquarters of Glamorgan Cricket, The SSE SWALEC in Cardiff, which have helped to ensure that the actions and deeds of these sportsmen and women – either at home, or on foreign fields – are fittingly remembered and not forgotten in the mists of time.

The book follows a thematic and chronological order, telling the story of the lead-up to the start of hostilities in 1914, as well as chronicling the various battles and other major actions of the War, through the actions and, sadly in many cases, the deaths of these servicemen on the bloody battlefields of Europe. It also recalls the return to normal life and what happened to those who survived and returned home at the end of the War in November 1918, as well as those who came back to Wales permanently affected by what happened.

Andrew Hignell
August 2017

1

BUSINESS AS USUAL?

The summer of 1914 began for the cricketers of south Wales no differently to those years which had gone before. It seemed to be very much a case of business as normal as the season began on the first Saturday in May. Whilst the local newspapers carried articles about Home Rule and Ulster, plus stories about improving safety in coal mines, Swansea CC had a trial match at their St. Helen's ground.

George Cording and Billy Spiller – two of Glamorgan's batsmen – performed well for St. Fagans, whilst Eddie Bates, the former Yorkshire batsman who had been qualifying for the Welsh county, scored a fine century for Briton Ferry Town against Newport at Rodney Parade. At Stradey Park in Llanelli the town club met a team of Colts chosen from clubs throughout Carmarthenshire by CP Lewis, the former Oxford University and South Wales CC cricketer, whose exploits on the sporting fields during the late 19th century had marked him as one of the greatest all-round sportsmen that Wales had ever produced.

Prestatyn Cricket Club – 1912.

The first week of May saw Lord Tredegar – one of the great patrons to cricket, and sport in general, in Newport – in Cannes enjoying a yachting party in the South of France with members of his family plus other socialites and debutantes, whilst Wednesday May 5th saw the first match of the season take place at Cardiff Arms Park – involving the Central club against an XI from the Jewish Institute. As Cross Brothers, the Cardiff ironmongers, advertised a special offer for rustic summer houses reduced from £59 to just £22, and James Howell, the city's leading drapers, announced that the latest range of English and Continental hats and bonnets were now in stock, Cardiff CC were in action again three days later against Penarth, with Norman Riches, the Cardiff-born dentist who was one of Glamorgan's most prolific batsmen, starting the season in style by making a brisk half-century.

At Dinas Powys, a new golf course was opened on land owned by Colonel Gore, whilst the town's cricketers suffered a massive defeat in their away match at Pentrebach in Merthyr as the Hill's Plymouth side dismissed them for just 29 before posting 224-5 in reply. In Ebbw Vale, where local mine workers were in dispute with the colliery owners, morale was boosted by a fine performance from Frank Pope, a new acquisition from the Sussex area, who posted a handsome half-century in their draw against Abercarn.

Bill Bestwick (standing).

With newspapers carrying reports about the creation of a Federation of Trades, plus coverage of a joint conference between colliers, railwaymen and transport workers, Bill Bestwick, the former Derbyshire fast bowler who prior to being a professional cricketer had been a coal miner, made a decisive statement of his own as he began the new summer by claiming 8-15 as Neath opened their season with a crushing 151-run victory over Clydach. However, a few days later at St. Helen's, the Gnoll-based club were brought back down to earth as a century from James Maxwell saw Swansea to a comfortable win as Harry Creber, the Glamorgan spinner, celebrated his call-up to play for the Minor Counties representative side against the MCC with figures 6-19.

As the House of Commons discussed Lloyd George's budget proposals, there was plenty of talk as well about money at some cricket clubs in south Wales with an ongoing dispute over unpaid fees at Briton Ferry Steelworks CC involving Arthur Webb, the former Hampshire batsman. May Day saw many south Walians take advantage of Campbell's Steamers to the beauty spots on the north Somerset and Devon coast, whilst others travelled on the special excursions organised on the Taff Vale, Rhymney and Cardiff Railway lines to Weston-super-Mare. In Bridgend, festivities took place at the opening of a new Recreation Field whilst in Monmouth an exceptionally large supply of animals was available for auction at the town's May Fair.

In mid-May, the committee of the Monmouthshire County Cricket Club held their annual meeting in Newport, and whilst bemoaning a falling off of gate receipts in Minor County matches at Rodney Parade, they noted an increasing interest in the game in the manufacturing and mining valleys

A group of spectators watching a match in Pembrokeshire, circa 1909.

whilst discussions took place about more games being staged at Ebbw Vale in order to tap into this growing enthusiasm for the summer game.

Shortly afterwards, the regional newspapers carried details of potential new collieries that might be shortly opened in the Vale of Neath where hitherto untapped seams of coal existed, whilst the Great Western Railway announced plans for new branch lines. In Cardiff extensive discussions took place about widening Duke Street and the area in front of the castle which had become a bottleneck for horse-drawn trams and people alike, whilst in Maesteg a special presentation was made to Canon Kelly, the cricket-loving priest-in-charge of the town's Roman Catholic Church, to thank him for a dozen years of service to the spiritual and recreational needs of the townsfolk following his move from a parish in Swansea where he had regularly turned out for the town's side at St. Helen's.

The ground overlooking Swansea Bay witnessed a keenly fought match in mid-May against Briton Ferry Town. With flags at the ground flying at half-mast in honour of Tip Foster, the great Worcestershire and England cricketer who had died earlier in the week, Swansea's batsmen were in trouble at first against the accurate bowling of Jack Johns, who eight years later marked his one and only appearance for Glamorgan by taking a wicket with his first-ever ball in Championship cricket. On this occasion in 1914,

Canon Kelly (standing, far left) with the Swansea side at Maesteg in 1905. Billy Bancroft, the Welsh rugby international and Glamorgan cricketer, is also seated (left, on the front row) wearing the white hat.

he caught and bowled Edgar Billings, the free-scoring batsman wicket-keeper who played regularly for Glamorgan before catching Billy Bancroft, the former Welsh rugby international, who back in 1895 had become the Welsh county's first home-grown professional.

Swansea eventually mustered 139 but Briton Ferry's hopes of victory were dashed towards the end of the home team's innings as Bates badly dislocated a finger and departed the ground for medical attention. Without their crack batsman, the visitors struggled against the nagging accuracy of Creber and Maxwell, and they were bundled out for just 50 with the former claiming 5-18. However, as far as cricket in south Wales was concerned on May 16th, it was Bestwick who produced the performance of the day as at The Gnoll, he claimed a hat-trick in their victory over Cardiff. During his thirteenth over of the afternoon, the fast bowler removed Webster, the city club's new professional before dismissing John Chandless and the veteran James Horspool, who had each appeared for Glamorgan, with the next two deliveries. John Walter Jones, another county batsman, together with Billy Allin then shared a match-winning stand to see Neath to a fine victory by three wickets.

The following weekend Cardiff went down to another defeat as they lost against Newport at Rodney Parade with Arthur Silverlock, their long-serving and talented professional taking five wickets and sharing a match-winning

A view of the St.Helen's ground in Swansea, shortly before the start of the Great War, with the groundsman – far left – cutting the outfield with a horse-drawn lawn mower.

stand with Edward Stone Phillips, the captain of the Monmouthshire county side, as Newport secured a four-wicket victory. At Stradey Park, Swansea's decent run of form was smartly ended by a return of 7-51 by Ernie Gee, the Manchester-born schoolmaster at Gowerton County School. The excellent bowling of the Carmarthenshire bowler, plus a vibrant opening stand between Percy Rees and Claude Warner saw Llanelli's batsmen take just over an hour to surpass Swansea's modest total of 112.

A few days later attention was focussed on Swansea again as the town hosted the Bath and West Show. Despite heavy showers, a large crowd turned out at St. Helen's to watch the various equestrian displays and show jumping. With their ground in use, the town's cricketers headed to the Arms Park to meet Cardiff. But the bowling of Ernie Vost, the former Lancashire and Staffordshire cricketer proved to be too much of a handful for the visitors with Vost taking 5-30 as Swansea were dismissed for 81.

With James Howell's department store in Cardiff announcing their special show of 'Ladies and Gentlemen's requisites for Travelling and other Holiday requirements', full of smart dresses for the holidays and other ready-to-wear millinery, plus Cardiff City FC also announcing during the penultimate week of May their fixtures for the 1914-15 season, all therefore seemed well in the world as the committee of Glamorgan CCC met to confirm the arrangements, and likely personnel, for their forthcoming fixtures in the Minor County Championship, starting with an away match against Surrey 2nd XI at The Oval on June 1st and 2nd.

A photograph of the Neath 2nd XI in 1914.

Few in the smoke-filled rooms of the Angel Hotel, where the meeting was convened, could have imagined, though, that events on the world stage would take such a dramatic turn, causing the matches scheduled on August 17th and 18th against Wiltshire at Trowbridge, and against Essex 2nd XI at Leyton on August 19th and 20th to be cancelled following the declaration of War by Britain on Germany on August 4th, 1914, and that no more inter-county fixtures would be staged for almost six years.

A family enjoy their seaside holiday on the beach near Tenby during September 1914. Other things were soon on their minds.

2

THE DETERIORATING SUMMER OF 1914

Glamorgan began their 1914 season, against Surrey's 2nd XI at The Oval on June 1st with all concerned eager for success so that the Welsh club's bid for first-class status and higher recognition in the cricket world would, at long last, be achieved. The club, though, had already been dealt a blow as Tom Whittington, the captain of Neath and one of the county's leading amateur batsmen announced that owing to pressures of work at his solicitors office in Neath, he would more than likely have to decline invitations to turn out for Glamorgan. He had already said no to an approach from the MCC to play in their games against Hampshire and Yorkshire, although he did accept an invitation to lead the Minor Counties in their annual encounter against the MCC at Lord's.

The omens did not look good for Glamorgan in the opening passage of play at The Oval as, without the services of Whittington, they plummeted to 93-9. But Norman Riches boosted morale by sharing a rousing stand of 125 for the final wicket with Harry Creber, with Riches posting a superb 109 in three and three-quarter hours of defiance. Stamford Hacker, the former Gloucestershire bowler then claimed two early wickets before Andy Sandham launched a recovery mission with Arthur Rutty, as their side secured a slender lead on first innings. Sadly, when Glamorgan batted again, Riches could not repeat his first innings heroics and despite some forthright blows by fellow Cardiffian Edward Sweet-Escott, the Welsh hockey international, Surrey reached their target with four wickets in hand shortly before the close of play, which by mutual agreement had been brought forward to five o'clock.

The reason for the early finish in London was that Glamorgan were due to travel by train to Durham where they were engaged for the next two days at Sunderland. The long journey allowed many of the Glamorgan party to catch up on some sleep, though some of the amateurs no doubt opted to read the newspapers, several of which carried photographs of the wedding of Prince Oscar of Prussia, the German Emperor's fifth son to Countess

Ida Marie von Vasewitz, a lady-in-waiting to the Empress. As they headed north on the overnight express, few could have imagined how the Kaiser would play such an important role in their lives during the course of the next few months.

After their long and tiring journey, Glamorgan were relieved to win the toss and bat first, but only Riches and Billy Bancroft batted with any comfort against a persevering home attack as the Welsh county were bundled out for 186. The home batsmen then feasted on a weary attack, racing to 241-4 by the close of play. The home batsmen then added a further 176 the following morning before declaring and hoping to cheaply dismiss the Welshmen again. But Riches and Jock Tait, the Scottish football international and Cardiff businessman, shared an opening stand of 108, and with John Walter Jones of Neath making a patient half-century, Glamorgan secured a well-earned draw.

A four-week break then followed before the next inter-county match as the club season took centre-stage. Many of these games in the larger settlements attracted decent crowds, with the cricket supporters of south Wales in 1914 – a summer lacking any Test Matches or touring teams – heading to Cardiff, Swansea, Newport, Llanelli or Merthyr to watch the county stars in action for their clubs. A few cricket fanatics also made their way to Bristol, Gloucester and Worcester to watch County Championship games, especially over the Whitsun Bank Holiday when a number of excursion trains were running with specially reduced ticket prices.

Indeed, Whitsun saw some clubs undertake their annual tours, with the Mackintosh club of Cardiff, based at the well-known welfare institute in Roath, travelling to Somerset to play Bridgwater and Weston-super-Mare, before returning home to Wales on a Campbell's steamer. Glamorgan Nomads also enjoyed an unbeaten tour of South Devon, playing against the United Services at Devonport, South Devon, Chudleigh, the Royal Naval College at Dartmouth, Paignton and then Wellington in Somerset on their homeward journey by train.

In the Cardiff and District League, the Riverside club continued to lead the table after emphatic wins over the Wood Street Congregationals and the Saltmead club from Grangetown. Formed during the late 1880s, the Riverside cricket club had also been the founding fathers of Cardiff City FC, who played originally as Riverside FC before changing their name and then in 1910 securing the use of Ninian Park for their football matches.

As June unfolded, the leading cricketers in south Wales continued to enjoy success for their clubs. Arthur Silverlock scored an unbeaten 116 as Newport defeated Cheltenham by eight wickets, whilst Eddie Bates struck an undefeated 152 as Briton Ferry Town won the local derby against the Steelworks team. For Llanelli, their two Ernies – Messrs Gee and Vogler – shared nine wickets between them as the Stradey Park club defeated Hill's Plymouth. The following week, the Merthyr club also lost by just a single run to the students of Llandovery College.

Mid-June saw Norman Riches complete an unbeaten century for Cardiff against Barry and then post-match pay tribute to the efforts of Mr. Lofill, the Arms Park's new groundsman who seemed to be getting the wickets back into good order following the decision in 1911 by Jack Nash, the previous incumbent to accept a post in Lancashire. Another Cardiff-born cricketer excelled during June, with the former Welsh rugby international Billy Spiller firstly completing a match-winning performance for the Glamorgan Police against Penarth's Wednesday XI. After posting an unbeaten 68, the man who seven years later would enter Glamorgan's record books as their first-ever Championship centurion also claimed five wickets at no cost with his off-spin bowling. The following week, Spiller added another century to his tally as the Glamorgan Police defeated Barry's Wednesday XI.

Another star of the oval-ball game was in the news as Billy Bancroft posted a superb hundred for Swansea as they defeated Llanelli at St. Helen's. At St. Fagans, another Glamorgan cricketer was in the headlines as Trevor Preece struck a fine century for St. Fagans against Whitchurch whilst at The

Riverside Athletic Cricket Club in Cardiff, seen at Ninian Park in 1919.

Gnoll, Bill Bestwick, was rubbing his hands with glee as a crowd in excess of a thousand turned up for his Benefit Match as Neath met Briton Ferry in a keen-fought local derby. Monmouthshire's cricketers though were less delighted later in the week when a heavy thunderstorm washed out their Minor County Championship match with Kent 2nd XI at Folkestone, just when they seemed to be getting into a decent position.

Cricket in south Wales though was dealt a massive blow when it was confirmed on Saturday, June 27th that Jack Brain, the man who had master minded Glamorgan's rise from a lowly third-class county into an outfit with first-class aspirations had died of a heart attack following complications after an acute attack of bronchitis which had caused the manager of Brain's Brewery to be housebound for several weeks. During this time, he was constantly attended by Dr. Hastings Torney of Cowbridge who feared that a fatal seizure was imminent. His prognosis proved correct as tragically on Thursday, June 25th Jack suffered a massive stroke before quietly passing away the following morning at Bonvilston House.

Cardiff's players duly wore black-arm bands and flags flew at half-mast on Saturday, June 27th at the Arms Park as the city club met Neath. A few days later there was a massive attendance at the village church for Jack's funeral which was conducted by his brother-in-law Canon Bevan of Babbacombe, near Torquay. The great and the good of the cricketing and political world of south Wales were in attendance, and a host of fitting tributes were paid to the former Glamorgan captain with the *Western Mail* saying 'his prowess at the wicket and in the field won him friendship; his generous patronage of the game won him gratitude.'

News of Jack's death duly displaced stories in the Saturday morning editions of the local newspapers about the trade union unrest, the threats of dock workers and miners going on strike plus the heated question of Home Rule for Ulster. Also briefly put to one side were stories of concern about the Suffragette Movement which had continued to mount various displays of defiance during the summer. Earlier in the month, an evening service at St. Augustine's Church in Penarth had been disrupted when a group of women stood up and offered prayers for the groups of Suffragettes who

Jack Brain, seen in a team group from 1886.

were in prison in London. Their action followed newspaper reports that several women in prison in Holloway Gaol in London had claimed that they had been drugged by prison wardens prior to being force fed.

A few days later various bombs and incendiary devices had exploded in various churches in London where society weddings took place, whilst a lady attempted to jump into the ring at Olympia at the International Horse Show. Another also disrupted the equine show by repeatedly shouting at the King "Sir, why do you allow women to be tortured?" During the month, various fetes and garden parties in south-east Wales were also held in aid of the Suffragette cause, and certain figures in Welsh public life spoke out in favour of the women.

With further disruptions being talked about, increased security accompanied the races at Ascot, as well as the Wimbledon Lawn Tennis Championships, but thoughts of Suffragette disturbances were far from the minds of those in Pembrokeshire, who had gathered to play in, or watch, the annual match on the Garrison Ground in Pembroke Dock between the gentlemen officers of the 2nd Battalion of the Border Regiment and a side comprising the wives and lady friends of the officers. The gentlemen had to bat, bowl and catch only with their left hand as the Regimental Band provided suitable music for the amusement of a decent crowd.

As the gentlemen successfully chased a target of 113 to win under the summer sun, with a variety of unorthodox and lusty blows against the valiant ladies, it seemed as if everything in Edwardian life was proceeding as normal, but a few days later, on Sunday June 28th, thousands of miles away an event of cataclysmic importance occurred in Sarajevo which was to bring an end to these joyful summers for the military men, their spouses and so many others as Archduke Francis Ferdinand, the heir to the throne of the Austro-Hungarian empire and his wife Sophie, Duchess of Hohenberg, were assassinated.

His death dominated the newspapers the following morning, with stories of further Suffragette disturbances in Hyde Park and at Llandaff Cathedral sidelined as the newspaper editors focussed their attention on events in Sarajevo – 'there is no longer any doubt that the crime was the result of a pan-Servian plot,' proclaimed the *Western Mail*, 'conceived with diabolical cunning and carried out with callous determination.' With feelings against the Serbs running high, and several demonstrations taking place in Austria, martial law was duly declared in Sarajevo. For the next few days, the same paper carried details of the funeral arrangements in Vienna, as well as news that the Secretary of the Austro-Hungarian Legation at Belgrade had sent a despatch to Vienna accusing Serbian complicity in the assassination.

Relations between the two nations swiftly deteriorated and on July 20th

Austria-Hungary sent troops to the Serbian border. Serbia's response was to mobilise its own troops, whilst its ally Russia arranged for troops to be stationed on its frontier with Austria. On Monday, July 27th the Editor of the *Western Mail* summed up the ever-worsening situation by stating that 'the Austrian ultimatum and the Serbian rejection thereof have produced a situation which engages

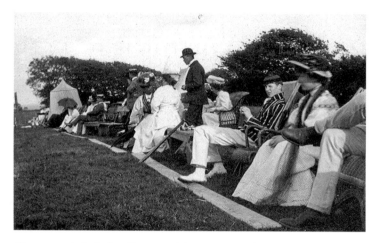

Players and their families watching a match from the boundary at Cresselly in 1910.

the alarmed attention of the whole of Europe … The determination expressed in the Austrian ultimatum and in the Austrian war preparations on the one hand, and the departure from Belgrade of the government and the garrison on the other, leaves little hope for a peaceful result … While Germany is equally determined to stand by her ally, the next move will lie with France and should France be unable to keep her frontier intact it will be Britain's turn to be concerned.'

Whilst matters were escalating in Eastern Europe during July 1914, back in south Wales, events had largely been continuing as usual. The month had witnessed the annual match between Christ College, Brecon and Llandovery College, which saw the latter win by 104 runs, as well as Glamorgan's cricketers embarking on a trio of back-to-back matches at the St. Helen's ground in Swansea, against Northamptonshire, Durham and Essex 2nd XI. The first game against the East Midlands county, who had been admitted into the County Championship in 1905, gave the Welsh side a chance to assess their talent ahead of what the county committee hoped would soon be a renewed bid for elevation to first-class status. But after being put in to bat on a damp wicket, the home side's batsmen struggled in their first innings. Harry Creber however prospered on his home wicket, and after being set 240 in two and a half hours, the visiting batsmen opted a safety first approach against the spinner as the game ended in a draw.

The weather interrupted the following match against Durham, but Jock Tait and Norman Riches each posted half-centuries. Creber and Bestwick also shone with the ball as Durham's batsmen opted against a helter-skelter pursuit of a target of 213 in two and a half hours. Despite the draw, the Welsh officials were delighted as Essex confirmed that they would be sending a strong side for the match starting the following day, including Charles McGahey, one of their most prolific batsmen. First honours, though, went to the visiting bowlers, before the Swansea pair of Percy Morris and James Maxwell led a counter-attack. Stamford Hacker then made inroads with the new ball before Creber again spun his way through some modest resistance as Glamorgan secured a decent first innings lead of 93.

The following morning, to the delight of a crowd in excess of one thousand, Billy Bancroft raced to an unbeaten hundred, before Glamorgan declared, and with three hours left to play, ended their Swansea week by dismissing the visitors again. But McGahey led a stout rearguard action and left the Glamorgan officials to rue the fact that Neath had failed to release Bestwick for the match with Essex. Just to rub salt into the wounds, as the Glamorgan bowlers were thwarted by the Essex batsmen, the fiery pace bowler duly took 8-19 against Briton Ferry Steelworks at The Gnoll.

After some rest on the Sunday, Glamorgan were then back in action against Wiltshire at the Arms Park, with Stamford Hacker taking 6-17 as the visitors were dismissed for 71. Reggie Gibbs made an attractive half-century as Glamorgan secured what proved to be a decisive first-innings lead. Hacker added another five-wicket haul to his tally as Glamorgan were left with a target of 99. Their hopes of an easy victory were dealt a blow as Riches and Gibbs soon departed, but Edward Sweet-Escott and Maxwell shared a morale-boosting stand before Frank Bennett and Tom Morgan saw Glamorgan to a thrilling two-wicket win.

Harry Creber.

There was further good news later in the week for cricketers in south Wales as Monmouthshire defeated Cornwall at Camborne by 131 runs with Arthur Silverlock making 139 and sharing a fine opening stand with Edward Stone Phillips, who continued his run of good form with the bat having the week before made a fine century for Newport in their victory over the Gloucester City side. Monmouthshire also enjoyed the better of their game with Glamorgan at the Arms Park before rain washed out the final afternoon's play.

Cricket had also been given a boost in Carmarthenshire, who had briefly had a foray in the Minor County Championship as an all-amateur side representing the county defeated a similar eleven from Monmouthshire at Llandovery College. The officials in the county had also organised matches in mid and late July against an all-amateur side from Glamorgan at Swansea and Llanelli, with the latter seeing the West Walian side win by eight wickets.

But the latter match at Stradey Park took place as the *Western Mail* carried headlines proclaiming 'the War Cloud in Europe' with the report underneath starting off as follows – 'Europe is in a state of suspense, with the shadow of war overhanging.' Thoughts of Carmarthenshire returning to the Minor County Championship and Glamorgan mounting a campaign for first-class status swiftly evaporated as, on July 28th, Austria-Hungary declared war on Serbia, and within a month, British troops were on French soil as the First World War began.

The Monmouthshire side of 1909 with E.S. Phillips (front row, centre) and Arthur Silverlock (far left, standing).

3

THE OUTBREAK OF WAR

"It must be obvious to any person who reflects upon the situation that the moment the dispute ceases to be one between Austria-Hungary and Serbia, and becomes one in which another Great Power is involved, it can but end in the greatest catastrophe that has ever befallen the continent of Europe in one blow." The words of Sir Edward Grey, the British Foreign Secretary, speaking in the House of Commons on Monday, July 27th whose speech was quoted verbatim in the *Western Mail* the following morning.

If the newspaper was an accurate barometer of feelings in Wales, the mood amongst the eight pages of the daily publication had dramatically changed by the final week of July. Maps of Eastern Europe as well as photographs of the area around Vienna, Budapest and Bucharest filled the column inches which hitherto had been occupied during the previous weeks by photographs of the summer fetes and galas across south Wales, plus pictures of the great and good of local society frolicking in the summer sun.

Besides in depth coverage of the debate in Parliament, prominence was also given to accounts of the attempt by Sir Edward Grey to convene a conference in London with the Ambassadors of France, Germany and Italy in a bid to arrange a peaceful settlement. Other stories about the escalating events on the European stage replaced

JM Staniforth's cartoon from the Western Mail newspaper on July 28th, 1914.

those about Home Rule, the Ulster situation and the threat of a National Strike, whilst on the sports pages there were only perfunctory and truncated reports on both Cardiff's victory over Newport as well as Neath's success against Swansea.

The following day there was confirmation that German officials were unwilling to participate in talks with the British Foreign Secretary and other diplomats. Consequently, a warning was issued by Great Britain to Germany that it could not remain neutral, but matters swiftly escalated as Austria declared war and attacks took place on the Serbian capital of Belgrade. The chain of events duly saw German patrols cross the French border and on August 1st the French authorities ordered the mobilisation of their military. On the authorisation of the Tsar, Russian troops also moved to defend Serbia, and Germany formally declared war on Russia.

In the dockland communities of south Wales, French nationals swiftly tried to make contact with friends and families back home as talk increased of a German advance across the Continent. But it was not just in the French Diaspora that there was talk of a German invasion as in the bars, clubs, offices and other organisations throughout Wales, there was excited chatter about what would happen next, and the prospect of an invasion by German troops and ships.

The talk of the gossip-mongers was fuelled by the hurried movement of troops across the region, with engineers and other artillery personnel at Milford Haven summoned to Aldershot, whilst orders were given to members of the 3rd Welsh Regiment to convene at Newport Barracks. Officers and soldiers were also sent to the Docks at Cardiff and Newport, whilst additional look-outs were sent to the Severn Tunnel. Shortly afterwards, all naval personnel in the counties of Glamorgan and Monmouthshire received telegrams to immediately return to their vessels whilst at Barry Docks, precautionary measures were also taken with soldiers on duty with fixed bayonets and loaded rifles.

In Brecon, orders were issued to all those out of Barracks to hastily return back to camp, and almost every train leaving the Great Western Railway station in Cardiff had small contingents of soldiers travelling to various destinations to rejoin their regiments. The 2nd Battalion, The Border Regiment, stationed at Pembroke Dock at the outbreak of war, travelled to take up positions guarding the entrance to Swansea Docks. Colliery owners at Cardiff Coal Exchange also received orders from the Admiralty that emergency orders for Welsh coal might soon be placed. For once, it was a very quiet day on the trading floor as across the mining communities of the region, companies set in motion emergency plans to get as much steam coal as possible to the coastal ports for the Royal Navy. In a bid to quell any panic, the government issued a statement saying that 'the military movements which have taken place are of a purely precautionary nature,' but there was no denying that by July 29th the country was definitely on a war footing.

July 29th was also the date of the first day of a two-day friendly which Glamorgan's officials had organised at The Gnoll in Neath against a combined Briton Ferry XI, largely as a means of thanking the Town and Steelworks clubs for their help in releasing players for Minor County matches, and also as a means of helping to raise funds for the two organisations. The match also promised to give some decent practice to the county's players ahead of the next batch of scheduled games in the Minor County Championship, but with talk of impending invasion by German troops, several of the amateurs who worked in the Cardiff area and had initially agreed to turn out for Glamorgan were now unable to take time off from their jobs as their employers started to make contingency plans for the country going to war.

The upshot was that several players dropped out the day before the match at Briton Ferry and, although replacements were sought, another player withdrew on the morning of the game, as Glamorgan turned up with only ten men, chiefly from the Swansea and Neath clubs. Harry Creber was again in fine form with the ball and the Swansea spinner duly led the Glamorgan XI to a 50-run victory over the combined side.

It was a case of business as usual in the first-class world as well, as over the gloriously warm August Bank Holiday 14,555 people flocked to The Oval to see Jack Hobbs score what at the time was a career-best score of 226. His colleagues in Surrey's 2nd XI headed to south Wales for the Bank Holiday period with Glamorgan engaged in back-to-back games at Rodney Parade and the Arms Park with Monmouthshire and Surrey 2nd XI.

At Old Trafford, 'Monkey' Hornby was called from the field where he was leading Lancashire in The Roses match against Yorkshire and was summoned to the War Office. A few hours later Sir Archibald White, the Yorkshire captain, was also heading south to join his regiment, leaving George Hirst – a professional – to lead the Yorkshire team. At the time, it was extremely rare for a paid player to lead the side, but Hirst fulfilled the same role in six out of seven further games as, encouraged by the government to main a feeling of normality, the County Championship continued.

Some of the Glamorgan amateurs also had commitments with the Territorials and county Militia so the Glamorgan committee called up William Gibson of the Alpha club, based in the Canton suburb of the coal metropolis, plus Harry Arundale from Briton Ferry for the two Bank Holiday contests. Each duly made their county debuts, but as it turned out rain severely curtailed play on both days at Rodney Parade and there was, quite understandably, plenty of chatter in the pavilion and enclosures at the Newport ground about the grave situation as a State of War was formally declared by Germany on France.

'The dreadful drama of War is now being enacted over five countries of Europe,' proclaimed the editorial in the *Western Mail* on Monday, August 3rd, 'and before long, possibly before these lines are read, it may have extended to another country – our own.' Prophetic words indeed, as the following day a State of War was declared against Germany and orders were given for troops to mobilise. The momentous news swiftly filtered out from the newspaper offices close to the Arms Park where Glamorgan's cricketers were engaged on the second day of the Minor County Championship match with Surrey 2nd XI.

The match duly continued with Norman Riches posting a century as the home side set the visitors a target of 184 to win. However, there were concerns amongst the visiting team over both how, and when, they might travel back to Paddington, as the Great Western Railway announced that it was cancelling several planned excursion trains, and with troop movement now a necessity, a revised timetable was drawn up. It may have been no coincidence that Harry Creber swiftly worked his way through the Surrey line-up as Glamorgan secured a facile victory by 81 runs, with the visiting players and officials hurriedly departing the Arms Park and heading to the railway station to catch the next available service back to London.

Perhaps sensing that it might be the last match of the season, a decent crowd had turned up at the Arms Park to cheer on the efforts of Norman Riches and his team. Elsewhere in Cardiff, there was hectic activity at the City Hall where a recruiting station was swiftly opened, with the *Western Mail* proudly reporting how 'a hundred men of first-class type and splendid records in the field were enrolled.' The newspaper also received a telegram from the Pontypridd Veterans Association saying 'Veterans offer their services – all ex-soldiers. Fifty strong – to go anywhere.' Hectic activity was also reported at recruitment stations in Ebbw Vale, Merthyr, Maesteg, Abergavenny, Neath, Llanelli and Newport, whilst a group of Frenchmen, holding high the Tricolour flag and singing the Marseillaise, proudly marched through Cardiff before heading to the General Station to board a train to Dover.

By the following day, four German vessels were seized at Cardiff Docks, plus two at Swansea and one apiece at Barry and Newport, whilst old soldiers, Reservists and Territorials had continued to sign up in droves. Another show of patriotism came at Pentrebach, to the south of Merthyr where the members of the Hill's Plymouth club gathered up all of their kit and equipment and donated it to the Army, believing that those heading off to military camps and foreign shores could keep both their fitness and their spirits up by playing cricket.

By August 5th, the first of a wave of military detachments had marched through the main streets of Cardiff before boarding trains at the city's railway station to travel to Bordon Camp in Aldershot. 'The streets of Cardiff remained crowded up to a late hour at night,' reported the *Western Mail*, 'and before the trains steamed out, there were some affecting scenes as wives and sweethearts took farewell of the soldiers. Cheers echoed through the station and were taken up by the dense crowds who had congregated.'

As similar patriotic scenes took place at other railway stations throughout the region, there was some panic buying, with two shops in Swansea having to temporarily close, having completely run out of provisions. A few days later, when several grocery shops in the town raised their prices, shoppers responded in an angry way by smashing windows and throwing stones at shopworkers as they desperately tried to build their stores ahead of the anticipated invasion by German forces. Similar concerns were raised about the presence of German sailors, plus businessmen and their families in the various towns in the region, and so grave were these worries that in Cardiff the Chief Constable wrote to all German nationals living in the city who owned motor cars saying that they needed his written permission to use their vehicles. He also warned all garage proprietors not to lend cars to aliens.

Anti-German feelings were also high in the valley communities with a German-born engineer called Francis Barr, who had lived in the Pontypridd area for 33 years, being arrested for being drunk and disorderly and then being told by the local magistrate that he would only be allowed to remain in the area if satisfactory reports were made about his recent behaviour. In Barry and Penarth, 50 German sailors who had been taken from vessels in the two harbours were told that they would be taken to a detention camp either on Flat Holm in the Severn Estuary or at Alton Towers in Shropshire.

On August 5th Lord Kitchener had been sworn in as the government's War Secretary, and the following day he made his now famous appeal for raising a further 100,000 men for the Army with the slogan that 'Your Country Needs You'. Shortly afterwards, a series of patriotic and tub-thumping speeches were made at recruitment drives across the region, whilst the editor of the *Western Mail* did his bit, writing on August 7th that 'Wales is a country of proud military traditions. Long before the present military system arose, the Welsh people were distinguished for their warlike spirit and valour. Patriotism has, with them, never been a sentiment merely. It has been a virtue and an impulse; a deep-seated and enduring principle.'

Several leading figures in the world of cricket, the military and Conservative politics were prominent amongst the recruiting operations which took place in August 1914. Amongst these was Tom Pearson, who had served in the Royal Engineers besides winning thirteen Welsh rugby caps, playing hockey for Wales and appearing for the Glamorgan Colts team of 1893. Another prominent figure was John Nicholl of Merthyr Mawr House who had played for the full Glamorgan side between 1893 and 1895. The Old Etonian was the son of John Cole Nicholl, the former Tory MP for Cardiff, and was prominent in a number of recruitment and training initiatives in the Vale of Glamorgan and at Lavernock where various Territorial groups took part in regular summer camps.

Both had the support of Colonel Morgan Lindsay, a fellow former Royal Engineer who had served in the Boer War, and who was the grandson of Lord Tredegar. In his younger days, Lindsay had also played for the South Wales Cricket Club and the fledgling county teams representing Glamorgan and Breconshire, before setting up home at Ystrad Mynach and serving on the Glamorgan County Council. Indeed, the summer of 1914 had initially seen Lindsay oversee cricket games at his home, as well as infrastructure improvements in the locality before helping to organise the recruitment of Kitchener's New Army, and then departing himself later in August with the British Expeditionary Force (BEF) to the newly-formed Western Front in France.

The first members of the BEF had landed on French soil on August 7th in France, just twenty-four hours or so after the first British casualties had been sustained as HMS Amphion, a cruiser built at Pembroke Dock, had struck a German mine whilst in the North Sea, causing the death of 150 sailors, some of whom were from the Pembrokeshire military base. The day after the sinking of the naval vessel, and just a week after the jolly Bank Holiday festivities across south Wales, the *Western Mail* carried a letter – written in both English and Welsh – from the Right Hon. David Lloyd George appealing for everyone to play their part in the War Effort. With more than half an eye on the union unrest in previous weeks, the Chancellor of the Exchequer wrote, 'Let us who have to remain at home, on the land, in the mine or the quarry, do their duties faithfully, and that in the spirit of courage and self-sacrifice which must be the inspiration of our brothers in the field.'

Colonel Morgan Lindsay.

Yet county cricket continued with the MCC issuing

a statement on August 6th that 'no good purpose can be served at this present moment by cancelling matches, unless the services of those engaged in cricket, who have no military training, can in any way be utilised in their country's service. If it can be shown in what way their services can be used, the MCC would close their ground and the cricketers of England would be sure to respond to any definite call.' Mirroring the trends in England, the cricketers of Monmouthshire duly commenced their Minor Counties match against Cornwall at Rodney Parade, although the second day was washed out by heavy rain, whilst the following week the Rodney Parade ground hosted a match between Monmouthshire and Kent 2nd XI.

There were also calls for recreation grounds across the region to be used as venues for drill parades and other military gatherings with the Rev. Thomas Price, the Rector of Coity, catching the mood at large by stating how 'each night in Bridgend hundreds of young men are wandering up and down, anxious as to what is happening and ashamed of themselves that they are not having a share in their country's defence. Could not old Volunteer officers who know all about drill get these young men into shape… Cardiff with its parks, the multitude of townships in Glamorgan each with its sports ground, all offer opportunity of place.' The Marquess of Bute had already given the use of Cardiff Castle, Bute Park and the Sophia Gardens Recreation Field to the military authorities, with the latter ground being used to train cavalry officers, with over 350 ex-Service men all undergoing training ready for action with the British Expeditionary Force.

Similar calls were made in England, with The Oval being requisitioned by the Army, forcing Jack Hobbs to switch his Benefit Match from the South London ground to Lord's. It was quite novel for the Surrey cricketers to play a home match in St. John's Wood, but the sight of cricketers carrying on almost as normal enraged many people and in a letter to the *Daily Mirror,* 'A British Woman' asked 'cannot something be done to persuade the cricketers to turn their time and thoughts to more serious matters than playing matches?'

But county cricket continued for a few more weeks, although some Minor County sides, more reliant on amateurs than the first-class sides, struggled to raise a decent side and Monmouthshire's match in mid-August against Devon was cancelled when the visiting county's secretary informed the Newport officials that they would not be able to raise a team, with many of their amateurs having military commitments.

Despite the previous encouragement to play on from government officials, on August 13th, the MCC announced that it was cancelling all of its club matches, including the games planned to take place at Lord's during

September as 'every sound man of England will be performing some kind of duty on behalf of his country.'

Other clubs across England and Wales soon followed suit and on the day that over 200 German prisoners, largely from vessels impounded at Welsh ports, were marched by an escort of officers from the King's (Shropshire Light Infantry) from Cardiff Gaol to temporary accommodation at Cardiff Castle, the officials of Glamorgan CCC announced that their concluding away matches against Wiltshire at Trowbridge on August 17th and 18th, plus the matches with Essex 2nd XI at Leyton on August 19th and 20th, as well as the game against the MCC at the Arms Park on August 21st and 22nd had all been cancelled. Other sporting events and annual gatherings such as the Welsh Amateur Golf Championships, scheduled to be held at Pembrey were also cancelled as matters of honour and patriotism took precedence over sporting endeavour.

Nevertheless, a number of first-class matches continued to be staged in England, whilst in Wales, games continued to be staged in several towns and villages. There was also one last hurrah for a group of county cricketers from south Wales, as following the cancellation of the match at Lord's, a game took place on August 21st and 22nd in Cardiff between a Glamorgan Amateur XI, led by Norman Riches, against an XI of Weston-super-Mare and District. The Glamorgan side included Trevor Preece, Edward Sweet-Escott, George Cording and Reggie Gibbs, and the gentlemen cricketers from south Wales travelling – like so many trippers before them – across the Severn by steamer to the Somerset resort. Gate receipts from the contest went to local War Charities – and giving the participants a good feeling as they enjoyed themselves under the late summer sun. The Welsh side duly won by an innings in what was to be the last game of note under the county club's name for many years.

The day after returning from Weston-super-Mare, Riches led a Cardiff side against the Earl of Plymouth's XI at St. Fagans, but with the city side on 30-0, a downpour forced the players off the Crofft-y-Gennau ground and washed out the rest of the game. A few matches involving junior clubs in Cardiff and Newport were also abandoned, with much of the talk in the pavilion being about the German advance in Belgium and France. Other matches were also staged, largely to entertain troops as they gathered at various military camps in south Wales ahead of active service. An example was the match in late August at Monmouth between a scratch XI of players from the town against a team from the Royal Monmouthshire Royal Engineers who had just recently moved into the area.

Late August and early September saw the arrest, and charging, of further people of Germanic background who were living in south Wales without residence permits and were therefore deemed to be unregistered aliens. It also saw the start of the Football League season as clubs opted for a 'business as usual' approach, but it met with disapproval in some quarters, as gauged by the following letter in the *Western Mail* on August 26th:

'Sir – there is a football match [Cardiff City v Tottenham Hotspur] to be played here on Wednesday next. In all seriousness, I suggest to the footballing authorities that this game is cancelled, that these 22 well-trained young athletes should enlist, and that the directors of these footballing clubs should hand over their grounds as training fields for young recruits free of charge. Business as usual is a fine motto at the proper time, but today is not the accepted hour for so-called sport. If sport is what they hanker after, let them pay a business visit to the plains of Belgium with a rifle in their hands....'

In contrast, the rugby clubs in Cardiff and Swansea, as well as the London Welsh club cancelled their forthcoming fixtures – a decision described in the local Press as demonstrating their loyalty and patriotism. But other sports continued with the Powderhall Sprints taking place in Taff Vale Park in Pontypridd, and as well as League football and some horse-racing, fixtures in the County Championship, as well as in the Cardiff and District League continued. In late August, Neath travelled to Newport whilst Norman Riches also led a Cardiff side at St.Helen's in a Benefit Match against Swansea in aid of Billy Bancroft.

But the mood towards the playing of cricket dramatically changed following the publication of an article in *The Sportsman* by W.G. Grace, with the legendary doctor writing that 'I think the time has arrived when the county cricket season should be closed, for it is not fitting that at a time like this that able-bodied men should be playing cricket by day and pleasure-seekers look on. I should like to see all first-class cricketers of suitable age set a good example and come to the help of their country without delay in its hour of need.'

On Friday, August 28th, sensing the mood of many against the playing of sport, the *Western Mail* also carried a cartoon called The Slackers showing a cricketer and footballer turning their backs on a billboard calling for young men to enlist and join Kitchener's Army. It prompted further letters with one correspondent saying

'Sir – I trust the cartoon will serve to instil a sense of shame in all those slackers who think more of sport than the welfare of their country. I also think it would materially assist in bringing home to

JM Staniforth's cartoon from the Western Mail on August 28th, 1914.

these slackers their utter lack of patriotism, now that the very existence of this country is at stake, if the press were to boycott all cricket and football matches, and refrain from publishing any information whatever concerning them.'

In London, Lord Roberts addressed a newly-formed Battalion of the Royal Fusiliers (City of London Regiment), praising the recruits for enlisting and saying "how very different is your action to that of the men who still go on with their cricket and football as if the very existence of this country were not at stake. This is not the time to play games, wholesome as they are in days of peace."

A further cartoon called Two Britons followed in the *Western Mail* on August 31st, together with letters from amongst others various directors of companies at Cardiff Docks and the Headmaster of Cardiff Municipal Secondary School in Howard Gardens urging those of the requisite age and health to enlist as soon as possible. There was also a letter from Lady Bute urging 'every young able-bodied man in Cardiff, Cowbridge and Llantrisant to come forward and give his service for the glory of the Empire.'

The following day, Billy Bowden, the influential secretary of Cardiff CC, hastily convened a committee meeting at which it was unanimously resolved 'that owing to the present war disturbances, the remaining fixtures for this season, together with all practices, be abandoned and that we, jointly with Cardiff Rugby Football Club, hand over the pavilion to Lord Bute to be used by him for whatever military purposes as he wishes.' The same day the representatives of the Cardiff and District Rugby Union met in the Cottage Hotel and cancelled all of their forthcoming fixtures.

During the course of the next few days, the newspapers carried further stories about the German advance through France, plus lists of the first members of the British Expeditionary Forces to be killed. There was plenty of coverage about the hectic activity at recruiting stations as thousands of

TWO BRITONS.

JM Staniforth's cartoon from the Western Mail on August 31st, 1914.

men enlisted, besides the meetings organised by various sporting clubs at which their players and members agreed to sign up *en masse*. By the end of the month, various Sportsmen's Battalions had been formed, whilst the cricket pavilion at the Arms Park was being used as a recruitment station with the gymnasium at the rear of the impressive building together with the balcony and scorer's box being converted into accommodation and bedrooms for 200 Belgian refugees. Temporary washrooms were also created by the erection of canvas tents near the river, whilst wooden boarding was also placed in the rugby grandstand to provide additional space for the refugees.

In Cowbridge, nine members of the club's 1st XI, including their professional, who a month before had enjoyed a jolly tour in North Somerset all enlisted and soon afterwards made their way to Neyland for military training, whilst on Saturday, September 12th, members of the so-called Cardiff Pals Battalion paraded through the streets of the city to rousing cheers from on-lookers, friends and families, before also proceeding by train to various training camps in southern England. Within a day, a Red Cross ambulance train had also arrived at Cardiff General Station bringing 120 wounded soldiers from the front who were to receive treatment at the city's hospitals. The arrival of these invalids was also covered by the local newspapers with the correspondent of the *Western Mail* taking great delight in saying how 'some of the less severely wounded had secured German helmets as trophies, and these were waved aloft in an exhibition of a somewhat grim humour. One of the gallant fellows who possessed such a

ST. JOHNS CRICKET CLUB SKEWEN - SEASON 1914

souvenir shouted that he was not going to stay here long, but was going back to the Front to collect some more.'

As further contingents of British troops headed across the Channel, and further ambulance trains arrived in south Wales, the mood in the country remained quite upbeat with most people believing that the War would be over by Christmas. The cricketing contingent were not too distraught about the cancellation of the concluding matches of the season in August and September as, like almost everyone else, they believed that everything would be swiftly sorted out and that they would be back home playing in the late spring of 1915. But these games in August and September proved to be the 'last hurrah' of the so-called Golden Age, and the final hours of joyous cricketing activity before five long and dark years dominated by death and depravity. Not even in their very worst nightmares could anyone have foretold what dreadful events would unfold.

4
1914 – MONS

The Battle of Mons was the first military engagement in which Allied troops were involved following the declaration of War by Britain on Germany on August 4th, 1914. Five days later the British Expeditionary Force (BEF) had begun embarking for France, although the term 'Force' remains something of a misnomer as whilst the German and French armies mustered over a million men each, many of whom were conscripts, the BEF comprised about 80,000 soldiers, the majority of whom were professionally-trained soldiers and who had answered the calls earlier in the month to return to action for King and Country.

The Battle of Mons was part of the Battle of the Frontiers, in which the advancing Allied army met their German counterparts along the borders of France with Belgium and Germany, with the battle lines stretching from Alsace-Lorraine to Mons and Charleroi in southern Belgium. The task of the BEF, despite its small size was to try and hold back the advancing German First Army as well as preventing any manoeuvres which might out-flank the Allied forces.

The BEF reached Mons on August 21st as the French Fifth Army was heavily engaged with the German Second and Third armies at the Battle of Charleroi. At the request of the Fifth Army commander, General Charles Lanrezac, the BEF's first task was to try and hold positions along the line of the Mons-Condé Canal. The first contact between the two armies had occurred earlier in the day when a British bicycle reconnaissance team encountered a German unit near Obourg. One of the cyclists, Private John Parr, was killed, thereby becoming the first British fatality on the Western Front.

The first substantial action occurred on the morning of August 22nd when at 6.30 am, the Fourth Dragoon Guards laid an ambush for a patrol of German lancers outside the village of Casteau, to the northeast of Mons. When the Germans spotted the trap and ran back, a troop of dragoons, led by Captain Hornby, gave chase on horseback, all with sabres drawn. The retreating Germans led the British to a larger force of lancers, who they promptly charged, and Captain Hornby became the first British soldier to kill an enemy in the Great War. After a further pursuit, the Germans turned and fired upon the British cavalrymen, at which point the Dragoons dismounted and opened fire. Drummer Edward Thomas is reputed to have fired the first shot of the War for the British Army, successfully hitting a German trooper.

The following morning the Battle of Mons began at dawn with German artillery bombarding the British lines. At 9.00 am, the first German infantry assault began, as they attempted to cross four bridges over the Mons-Condé canal, advancing in close columns and being relatively easy targets for the well-trained British riflemen. This initial attack was repulsed with heavy losses, before a second assault in a less closely-knit formation resulted in the capture of the bridges at Nimy and Ghlin, but with a heavy loss of life as well as having hundreds of other wounded troops.

But further reinforcements helped the Germans to maintain the attack, and as a result in mid-afternoon the British leaders decided to retreat and by nightfall Allied forces had established a new defensive line running through the villages of Montrœul, Boussu, Wasmes, Paturages, and Frameries. But having secured the bridges, the Germans had swiftly constructed other pontoons over the canal, and as a consequence were able to attack the new Allied lines in great strength and inflicted further heavy losses. By nightfall on August 24th, the British had successfully retreated to what was expected to be their new defensive lines on the Valenciennes to Maubeuge road, but significantly outnumbered by the German First Army, and with little support from their French allies, the BEF had to retreat even further, back to Landrecies and Le Cateau.

In all, the British were outnumbered by as much as three to one, and it was to their credit that they managed to hold up the German First Army for two days, whilst also inflicting heavy casualties on their enemies. In what was the first battle on European soil by British troops since the Crimean War almost 60 years before. For the Germans, the Battle of Mons was a tactical defeat, but nonetheless it was also a strategic victory as they successfully crossed the barrier of the Mons-Condé Canal and advanced further into France. In time, the German's drove the 'Tommies' of the

Archer Windsor-Clive.

BEF and their French colleagues almost back to the outer suburbs of Paris before finally being stopped at the Battle of the Marne.

Archer Windsor-Clive was one of the first British officers to be killed in the Battle of Mons, and he was also the first prominent cricketer to lose his life in the Great War. He was the third son of the Lord Robert George Windsor-Clive, the Earl of Plymouth who lived at St. Fagans Castle, some six miles west of Cardiff. As lords of the manor, the Windsor-Clives had a long and close association with St. Fagans CC, which had been formed in 1862 by the local vicar, who was a proponent of Muscular Christianity, believing that playing was a manly and healthy exercise. It soon became the archetypal village club with their side including the sons of the village priest, as well as the village's schoolmaster, shoemaker and carpenter. On many occasions, the Earl himself turned out for the club – on these occasions, the side became known as The Earl of Plymouth's XI, rather than St. Fagans CC – and as a keen sportsman himself, he relished the opportunity to play alongside the local residents and estate workers.

During the late 1890s, the Earl increased his involvement with the village cricket club, not least because his three sons – Other, Ivor and Archer – were

The St.Fagans team of 1907 with Archer Windsor-Clive in the middle row, sat second left with his brother and father to his left.

all enthusiastic cricketers and decent players in their own right. In 1898 he became the club's President and from 1900 provided land for the club to develop their own ground, as well as providing over £2,000 towards the construction of a decent pavilion. As a measure of his ambitions for the St. Fagans club and, *inter alia* his sons, the Earl also hired a county professional to look after the ground and coach the playing members, whilst he also created a St. Fagans Boy's team so that the young gentlemen could further their cricketing education and expertise.

Around this time, the Earl also became involved with many organisations in the Cardiff area and served as Lord Mayor in 1896, besides overseeing the development of Penarth as both a thriving port and genteel resort, away from the hustle and bustle of the coal metropolis at the mouth of the Taff. The Earl also became actively involved with Glamorgan CCC, serving as the club's President from 1901 until 1922 – a period when the club metamorphosed from being a Minor County to a first-class side, with the Earl taking great delight in seeing Archer turn out for the county side. Indeed, many believed that Archer would become a future captain of Glamorgan CCC, thereby emulating the achievement of Edmund David, the son of the vicar of St.Fagans in leading Glamorgan in their inaugural game in 1889. Given his great interest in cricket, and wanting to see his son do well, the Earl would have greatly approved of Archer becoming a leading figure with the county club as they entered the County Championship – tragically, it was not to be.

Archer was born in November 1890 at Hewell Grange in Redditch, Worcestershire – the home of Lady Harriet Windsor – and subsequently attended Eton and Trinity College, Cambridge. Having played for St. Fagans from his early teens, it was no surprise that he made his debut for the Eton XI in 1907, and the following year struck a fine 105 in the annual match against Winchester. This century, together with some other decent innings for St. Fagans plus his family's connections, led to his selection in the Glamorgan side which met Monmouthshire at Cardiff Arms Park in early August 1908. The schoolboy, though, met with a modest debut at county level making 5 and 0 as Monmouthshire won by an innings.

Further promising performances for Eton in 1909 saw Archer win selection again for Glamorgan against Cornwall at Swansea and against Nottinghamshire 2nd XI at the Arms Park. There was a strong St. Fagans contingent for this latter game, which was the semi-final of the Minor County Championship, with Ralph Sweet-Escott, the son of the vicar of St. Fagans opening the batting and Trevor Preece, a prolific run-scorer, batting at number four. Archer occupied the number five berth, but again he met with little success scoring 4 and 0 in the drawn contest.

During the Autumn of 1909, Archer went up to Cambridge and the following summer appeared in the Freshman's Match where he took 7-49 with his left-arm medium-pace bowling, besides making 33 and 110 for the Perambulators against the Etceteras. He duly made his first-class debut for the University in early May against Essex, making 13 and 15, besides taking three wickets, and he kept his place for the following match against Surrey, against whom he made 3 and 11. As promising as these performances were, Archer failed to win a Blue and made just one further appearance that summer for the Light Blues, against Kent at Fenner's.

In 1911 Archer again impressed in the early season trials, making 45 plus an unbeaten 80 in the Seniors Match, but he failed to appear that summer for the University XI, and instead won the first of two tennis Blues. He met with more success on the cricket field in 1912 appearing, in all, in four further matches for the University, but after bagging a pair against Sussex, the left-hander was overlooked for the Varsity Match and yet again missed out on a Blue. Lady luck was also not on his side when he appeared again for Glamorgan in August 1912 at the Arms Park against Surrey 2nd XI. His call-up followed a decent series of scores for both St. Fagans and I Zingari, but after taking a wicket and making a catch, he did not get the chance to display his batting skills as rain washed out the remainder of the game.

The following month Archer began his military career and joined the Coldstream Guards as a Second-Lieutenant, attracted no doubt by the chance to further develop his latent leadership skills as well as playing a decent standard of cricket. Indeed, in June 1914 he appeared for the Household Brigade against the Band of Brothers in their two-day match at Burton's Court in Chelsea. He opened the batting, making 0 and 34, besides claiming three wickets in what tragically proved to be his last major game of cricket.

On August 12th, 1914 he was amongst the first wave of British troops to head across the Channel to fight on foreign soil. As a Lieutenant in Number 2 Company of the 3rd Battalion he left Chelsea Barracks and travelled by train to Southampton before crossing with the other Guardsmen on the SS Cawdor Castle before proceeding on to Harveng where defensive positions were dug on 23rd August.

The following day, other troops in the BEF began their retreat from Mons, so half of Archer's battalion were instructed to head back via Malgami to Landrecies where they were positioned as outposts in a bid to delay the advancing Germans. Around dusk on that evening, a column was seen heading up the Le Quesnoy road, and an officer then appeared in French uniform who, speaking in French, announced that a large body of French troops were approaching, and added that he had come in advance to alert the 600 or so Coldstream Guards so that they did not fire on their allies by mistake.

Sadly, it was a cruel trick as shortly afterwards, the column duly appeared, singing French songs and those at the front wearing French and Belgian uniforms. But those at the back were German and they opened heavy fire on the Coldstream Guards, with Archer being struck by a shell as he and his men defended an important bridge. Archer never recovered from the awful wounds he sustained and he was one of three Guardsmen to be killed in the initial skirmish. A further eighteen were wounded, whereas around 500 of the French and German troops were killed, and a further 2,000 wounded. The action of the Coldstream Guards did allow the retreating BEF to retire from the area in relative safety, and Sir John French, their Commander in Chief, duly mentioned the battalion in his despatches on September 7th.

News of the death of the popular and much admired young gentleman came as a huge shock to the residents of St. Fagans, and his many friends in both Cardiff and London. The Earl was mortified by the news of Archer's death, and the day after he had relayed the tragic details to the rest of his household, he presided over a recruitment meeting in Cardiff. Shortly afterwards, on September 3rd, *The Times* reported the grim details of what had happened at Landrecies, with the headline 'The Toll of War - A First List of British Losses', whilst a leader article stated: 'The nation has learned of its losses with mingled pride and grief, and its determination to avenge its dead, and to carry to victory the sacred cause for which they died, has hardened like steel.'

Three weeks later, the Earl chaired a packed public meeting held in the Queen's Hall, London, attended mainly by members of the London Welsh as well as by David Lloyd George. No direct reference was initially made to the poignant loss which the Earl had

IVOR   WINDSOR   ARCHER

1910

The Earl of Plymouth and his sons.

recently sustained, but the death of the Hon. Archer Windsor-Clive, was in everyone's thoughts as the Earl addressed the meeting and spoke of the heavy sacrifices that would have to be endured in the maintenance of the honour of the nation. "We must learn," he said, "to say with Mr Rudyard Kipling, and say it with deep conviction: *Who dies if England live?*" There was another moving moment towards the close of Lloyd George's speech when he turned to the Earl and said "Some have already given their lives. Some have given more than their own lives – they have given the lives of those who are dear to them. I honour their courage, and may God be their comfort and their strength." Tears came into the eyes of the Earl as the audience spontaneously applauded. It was many weeks before the Earl got over the tragic loss, although contemporaries say that life was never the same either at the cricket club or in the house following Archer's death, with his bedroom being left untouched as a tribute to the loss of a favourite and favoured son.

5

The Last Hurrah

The death of Archer Windsor-Clive, one of the 'bright young things' of cricket in south Wales, and a man tipped to become one of the captains of Glamorgan, brought home the stark realities of war and, as the list of fatalities in local newspapers grew longer and longer by the day during the autumn of 1914, it became evident that those who thought it would all be over by Christmas had been wrong.

Officials of cricket clubs, like other sporting organisations, therefore held meetings during the autumn and winter months to put in place a range of measures, establishing holding committees to ensure that their club's assets were protected. With uncertainty about how long the War would continue, their principal concern was ensuring that their club's finances were being properly looked after. Making arrangements for fixtures for the 1915 season, and arranging pre-season nets, was out of the question for most clubs as the playing members who would normally have attended the practices were amongst the growing platoons of troops heading for France and Belgium. In fact, playing games was completely out of the question for many clubs as their grounds had been taken over by the military authorities. Swansea Cricket and Football Club was one such example as a series of rifle ranges had been established across the outfield at St. Helen's, with the facility being used by the Swansea Battalion Voluntary Training Corps.

Some forms of recreation had continued during the winter of 1914-15 with soccer and rugby being played, whilst horse racing continued at a number of racecourses in Britain and Ireland. However, by the spring of 1915, even these meetings were curtailed and the races planned at Cardiff racecourse over the Whitsun Bank Holiday period in late May were amongst those to be cancelled by the authorities. Indeed, the Whitsun weekend usually marked the first high point of the cricket season with a plethora of fixtures across south Wales, as well as further afield with some clubs venturing on short tours of the West Country, the West Midlands or the Home Counties.

Nothing of the sort took place at Whitsun in 1915 and instead a variety of civic and military sporting contests took place over the holiday period. A variety of athletic events were held on the beaches at Aberavon, Porthcawl and Tenby, whilst horse and whippet racing was arranged at Aberdare and Llanelli. At Pontypool, the military authorities organised a tug-of-war tournament and a boxing contest, whilst in Caerphilly, there was a walking race to Machen and back, followed by wrestling matches, a tug-of-war contest and military parades, with the *South Wales Echo* also reporting how 'Watson the Wizard gave his conjuring performance within the castle walls, together with a concert by the Caerphilly Ladies Choir.'

However, there was some cricketing activity as Barry Athletic Club organised matches at their Barry Island ground including a one-day match in August 1915 against a Glamorgan XI in what is believed to be the only game, under the county's name, which took place during the War. Barry Athletic Club had been one of the thriving teams in the years before the War, and several of their members had played for the county side.

Most prominent amongst these was Arthur Osborne, who had been born in South Shields in December 1876 and, in 1895, had appeared for the Durham Colts. His father, Herbert, was a master coppersmith and in 1900 both he and Arthur, who by then had completed his apprenticeship, moved to Barry. Arthur's graceful batting as well as his clever seam bowling won him a regular place in the line-up, besides attracting the attention of the Glamorgan talent scouts. He duly made his debut for Glamorgan against

Playing members of Barry CC gather in front of the pavilion with their friends and family in 1913.

Surrey's 2nd XI at The Oval in 1901, and opened the batting for several seasons in Minor County cricket. During his first season of county cricket he scored 110 in a high-scoring contest against Monmouthshire at Cardiff, whilst two years later he took 6-40 against the touring Philadelphians, again at the Arms Park.

Despite having retired from county cricket at the end of the 1911 season, Arthur was still captaining the Barry club in 1914 and was amongst the chief mourners, in late August, at the memorial service for Archer Windsor-Clive, the cricket-loving son of Lord Plymouth, who owned the land on Barry Island where the Athletic club was based. By the time other leading members of the Athletic Club gathered to mourn the loss of the gifted young batsman, Barry had become a hive of activity. As one of the country's major coal-exporting ports, it was likely to be attacked if a German invasion were to take place and, by September 1914, Barry bore the hallmarks of a garrison town with artillery personnel travelling from Portsmouth to supplement the gunners protecting the docks. The Athletic Club's members were also very prominent in the recruitment drives which took place in the early autumn with an estimate of 600 men attending the Drill Hall to answer Lord Kitchener's call to arms.

The horrors of War were also, quite literally, on the doorstep of Barry when passengers were landed at the town's docks from a vessel attacked by a German submarine lurking in the waters off Ilfracombe in North Devon, whilst wounded soldiers started to arrive almost on a daily basis by train or boat, prior to transfer to local convalescent homes. With talk of further attacks by German submarines, and a possible invasion, the local authorities could ill afford any panic or mass hysteria. There had already been an element of civil unrest when, shortly after the announcement of War, German merchant seamen visiting vessels in the Docks had been attacked, and others in the local area were rounded up and accused of being spies. It was as much for their own protection that groups of German nationals were transferred to Flat Holm, prior to transfer to internment camps in Hampshire.

Anti-Kaiser feelings were still high in May 1915 as around 150 tippers and coal trimmers at Barry Docks went on strike as a protest against the employment of naturalised Germans. It was against this background and a need to preserve an air of normality that Barry Athletic Club held their Annual General Meeting on April 16th. Whereas other cricket clubs and sporting organisations in other towns had decided not to continue their activities, Barry was a port full of military personnel and others who were looking for something to take their minds off the horrors of war, so the Athletic Club's committee unanimously passed a motion that the cricket, bowls and tennis sections would all continue their activities in 1915.

Consequently, matches took place during 1915 at the club's ground on Barry Island, against the University Settlement XI from Splott in Cardiff, a Royal Garrison Artillery XI, a team representing the Royal Engineers, the side from St. Andrew's Church in Dinas Powys, plus a scratch XI raised by Cardiff schoolmaster George Cording, a man whose brother had been a leading figure with the Barry club. At first the club found it quite difficult to raise funds to meet the costs of staging these games, as well as covering any expenses and the sundry costs of the upkeep of the playing facilities and the wooden pavilion. An ingenious solution was mentioned for a fund-raising match against a Glamorgan XI so an approach was made to the county club who themselves had appointed a temporary committee to oversee the financial administration until, at least, the end of hostilities.

Norman Riches, the prolific Glamorgan batsman, who served as an Army medic.

Norman Riches, the Cardiff-based dentist who was chairing the club's emergency committee, agreed to the proposal and the outcome of the discussions was a game at the Barry Island ground on Saturday, August 28th, starting at 2 pm, with admission, by ticket only, at sixpence with tea in the Pavilion for an additional ninepence.

The *Barry Dock News* report of the game at Barry Island in August 1915 records the scores as:

Glamorgan County XI		Barry	
GE Cording	8	A Deacon	17
TR Preece	16	S Beaumont	17
TR Morgan	0	RV Williams	6
AI Dunn	17	AR Osborne	3
WA Hardman	0	R Norman	5
J Chandless	2	F Williams	1
HAF Dunn	1	B Cording	0
RW Price	0	AW White	9

WL Ferrier	9	G Waters	2
WT Braddon	0	W Kinsley	2
AC Chandless	0	WT Llewellyn	2
Extras	6	Extras	11
Total	59	Total	75

A decent-sized crowd duly watched the game which Barry, with Arthur Osborne in their ranks, winning the contest by sixteen runs. The Glamorgan side contained a handful of men with county experience including George Cording, who subsequently kept wicket in Glamorgan's inaugural County Championship match against Sussex at the Arms Park in 1921, Tom Morgan, Trevor Preece and John Chandless, another stalwart of the Cardiff club who worked as an insurance clerk.

Several lesser-known players also turned out for the Glamorgan XI, including John Chandless' brother Arthur, and Warren Ferrier, a fellow insurance agent who also played for the Cardiff club. Also in the line-up was Billy Hardman, a teenager from Lancashire, but sadly this proved to be his only game of note. Born in Bootle in 1897, he was serving with the 7th North Lancashire Regiment and owed his selection for the Glamorgan side to being stationed in the area. After some decent performances in games between the various service teams, George Cording decided to include the youngster in the Glamorgan line-up in the hope that he might opt to throw in his lot with the Welsh county once the War was over. Tragically, he departed for northern France later in the year where he was killed in action on October 25th, 1916.

The Glamorgan side also included Augustin Ivor (or Guy) Dunn and his brother Hugh Aubrey (or Tom) Fairfield. Together with their other brothers, Frank and Jack, they had been leading lights with the Cowbridge club, and had played with distinction for many years for the club from the Vale of Glamorgan. Taking part in this match was a bitter-sweet moment for Guy and Tom as the match took place only a few weeks after the news that their brothers had been killed at Gallipoli. Tragically, for Tom, it also proved to his last major game as he – like team-mate Billy Hardman – joined the long, long list of men who died during the War.

The ill-fated Tom Dunn

6
1915 – GALLIPOLI

Between April 25th, 1915 and January 9th, 1916 the Battle of Gallipoli took place on the peninsula of that name in modern day Turkey – then part of the Ottoman Empire, who were aligned with Germany. It also saw an operation, also involving many troops from Australia and New Zealand, to capture the Ottoman capital of Constantinople (Istanbul) in order to preserve the sea route to Russia. Following an unsuccessful naval campaign to force a passage through the Dardanelles, an amphibious landing was undertaken at Gallipoli. Sadly, it failed, and after eight months of heavy fighting and many casualties on both sides, the Allied troops were evacuated.

The campaign is now regarded by military historians as one of the greatest victories by the Ottomans during the Great War, besides being one of the major failures by Allied forces. It was also the first major battle involving Australian and Kiwi troops, whilst in Turkey, the campaign is perceived as a defining moment in the history of the country and its people, laying the groundwork for the Turkish War of Independence and the creation, eight years later, of the Republic of Turkey under Mustafa Kemal.

The background to the attacks at Gallipoli stemmed from Allied concerns at the lack of progress on the Western Front and the need to secure a safe supply route into Russia via the Black Sea and into the Mediterranean. Their land trade routes into Europe had already been blocked by the German Empire and the Austrian-Hungarian alliance, whilst other ports were either too distant or ice-blocked for many months. While the Ottomans were neutral, supplies could pass through the Dardanelles, but following their entry into the War, this vital route was cut.

The first proposal to attack the Ottoman Empire was made by the French Minister of Justice in November 1914. This was rejected before an attempt by the British to persuade the Ottoman leaders to join the Allies also failed. Later that month, Winston Churchill, then the First Lord of the Admirality, proposed a naval attack on the Dardanelles, based on what subsequently turned out to be erroneous reports regarding the strength of Ottoman troops. Churchill reasoned that the Royal Navy had several obsolete battleships which could not be used against the Germans in the North Sea, but which could be useful in an attack on the Dardanelles.

The situation escalated on January 2nd, 1915 when Grand Duke Nicholas of Russia appealed to Britain for assistance against the Ottomans who were attacking their troops in the Caucasus. Planning for an Allied operation in the Dardanelles subsequently began, and on February 19th, the first attack began with a long-range bombardment of Ottoman artillery along the coast. A phase of bad weather slowed this initial phase but by February 25th the outer forts had been reduced and the entrance into the straits had been cleared of mines. A sense of impending victory was heightened by the interception of a German wireless message, which revealed the Ottoman Dardanelles forts were running out of ammunition.

The main attack by Allied and French troops then began on March 18th, 1915, with eighteen battleships plus a supporting fleet of cruisers and destroyers, targeting the narrowest point of the Dardanelles, where the straits are just a mile wide. Heavy losses were sustained, forcing the Allied vessels to retreat, and a change in strategy towards capturing the Turkish defences by land, thereby eliminating the Ottoman mobile artillery and allowing minesweepers to enter the straits in order to clear the way for the larger vessels.

Lord Kitchener, the British Secretary of State for War duly appointed General Sir Ian Hamilton to command a 78,000-strong Mediterranean Expeditionary Force, drawing on British troops augmented by Australian and New Zealand soldiers who had been encamped in Egypt ahead of being sent to France. Their destination duly changed as Hamilton prepared his plan for the land assault on the southern part of the Gallipoli peninsula. Bad weather and uncertain intelligence delayed the assault until April 25th. A series of bloody skirmishes then followed, with the Allied advance being hindered by the lack of decent maps as well as spirited counter-attacks by the Ottomans who, in places, having run out of ammunition turned to using their bayonets in a bid to repel the Allied troops. With their troops exhausted and unnerved by the battles for the beaches, heavy losses were sustained as the Ottomans swiftly called up reinforcements and the possibility of a swift Allied victory on the peninsula disappeared.

It then became a battle of attrition with further waves of Allied troops sent to the Dardanelles in order to try to secure them. The summer of 1915 duly witnessed a series of offensives including in August a plan by Hamilton to secure the Sari Bair Range and to capture high ground at Chunuk Bair. By this time, both sides had been reinforced, with Hamilton's original five divisions increased to fifteen, augmented by forty aircraft, while the six original Ottoman divisions had swelled to sixteen.

Operations began on August 6th and met once again with stiff resistance, with the summit at Chunuk Bair not being seized until two days later. But a massive Ottoman counter-attack on August 10th, led by Mustafa Kemal, swept away the Allied troops, and with Turkish forces having recaptured this vital ground the Allies' best chance of victory was lost. Elsewhere, Irish and Welsh troops began landing at Suvla, but they too met with heavy fire, and their assault also failed.

After the failure of another assault at Scimitar Hill, thoughts turned towards an evacuation, but the situation deteriorated further following the entry of Bulgaria into the War. In early October 1915 the British and French opened a second Mediterranean front at Salonika after redeploying three divisions from Gallipoli and reducing the flow of re-inforcements. But Bulgaria's entry into the War meant that a land route now existed between Germany and the Ottoman Empire, allowing the supply of heavy artillery into Gallipoli.

A decision to evacuate Gallipoli was taken by Allied commanders in early December, but the extreme winter weather, including torrential downpours and snowstorms led to many casualties being sustained. Rain flooded trenches drowned soldiers and washed unburied corpses into the lines, but despite these difficulties the last Allied troops had left the Dardanelles by early January.

Military historians are divided about their assessments of the overall campaign – some describe it as a closely-fought affair, others view it as stalemate, whilst others regard it as a disaster for the Allies, consuming large amounts of resources which otherwise could have been used on the Western Front. Whichever assessment is followed, there is agreement that the Allied attempt at securing a passage through the Dardanelles proved unsuccessful.

In total, there were nearly half a million casualties during the campaign, with the British Official History listing total losses as 205,000 British, 47,000 French and 251,000 Turkish. Many soldiers also became sick due to the unsanitary conditions, especially from enteric fever, dysentery and diarrhoea.

The failure of the landings had significant political repercussions in Britain, with the Prime Minister Herbert Asquith, ending his Liberal Government and forming a Coalition Government with the Conservative Party. Commissions of Inquiry were also set up to investigate the strategies of the military leaders and their actions, and the net result was that Asquith was overthrown and David Lloyd George became Prime Minister.

Douglas Parker Robathan (Radyr CC and Swansea CC)

Douglas Robathan was an enthusiastic cricketer and gallant officer who was killed during the landings at Suvla Bay on August 10th, 1915.

Born in Risca in January 1888, he was the youngest of five sons fathered by Dr. George Beckett Robathan, the town's G.P. who subsequently moved to Radyr, a prosperous suburb to the north of Cardiff. Douglas and his brothers duly grew up at Summerlands, a spacious villa in the well-to-do settlement and like his brothers, Douglas soon learnt the rudiments of cricket at Llandaff Cathedral School. He then attended Cranbook School in Kent, and in 1909 he duly played alongside his brothers Frank, Eric and Lionel in the Radyr cricket team. The following year Percy joined them but by this time Douglas had commenced his studies as a mining engineer at a colliery owned by the Insoles of Fairwater and his work allowed him to buy Ovid House in Radyr where he duly set up home with Frances, his Somerset-born wife.

The Robathan brothers – at the front are (left to right) Peter, Lionel and Frank, with Eric and Douglas standing behind.

Over the course of the next few years, his brothers moved away – Frank became a gold miner in Ecuador and Mexico, Percy became a chartered accountant, Lionel went into teaching, and Eric emigrated to Canada before becoming an Episcopalian Minister in Calgary and Oregon. In 1912 the tall and quite debonair Douglas also moved away, as he secured a position as under-manager and surveyor at the Tarenni Colliery in Ystalyfera. His move west saw a change of cricketing allegiance to Swansea CC, whilst he also helped to set up a cricket team near the Colliery at Varteg so that the staff and management could enjoy some healthy recreation together during the summer months.

For several years, Douglas had also been a member of the Territorial Force, having joined the Monmouthshire Volunteers in January 1908 before transferring to the 5th Battalion, Welsh Regiment Territorial Force, and obtaining his certificate in Musketry. When War was declared he dutifully joined the First Line of the 5th Battalion, which was largely drawn from recruitment meetings at Pontypridd. In November 1914, Douglas and his colleagues undertook training in Tunbridge Wells in Kent before being sent, in February 1915, to join the Forth and Tay Defences. After a couple of months in Scotland, the battalion headed back south for further training in Bedford, before heading to Plymouth in mid July, sailing at first to Alexandria on the SS Huntsgreen before proceeding to Port Said and joining other vessels for the journey to the Dardanelles.

The SS Huntsgreen arrived on August 5th at Mudros, Lemnos, as they awaited further instructions. Three days later, confirmation came through that they would be shortly landing at Suvla Bay to assist the 10th and 13th Divisions who had made the initial landings. In the early hours of August 9th his Battalion landed ashore, with plenty of fire from the Turkish troops greeting the Allied forces.

After some sleep, they attempted to head north and then east inland, but their progress was met with plenty of shelling by the Turks. Accompanied by the hissing and screeching of shells raining down from the surrounding hills, Douglas and his colleagues tried to move forward but they met with stiff resistance, and on the morning of August 10th Douglas was felled by a sniper. Despite being hit, he continued to cheer on his colleagues as they attempted to advance, shouting "Stick it, Welsh" until another round of fire from the Turks saw him struck for a second time and silenced by a wound, apparently to his lungs.

For a while, colleagues saw him lying still stunned on the ground, tragically too far away from Allied positions from which he might have been rescued. Soon afterwards, the Turks set fire to the area where Douglas and many others lay dead or wounded, and to the horror of his colleagues he was burnt to death, with the sounds of screaming, remaining with those who survived this bloody episode of the War. For his part, the loss of so many gallant men left the Commanding Officer of the Battalion Colonel Morgan Morgan a broken man and after collapsing, his state of mind necessitated his return to the UK and treatment for nervous exhaustion.

Douglas' death prompted a colleague to write, 'He led his men into one of the fiercest fights that has ever been fought on Gallipoli Peninsula. He was loved by his men and admired by all. He fought as gallantly as any as long as he was able to lead and I am expressing the thoughts of all Battalions when I say it has lost one of its best soldiers.'

The loss of Douglas was felt deeply by the Robathan family. Having no known grave, he is commemorated on the Helles Memorial as well as having an inscription in his memory in Llandaff Cathedral, close to the Epstein Arch. His brother Lionel – who had attended Epsom College – played for Glamorgan in 1910 and 1911, before becoming the first non-clerical Headmaster of Llandaff Cathedral School, serving from 1912 until 1919. He then moved to run a prep school at Newnham and duly appeared for Gloucestershire in three first-class matches during 1922.

Whilst not as talented a batsman as Lionel, there is no doubt that Douglas made up for this shortfall in energy and enthusiasm, yet far worse amateurs turned out for the Welsh county during the 1920s as they made their way in the first-class game. Had it not been for the horrors of Suvla Bay, Douglas Robathan might well have joined them in wearing the colours of the Daffodil county.

Frank Dunn (Cowbridge CC and Glamorgan)

Frank Dunn was a prominent amateur cricketer in the Vale of Glamorgan during the years leading up to the Great War. His father Frederick was a mining engineer, who after much business success in the Rhondda Valley, lived at The Cross, a large manor house in the village of Llanblethian. Frank had three brothers, as well as a sister, with all of the Dunn boys attending Cowbridge Grammar School where they shone in the classroom as well as on the sports field. Indeed, much to their father's delight, the Dunns were able to raise their own family XI which played at the Cowbridge ground with Frank's sister acting as scorer.

Indeed, Frank was one of the leading schoolboy batsmen in south Wales during the early 1900s, and after leaving Cowbridge Grammar, the tall and imposing young man attended Cardiff University whom he also represented with some success before training as an engineer. With Glamorgan CCC having ambitions of first-class status, the club's officials kept an eye on the youngster's progress with Cowbridge CC and in 1911 they selected him for the Minor County Championship match against Carmarthenshire at Stradey Park in Llanelli. It was, though, a fairly anonymous debut for Frank who did not bat or bowl, but did take a catch.

A fortnight later, Frank was included once again in the Glamorgan XI which met Staffordshire in a fund-raising two-day match at the Arms Park. Frank batted at number ten in the first innings and managed a single before being bowled by the legendary Sidney Barnes, but he met with less success in the second innings where batting at number nine he was dismissed for nought. It proved to be Frank's final appearance for Glamorgan but he continued to be a heavy scorer in club cricket for Cowbridge as well as other gentlemen's teams such as the Glamorgan Gypsies. Sadly, the game with Staffordshire was the last time his father saw him play in a major game as, at the end of August, Frederick Dunn died aged 67.

The outbreak of War saw Frank and his elder brother Jack, join the 5th Battalion The Welsh Regiment. They were initially stationed at Pontypridd, before moving in the autumn of 1914 for further training near Tunbridge Wells in Kent. February 1915 saw the Battalion move to Scotland to form part of the Forth and Tay Defences. After a month or so, they were transferred to Bedford where further training took place ahead of the campaign in the Dardanelles.

Frank and Jack duly departed on July 19th with their Battalion from Devonport in Plymouth and like Douglas Robathan, they were involved in the manoeuvres on Turkish soil at Suvla on August 9th. The day after landing at Suvla Bay, Frank – aged 29 – was killed during the heavy crossfire from Turkish positions as the Battalion tried to move inland. Just five days later Jack also lost his life in skirmishes with the Turkish troops as the Welsh Regiment attempted to consolidate their position near some wooded hills overlooking the Bay.

By the time the Brigade were evacuated from Gallipoli to Egypt in December 1915, it was estimated that they had lost around 85% of their full strength, and like so many others who lost their lives in the abortive campaign, neither Frank or Jack have any known graves and are also commemorated on the Helles Memorial.

Their younger brother Tom, who had played for the Glamorgan XI against Barry in 1915, was also badly injured whilst serving with the Royal Engineers. He returned home to recuperate from the physical and mental scars of warfare but, in May 1916, he died aged 28 near Monmouth in a drowning accident whilst swimming in the River Monnow. Together with Lieutenant David Williams, he had rowed a boat out into the river, with his friend being the first to dive in and swim back to the bank where his fellow officers were sat. Tragically, after diving in, Tom was soon in difficulty with his arms thrashing around and his head occasionally popping up out of the river. Seeing his distress others swam out to rescue him but, despite only being in sixteen feet of water, their efforts failed and Tom's body was recovered from the river fifteen minutes later by a boat-hook.

7

1915 – FLANDERS

The Flemish town of Ypres in western Belgium witnessed several grim and blood-strewn battles during the Great War. The first took place during the autumn of 1914, and before the following spring a second battle took place as Germany used poison gas for the first time on a large scale on the Western Front.

Ypres occupied a strategic position in western Belgium, with British troops eager to secure the town and its access routes to the English Channel ports, so vital to the British Army's supply lines. Indeed, the town represented the last major obstacle to the Germans as they advanced towards Boulogne and Calais.

The first major German offensive had begun in mid-October 1914 and resulted in the destruction of the so-called 'Old Contemptibles', the highly experienced and trained British soldiers who formed the British Expeditionary Force. The ranks of the 'Old Contemptibles' were soon replaced by a huge influx of conscripts, recruited following Lord Kitchener's call to arms.

The Second Battle of Ypres began in the spring of 1915, and had six distinctive elements, starting with the Battle of Gravenstafel on April 22nd and 23rd as the German Army released 168 tons of chlorine gas over a four mile section of the front held by French Territorial and colonial Moroccan and Algerian troops. It was the culmination of a massive logistical effort, with German troops hauling by hand 5,730 heavy cylinders of chlorine gas, before also opening them by hand and relying on the prevailing winds to carry the poisonous clouds towards Allied trenches.

The French swiftly noticed its distinctive smell, which was like a mixture of pineapple and pepper, before complaining about pains in the chests and a burning sensation in their throats. Approximately 6,000 French and colonial troops died within ten minutes at Ypres, primarily from asphyxiation after breathing in the gas, as well as subsequently from tissue damage in the lungs. Others were blinded by the chemical vapours, whilst because the chlorine was denser than air, it quickly filled the trenches and many British troops were shot as they tried to escape the acrid smelling gas by clambering out of the trenches.

German soldiers were also concerned about the effects of the chlorine gas, so they hesitated about moving forward in large numbers, allowing Allied troops to re-gather and fill the gaps which the dreadful vapours had opened up. Elsewhere, the Germans also used sulphur chloride which they had placed in front of their trenches. When released it caused a thick yellow cloud to be blown towards advancing French and Belgian soldiers. Unable to see what they were doing, the confused troops were then subjected to a series of charges by the Germans, forcing the French and Belgians back into their trenches.

The Battle of St Julien then followed from April 24th to May 5th with the hostilities starting when the Germans released another cloud of chlorine gas towards Canadian troops situated to the west of the village of St. Julien. As a result, German troops were able to take the village before a counter-attack from troops from the Northumberland Division in which they lost 1,900 men and 40 officers – equivalent to two thirds of its strength.

The next element was the Battle of Frezenberg between May 8th and 13th as the opposing armies fought either side of a ridge of high ground. Once again, chlorine gas was used, although it was not until the third assault that Allied lines were significantly breached. A fortnight later the Battle of Bellewaarde took place with, once again, British troops being forced to retreat as further clouds of chlorine gas were released by German troops.

Charles Donnelly (Hill's Plymouth CC and Glamorgan)

Charles Donnelly was one of hundreds of Allied troops to be killed by the poison gas during these battles on Flanders Fields.

Born in Nottingham in 1865 the seam bowler failed to secure a place on the Trent Bridge groundstaff before accepting a professional appointment with the thriving Hill's Plymouth club in Merthyr in the mid 1880s. These were heady years for the club as they secured a permanent ground at Pentrebach on land owned by Crawshay Bailey, the owner of the Hill's Plymouth works. Acquiring the services of Donnelly was another bonus, and his lively bowling brought success for the go-ahead club, as well as attracting the interests of the Glamorgan selectors.

Consequently, Donnelly was chosen for the two-day friendly against the MCC at Swansea, and after getting permission from the Works Manager to play in this prestigious fixture, Donnelly duly opened the bowling for the county side. However, he only took one wicket in the first innings and pulled a muscle which prevented him from bowling in the MCC's second innings, as the visitors completed a narrow three-wicket victory.

It proved to be Donnelly's sole appearance for the Welsh county, but he continued to enjoy much success at club level with Hill's Plymouth, including in the Glamorgan League, created in 1897 for teams in the Taff and Rhondda valleys, with the Merthyr-based club playing home and away matches against Pontypridd, Pentre, Treherbert, Treorchy, Porth, Ynysybwl and Llwynypia. Donnelly proved to be one of the leading bowlers in the Glamorgan League and played in their representative XI which met similar teams drawn from other leagues across south Wales.

In 1914 Donnelly switched from being a clerk at the Hill's Plymouth works to enlisting with the King's Royal Rifle Corps and by the time the 2nd Battalion were in Flanders he had been promoted to company sergeant-major. Sadly, he lost his life on May 9th, 1915 during a gas attack as part of the Battle of Frezenberg.

Edward Phillips (Newport CC and Monmouthshire)

The day before, the Battle of Frezenburg had claimed the life of another and more illustrious cricketer as Edward Phillips, a member of the Newport-based brewing dynasty lost his life aged just 32 years and 110 days

He was the son of Edward Phillips, who together with his brother William had developed the family's brewery in Dock Road. The Phillips family hailed from Northamptonshire where they ran a series of successful breweries, and from 1882 Edward senior oversaw the operation of the Newport plant, which supplied thirteen pubs in the town, besides instigating a series of improvements and extensions including a new malting plant.

E.S. Phillips.

Born in January 1883 Edward Stone Phillips was educated at Marlborough and Pembroke College, Cambridge where he furthered both his academic studies and his cricketing skills. Indeed, just days after leaving Marlborough, Edward junior made his debut for Monmouthshire in their Minor County Championship encounter against Wiltshire at Rodney Parade – the Newport ground where from his early teens he had batted with success for the town club. A few weeks later Edward gave a glimpse of his talents as a top order batsman by making a fine 69 in the return match at Trowbridge.

The following Autumn he went up to Cambridge where he duly made his first-class debut in May 1903 in the game against HDG Leveson-Gower's XI at Fenner's. Edward top scored with 22 in their first innings before being dismissed for a duck second time around as the students lost by an innings. Phillips won a regular place in the Cambridge line-up in 1904 – a summer which saw him score his maiden first-class hundred as he made 107 and 68 against GJV Weigall's XI at Fenner's, and a few weeks later he celebrated winning a Blue by making an assured 47 against the touring South Africans.

After coming down from Cambridge, Phillips enjoyed a prolific summer in 1905 with Monmouthshire, making an unbeaten 133 against Glamorgan at Cardiff Arms Park as they inflicted a crushing innings defeat on the home side. The flowing month he added to his tally with 111 against Berkshire and 162 against Devon – both at Rodney Parade – before being chosen for South Wales in their prestigious game against the Australians at the Arms Park.

His friend and fellow brewer Jack Brain, was the leader of both the South Wales team and Glamorgan, and had been instrumental in a campaign for Test cricket to come to south Wales in 1905. The campaign failed by a single vote as Trent Bridge was awarded the opening Test of the 1905 Test series with Australia, but so impressed were the MCC authorities that they awarded Cardiff a three-day match with the tourists. The cream of cricketing talent from Glamorgan and Monmouthshire formed the South Wales side,

The South Wales side which met the Australians at the Arms Park in August 1905. ES Phillips is sat second right, whilst to his right are the Brain brothers – Jack and Sam – whilst Norman Riches is on the far left of the front row.

and on each day a crowd in excess of 10,000 turned up to cheer on the local men against the Test stars from Australia.

Despite the best efforts of Phillips, the Australians ran out comfortable victors but the success of the game led to similar ventures for a South Wales side in subsequent years and, as he was still in fine form at club and county level, Phillips was chosen to represent the combined side against the 1906 West Indians, the 1907 South Africans and the Gentlemen of Philadelphia in 1908.

His success for Monmouthshire also led to his selection in the Minor Counties side which met the 1906 West Indians at Ealing. By this time, he had become a Director of the family firm, yet despite his increased business commitments he continued to play regularly for Monmouthshire. Indeed, some of his finest innings came on his home patch at Rodney Parade, with 130 against Glamorgan in 1909, an unbeaten 100 against Buckinghamshire in 1911 and 105 in the match with Glamorgan in 1913. Later that summer he also posted what proved to be his final century for his county, making 121 against Cornwall at Abergavenny before in August 1914 making 4 and 14 against Kent 2nd XI at Newport in what tragically proved to be his final match for Monmouthshire.

A week later he obtained a commission as 2nd Lieutenant in the 1st Battalion The Monmouthshire Regiment, Territorial Force, in August 1914, and underwent military training, before joining the Expeditionary Force in France and North Belgium during 1915. In early May, his battalion were engaged in the Battle of Frezenburg with their initial action, in conjunction with the London Regiment, being digging trench lines on the evening of May 2nd and 3rd, so that fire and support trenches were in place ahead of the battle. Their actions prompted heavy shelling by the German troops for several days, before on the morning of May 8th the order came to advance – it prompted a further pulse of shelling, plus gas attacks and heavy machine gun fire by the Germans, but Lieutenant Phillips and his battalion did not take a step backwards. Losses were heavy and as a captured British officer watching from the German lines subsequently recorded 'they came through a barrage of high explosive shells which struck them down by the dozens, but they never halted for a minute and continued the advance until hardly a man remained.'

So determined was the attack that German officers believed it could only have come from troops who were of sturdy and strong stature. Nothing was further from the truth, but the assault achieved its objective as rather than advancing further, the Germans dug in and reinforced their defences, adding further sulphur traps and machine gun positions. By the time they had completed this work, the Allies had regrouped and if the Germans had opted to move forward instead of consolidation, they could have made significant ground towards Ypres.

Edward, who was struck down by a combination of gas and machine gun fire, was given a battlefield burial where he fell near St. Julien, but in subsequent fighting, his grave was destroyed by shellfire. He therefore has no known grave and is commemorated on the Menin Gate. In a case of tragic coincidence, his younger brother Leslie Phillips, who was serving with the Welsh Regiment died at Frezenberg Ridge a fortnight later, within sight of the spot where his brother had been killed. He too is remembered on the Menin Gate, and one can only wonder at how their family dealt with such news in May 1915. Fortunately, their two other boys – Forrest and Herbert – survived the Great War.

Billy Geen (Newport CC and Monmouthshire)

Billy Geen was another talented sportsman from Monmouthshire to die in Flanders during 1915. Born in Newport on March 14th, 1891, William Purdon Geen was educated at Haileybury and Oxford University. He kept wicket for Haileybury from 1907 until 1910, and whilst still at school, he appeared behind the stumps in August 1909 for Monmouthshire in their Minor County Championship games against Carmarthenshire and Cornwall at Rodney Parade in Newport. He showed himself to be an adept wicket-keeper and a steady middle-order batsman, with a top score of 40 against Devon at Exeter in July 1912. This was his final summer of county cricket as by this time he had been studying at Oxford since October 1910, where he won three successive rugby Blues, as well as winning three Welsh rugby caps in 1912-13.

Indeed, rugby was Billy's main sport and he showed great dash in the centre or wing for Newport RFC between 1910 and 1914. Indeed, a contemporary of Geen's described how 'he used to zig-zag through most defences … He was essentially a player of moods, and rarely shone behind a beaten pack, though there were notable exceptions. He had an astounding power of quick side-stepping in a confined space that was bewildering in the extreme to his opponents. On his day he was so truly brilliant that one thought instinctively "only Geen could have done that"…'

Billy Geen.

Sport was very much in his family's blood as his uncle was Frank Purdon, the Irish-born sportsman who also won rugby honours with Wales and Newport, besides playing cricket for Monmouthshire and the South Wales CC. Billy had also been an outstanding schoolboy athlete, winning several boys races and putting his running and swerving talents to good use on the rugby fields for Newport, Oxford University, the Barbarians, Blackheath and Wales.

1912 was a headline season for the fair-haired centre as he played a leading role in Newport's 9-3 victory over the touring South African team. Due to his studies in Oxford at that time, he had not been Newport's first choice for the game, but when George Hirst failed to recover from an injury sustained at Leicester the previous week, Billy came into the starting line-up. He enjoyed a great game, and made what observers considered to be a match-winning tackle as he brought down Johan Stegmann when the Springbok was within sight of the try line.

Billy won rave reviews in the local newspapers after this and other eye-catching performances, so during mid-December 1912 he was called up by the Welsh selectors to play against the South Africans. He added two more Welsh caps to his tally, the first coming in January 1913 under the captaincy of Newport team mate Tommy Vile against England, and the second in March 1913 during a victory against Ireland at the St. Helen's ground in Swansea with his brilliant burst of speed, clever running and drop-kicks helped to create two tries in a closely-fought match which Wales won 16-13. Injuries in the 1913-14 season subsequently prevented him from winning further honours

In August 1914, Geen signed up to serve his country, joining, as 2nd Lieutenant, the Kings Royal Rifle Corps, part of the 14th (Light) Division. He undertook his initial training at Petworth in Sussex before being sent to the Western Front in May 1915 and for six weeks they fought in the Second Battle of Ypres. The battalion were then withdrawn from combat, but two days later they were sent back to support the 41st Brigade.

He was killed after being struck by a high explosive shell during heavy bombardment and an attack by German troops at Hooge, Flanders on July 31st, 1915, and was one of 350 casualties that day from his Battalion. Indeed, when recording events from that fateful day in the Regiment's records, Major John Hope wrote: 'Geen fought gloriously, and was last seen alive leading his platoon in a charge after being for hours subjected to liquid fire and every device the Germans could bring to bear to break through. Seventeen officers and 333 other ranks of this battalion were killed or injured in this engagement, in which officers and men showed themselves worthy of the best traditions of their Regiment.'

Valentine Davies (Crickhowell CC)

Valentine Davies was the son of Edward ('Teddy') Gratrex Davies, one of the leading cricketers of the late Victorian era and a man whose prowess on the cricketing fields of Wales won him fame and many friends. The son of the Land Agent of the Duke of Beaufort, Teddy Davies was born at Herbert Hall in Crickhowell and educated at Christ College, Brecon, before qualifying as a solicitor in 1871, and subsequently practising in Crickhowell for many years.

His cricketing prowess meant that Teddy Davies rubbed shoulders with the great and the good of the summer game. For example, when just fifteen years old, he appeared in July 1864, at Lord's alongside a similarly youthful W.G. Grace for the South Wales CC in their annual fixture against the MCC, whilst in July 1878 he was selected to play for South Wales CC against the Australian tourists at Swansea. Besides cricket, Teddy Davies was also very active with the Brecknockshire Volunteers as well as serving on the Breconshire County Council, but in 1899 he became unwell, suffering from cirrhosis of the liver followed by jaundice and he died in early June 1899 in Weston-super-Mare, where he staying at the time and hoping to recuperate from these various ailments.

Born in Crickhowell in October 1886, Valentine Llewelyn Gratrex Davies attended Felsted School in Essex where he showed great prowess as an all-round athlete, representing the school at cricket and also the Crickhowell club, though his father had passed away by the time he had progressed to the town's 1st XI, and for a couple of years Valentine Davies played important innings in the victories over Abergavenny, their local rivals and against whom a series of closely fought battles were staged each summer.

However, with his family having moved away from the Breconshire town, Valentine also decided to live away from Wales and in 1912 he emigrated to Canada where he became a cattle rancher in British Columbia. In September 1914 he was one of many men who enlisted with the Canadian Infantry, and in October 1914, Davies was a Private in the 7th Battalion Canadian Infantry, which arrived in the UK ahead of service on the Western Front.

In 1915 he and the rest of his unit were involved in operations in Flanders, with Canadian troops taking over from French troops a series of positions to the north of Ypres in April. By this time trench warfare had become deadlocked and in an attempt to change the position in Flanders the Germans decided to deploy poison gas. In the late afternoon of April 22nd, the German artillery concentrated its fire in a violent bombardment of the front line to the left of where Valentine and his colleagues were positioned. An hour later they opened the valves on 5,700 cylinders of chlorine gas, with long yellow clouds of asphyxiating gas being released to drift across into the French lines. The French colonial troops, who were on the immediate left of the Canadians, were swept back by the deployment of these poisonous fumes, with many of the French troops choking to death in their trenches, enabling three German divisions to pour into the gap which had been created.

This left the left flank of the Canadians completely exposed yet, despite being outnumbered by at least five to one, they continued fighting, realising that if they yielded their position, the whole of the British forces in the Ypres salient could be surrounded and captured, allowing German forces to reach the Channel ports. The Canadians held firm with two heroic, but costly counter-attacks, at Kitcheners' Wood and Mauser Ridge, giving the Germans the impression that the Canadians were a much larger force than they were. On April 24th the Germans attacked yet again in an attempt to obliterate the Salient once and for all, with an initial gas attack followed by waves of infantry. The fighting which followed saw Valentine Davies, amongst many others, lose their life, shredded by flying shrapnel and choking from the gas deployed by the German troops.

Yet the Canadian forces managed to grimly hang on and after three days of ceaseless fighting, they were relieved by other Allied troops who were able to quell the German advances, albeit at a massive loss of life, including the son of one of the most famous cricketers in Wales during the second half of the nineteenth century, who is commemorated at the Menin Gate memorial in Ypres.

Gerald Bailey (Usk Valley CC)

Lord Glanusk was a generous and kindly patron to cricket and other sporting activities in Breconshire, but during the Great War, Joseph Henry Russell Bailey and his wife lost two of their sons who were each on active service with the Grenadier Guards and the Royal Navy respectively.

Bailey was a member of the family whose wealth stemmed from the success of the Nantyglo ironworks. During the 1820s the ironmaster's grandfather purchased a number of country estates, including Glanusk Park in south-east Breconshire where he built a lavish mansion. Created the first Baron Glanusk in 1899, the Baileys' support for cricket included matches at Glanusk Park, always accompanied by plenty of liquid refreshment and a lavish post-match dinner or ball where the gentlemen could mix and mingle with the fairer sex.

During this period, Bailey also helped Crickhowell CC secure a regular home on his land at Glanusk, besides dipping into his pocket to financially

Lord Glanusk, leaning on a walking stick at a function staged at Brecon CC in 1908.

help the town club and to finance the creation of a pavilion at the ground for the use of the town club as well as the others – such as Usk Valley CC – who also played at the Baileys' ground and held fixtures against the likes of the Gentlemen of Worcestershire, the Gentlemen of Herefordshire, Oxford Harlequins and the MCC.

Born in November, 1893 the Hon. Gerald Sergison Bailey was the Baron's second son and, to his father's delight, showed much prowess as a hard-hitting batsman for the Usk Valley club as well as for the Crickhowell club. Lord Glanusk was also Commander of the Brecknockshire Battalion of the South Wales Borderers so he was also pleased when, after leaving school, Gerald opted for a military career, and joined the Grenadier Guards who were based at Chelsea Barracks. In mid-August 1914 the Guards were amongst the first wave of troops in the British Expeditionary Force, with Gerald and his colleagues arriving at Le Havre ready to do their bit for King and Country.

He survived on the Western Front for almost a year, before being killed – at the age of 22 – by a shell in Flanders on August 10th, 1915, with his body being laid to rest in the Guards Cemetery at Windy Corner, near Cuinchy. The following May, Lord Glanusk's third son – seventeen year-old Bernard Michael Bailey – was killed in the Battle of Jutland, whilst serving as a Midshipman on HMS Defence. He has no known grave, but is commemorated at the Plymouth Naval Memorial.

8

1915 – LOOS

The Battle of Loos was the largest British offensive mounted on the Western Front in 1915 and saw the use of specialist Royal Engineer tunnelling companies, who deployed mines underground in an attempt to disrupt enemy activities. It proved however to be a complete failure, with 60,000 British casualties and no ground being gained.

Before the advance, the British military commanders had high hopes for their troops, especially given the availability of gas. But their plans were thwarted by the initial shortage of artillery ammunition, and the preliminary bombardment, so essential for success in trench warfare, was weak. Prior to the British attack on September 25th, 1915, about 140 tons of chlorine gas was released. It met, though, with mixed success, especially as in many places it was blown back onto British lines. Through the inefficiency of the contemporary gas masks, many soldiers removed them as they could not see through the eyepieces, or could barely breathe with them on. Ironically, this led to some British soldiers being affected by their own gas.

Even worse followed when the call was give to start the attack, as British troops advanced across open fields within easy range of German machine guns and artillery. As a result, British losses were devastatingly high, although a group of British soldiers were able to break through weaker German defences and capture the town of Loos. It proved to be, however, only a temporary success as the next day, having drawn up formidable reserves, the Germans easily repulsed attempts to continue the advance. The fighting duly subsided on September 28th, with the British having retreated to their starting positions. There had been a heavy loss of life with casualties including three divisional commanders – George Thesiger, Thompson Capper and Frederick Wing – as well as Fergus Bowes-Lyon, brother to Elizabeth Bowes-Lyon, later the Queen Consort, of George VI and Queen Mother,

Further operations took place in October, with a British offensive on October 13th being thwarted by a lack of weapons, especially hand grenades. Military leaders considered another attack on November 7th, but the combination of heavy rain and accurate German shelling during the second half of October finally persuaded them to abandon the idea. The Battle also saw changes in the military leadership with Field Marshal Sir John French, who had already come in for much criticism before the battle, losing his remaining support in both the government and Army, and he was replaced by Douglas Haig as Commander of the British Expeditionary Force in December 1915.

The Battle was also the first time that the British troops used poison gas as a weapon to demoralize, injure and kill their opponents. The earliest uses of chemicals had been tear-inducing irritants, as opposed to fatal or disabling poisons, with the first large-scale use of the gas as a weapon coming on January 31st, 1915 when German troops fired 18,000 artillery shells containing liquid xylyl bromide on Russian positions to the west of Warsaw during the Battle of Bolimov. It had a limited effect as instead of vaporizing, the chemicals froze and did not have any major impact.

The first killing agent employed by the German military was chlorine – a strong irritant which inflicts damage to the eyes, nose, throat and lungs, whilst at high concentrations, can cause death by asphyxiation. It was first deployed to great effect by the Germans during the Battle of Ypres in April 1915 when the German Army had around 168 tons of chlorine deployed in 5,730 cylinders. Its use led to complaints from the Allied leaders who claimed the attack was a flagrant violation of international law. Germany, though, argued that the Hague Treaty had only banned chemical shells, rather than the use of gas projectors, and in subsequent exchanges in later May and early April, they used chlorine gas again. By this time, measures had been discovered by the Allied troops who covered their mouths and noses with a cloth, dampened by water or by urine, to counter the effect of the gases

Having expressed outrage at Germany's use of poison gas at Ypres, British troops responded by developing their own gas warfare capability. In the words of Lieutenant General Ferguson: 'Gas is a cowardly form of warfare which does not commend itself to me or other English soldiers... We cannot win this war unless we kill or incapacitate more of our enemies than they do of us, and if this can only be done by our copying the enemy in his choice of weapons, we must not refuse to do so.'

The first use of gas by the British therefore came at the Battle of Loos in late September 1915, but the use of chlorine proved to be a waste of time as the gas either lingered in no man's land or, in places, blew back on the British trenches. The situation was compounded when gas could not be released from all of the British canisters, and when German shells hit their lines, they released more gas amongst the troops. In subsequent battles, phosgene was used as unlike chlorine, it was a colourless gas with a less pungent odour, making it less easy to detect as well as being a more effective weapon.

However, it was often mixed with chlorine, which helped to spread the more dense phosgene, in a combination dubbed by Allied troops as White Star after the marking painted on the shells containing the deadly mixture. From 1917 mustard gas became the most widely used chemical weapon, largely because of the way it harassed and disabled its victims, whose skin quickly blistered, their eyes became sore and they began to vomit. Mustard gas also caused internal and external bleeding, and exposure to high levels of the gas led to a long and painful death, with perhaps four to five weeks of suffering.

Trevor Lewis (Garth CC)

Trevor Lewis was the youngest son of mining magnate Sir Henry Lewis who lived at Ty Nant House in Morganstown. Sir Henry had made his fortune by developing collieries in Ynyshir and Cilfynydd, as well as creating the Welsh Navigation Steam Coal company in the Ely Valley.

Sir Henry took a keen interest in cricket, and with the encouragement of neighbour and close friend Oakden Fisher, he laid out a cricket ground and pavilion in the southern part of the 30-acre estate of Ty Nant, largely for the use of Garth CC which had been created in 1893. Johnny Donovan, the professional who was attached to the Cardiff club, and who regularly appeared for Glamorgan, was hired as groundsman at Ty Nant which soon gained in popularity, aided no doubt by the fact that it lay next door to the local public house.

As a teenager, Trevor Lewis gleefully played for his father's club and enjoyed playing alongside some of the great and good in Cardiff society who staged matches in the grounds of Ty Nant. He also benefitted from some coaching by Donovan, and briefly harboured ambitions of possibly joining the town club and pitting his skills against the players of the other crack clubs in the region.

But thoughts of playing cricket became secondary at first to a career in mining, and he subsequently trained to become a mining engineer and secured a position in Bilbao in Spain. But his career – and tragically his life – was cut short by the outbreak of War, and he returned to the UK and joined the 5th Battalion South Wales Borderers, which had been formed at Brecon. Captain Lewis and the rest of the Battalion then undertook training at Park House near Tidworth, followed by periods at Basingstoke,

Burnham and Perham Down before heading to Le Havre in mid-July 1915 as preparations began for the Battle of Loos.

Tragically, Trevor was only to spend five weeks on the Western Front, during which his unit were engaged in the preparations for the Battle of Pietre, a diversionary action as the British troops readied themselves for the major action at Loos. On August 28th, 1915 Trevor lost his life as he tried to clear a group of unexploded grenades. One of them suddenly went off, killing the young engineer instantly. He was buried at the Merville Communal Cemetery in France.

Richard Davies Garnons Williams (Brecon CC and Breconshire)

Richard Davies Garnons Williams, the second son of Rev. Garnons Williams of Abercamlais in Powys, also lost his life in the Battle of Loos. Born in Llowes in Radnorshire on June 15th, 1856 Garnons Williams had been educated privately at Wimbledon School before going up to read Law at Trinity College Cambridge, where he showed great promise as a sportsman, playing both rugby and cricket for his college as well as the university, though he did not win a Blue in either sport.

During his summer vacations, Garnons Williams also played regularly for the Brecon Town and Garrison club, and in July 1875 he was chosen in the Breconshire side that met Glamorganshire at Brecon. Also in the Breconshire side were some other highly talented young sportsmen from Welsh public schools who were students at Oxford University, including Thomas Babington Jones from Christ College, Brecon, as well as C.P. Lewis of Llandovery College. Indeed, Jones and Lewis dismissed Glamorganshire for just 47 before Garnon Williams, batting at number eight in the order, top-scored with 34 before being run out as Breconshire amassed a first innings lead of 59. It proved to be a match-winning lead as well, as once again Jones and Lewis ripped through the Glamorganshire batting as they won by an innings and 14 runs.

After graduating, Garnons Williams opted to pursue a military career and entered the Royal Military College at Sandhurst before joining the Royal Fusiliers. His friendship with other sporting gentlemen in south Wales led to Garnons Williams joining the South Wales Cricket Club, who played

Richard Garnons Williams.

several matches each year against other gentlemen's clubs in the south-east of England, with the highlight of their cricketing calendar being an annual tour to London. In early June 1878 Garnons Williams was chosen to play in the two-day trial match held at the St. Helen's ground as the club's selectors ran their eye over the men who might be chosen for the away fixtures and the annual tour. Once again his batting impressed, being second-highest scorer in the first innings for the Next XVIII, and top-scorer in their second innings, but his military commitments prevented him from accepting invitations to appear for the South Wales CC.

Nevertheless, he continued to play a decent standard of club cricket, as well as rugby for whom he turned out for both Brecon RFC and Newport RFC. Indeed, his friendship with Richard Mullock of the Newport club in 1881 saw Garnons Williams chosen as one of the forwards in the Welsh team which Mullock assembled to play the first-ever rugby international against England at Richardson's Field in Blackheath. The team though was not fully representative of the nation's talent and it resulted in a crushing defeat for the Welsh side as the English side ran in thirteen tries in what proved to be Garnons Williams' only appearance at international level.

His military career continued to go from strength to strength, being promoted to the rank of Captain in 1885 whilst two years later he was appointed Adjutant of the 4th Battalion. He saw through his five years of service in this rank before retiring in May 1892 and returning to south Wales where he became a barrister, based in Brecon. He maintained his military links by serving with the 1st (Brecknockshire) Volunteers Battalion South Wales Borderers, where he was appointed to the honorary rank of Lieutenant-Colonel.

Garnons Williams rejoined the Army shortly after the outbreak of the Great War in 1914, rejoining the Royal Fusiliers as a Major, and was initially transferred to the South Wales Borderers to command the Brecknockshire Battalion. A year later he rejoined 12th Battalion Royal Fusiliers, and in September 1915 he led the battalion in actions at Loos, but sadly he lost his life during one of the assaults on German lines. Aged 59, Garnons Williams was the oldest of thirteen Welsh rugby internationals who were killed in the Great War, and is commemorated at the Loos Memorial.

Billy Hill (Briton Ferry Steel CC)

Billy Hill was one of the young men serving with the Royal Welsh Fusiliers whose role was to train, and arm, troops with the use of the poison gas. Billy, though, did not relish his role, and as a staunch chapel goer and

Billy Hill, sat on the front row, second right with his colleagues from the 13th Battalion of the Royal Welsh Fusiliers.

tee-totaller, he felt a certain amount of revulsion about what his duties entailed. 'He rarely spoke about his duties with the Royal Welsh Fusiliers,' said Billy's descendants, 'but he felt that he had to undertake these tasks out of a sense of duty.'

The perk of his job was representing the Battalion in cricket matches staged in Britain and also in France, as well behind enemy lines, matches were staged to occupy the minds of the troops and to boost morale.

Hill had made his debut for Briton Ferry Steel CC at the age of fifteen in 1910, before leading the club between 1928 to 1937. For much of his career, he was a competent batsman, an outstanding cover fielder and a very deceptive leg-break and googly bowler, besides being an outstanding hockey player, winning a place in a final Welsh trial as a centre-half, before rising to the position of Works Manager at the Briton Ferry steelworks.

Selwyn Biggs (Cardiff CC and Glamorgan)

Selwyn Biggs was a member of the well-known Cardiff brewing family who played county cricket for Glamorgan and rugby for both Cardiff RFC and

Selwyn Biggs in his Cardiff RFC blazer and rugby kit.

Wales. Whilst in his final year at school in Cardiff, Selwyn followed his elder brother Norman into the town's rugby team, before also winning a place in the Cardiff 1st XI where he showed rich promise as a lively opening bowler.

In 1891 the talented nineteen year-old made his debut for Glamorgan against the MCC in the august surroundings of Lord's, and for the next nine years he played, with some success, on a fairly regular basis for the county side. In 1892 he took 7-64 against Monmouthshire, before claiming ten wickets in the match against the same opponents the following year.

His wicket-taking abilities also won him a place in the South Wales side that played EM Grace's Gloucestershire XI in a fund-raising fixture at the Arms Park in 1894 as Glamorgan commenced their campaign for higher recognition as a Minor County. Biggs claimed another ten-wicket haul in 1896 against the MCC at the Arms Park, including a career-best return of 8-48 from sixteen overs. By this time, he had completed his legal training and his work as a solicitor subsequently prevented him from playing regularly for the Welsh county following their elevation to the Minor County Championship from 1897.

However, he found time in the winter months, to train and play for Cardiff RFC and after some impressive performances at fly-half for the town club, he made his debut for Wales in the opening game of the 1895 Home Nations Championship against England at Swansea. This was the first of nine caps which Selwyn won, in addition to captaining Cardiff RFC in 1897-98. He also played rugby for Richmond, London Welsh, Bath, Somerset and the Barbarians, whilst after retiring from cricket, he also proved to be more than adept at golf.

However, his sporting career and legal work came to an abrupt end as he was badly gassed during the Battle of Loos and was an invalid for the rest of his life.

Charles Gomery (Blaina CC)

The Battle of Loos also claimed the life of Charles Gomery of Blaina, a

A Biggs family photograph with Selwyn sat in the middle.

thriving club in the Monmouthshire valleys. Charles had enlisted in 1914 with the 6th Battalion the King's Shropshire Light Infantry shortly before the birth of his fourth child. By the time Reginald was born, Sgt. Major Gomery had completed his basic training at Blackdown Camp before, in April 1915, heading to Larkhill on Salisbury Plain for a final round of intensive training. In mid-July the Battalion went by train to the Kent coast where they subsequently completed a rough crossing to Boulogne, before arriving at 3 a.m. in torrential rain at Osterhove Rest Camp. After some sustenance from the Salvation Army, the Battalion marched over cobbled roads and through thick mud to Borre, where they were then introduced to life in the trenches by the West Yorkshire Regiment.

Charles and the rest of the platoon then took part in preparations for the Battle of Loos. Tragically, he was one of four officers and 59 other ranks from the Battalion to be killed during the battle, with Charles dying on October 2nd, 1915 at the age of just 41 from wounds received during a sudden German counter-attack.

News of his death duly reached Blaina where his wife Mary was left to bring up alone the four young Gomerys. Like the thousands of other war widows the next few years were very tough for the family, but thankfully John, who had barely been five when his father was killed, gave her plenty to smile about as he subsequently played a leading role with the town club during the inter-war period, acting as their captain in 1938 and 1939, as well as being their Secretary between 1934 and 1938.

9

1916 – THE SOMME

The Battle of the Somme took place between July 1st and November 18th, 1916 as the British Expeditionary Forces and the French Army mounted a joint offensive, and for the first time in combat, deployed the use of tanks.

The plan for the Somme offensive stemmed from discussions at the Chantilly Conference which took place between December 6th and 8th, 1915, chaired by General Joseph Joffre, the commander-in-chief of the French Army. The outcome was agreement that simultaneous offensives would be mounted on all fronts with the Russians attacking to the east, the Italians to the south in the Alps, whilst on the Western Front, the Anglo-French would attack near the Somme River.

Sir Douglas Haig, the Commander-in-Chief of the British Expeditionary Forces favoured an offensive in Flanders in an attempt to drive the Germans away from the Belgian coast and their U-boat base at Bruges. But as they were the junior partner in the alliance, they had to comply with French policy and the plan was subsequently amended with a combined offensive close to the Somme River, prior to a British offensive in Flanders. But in February 1916 the Germans began an offensive against the French at Verdun, and with heavy losses sustained by the French, the plans for the Somme were amended yet again with the British troops now assuming the main role for an offensive involving twenty-two infantry divisions after a relentless week-long bombardment by the Allied artillery with over a million shells.

One of the key areas in the middle phase of the offensive came between late July and late September at the village of Pozières where a chance existed to breach the Germans' northern defences. Several attempts had already been made by the Fourth Army as well as by Australian and New Zealand troops before the main assault started on the evening of July 23rd. After much shelling, the village was successfully taken, but the Germans then made three counter-attacks, before commencing themselves a prolonged bombardment of Pozières and the surrounding area. Further advances by the Allies into German occupied territory met with stiff resistance and further heavy loss of life ensued before the goal of taking Mouquet Farm was finally achieved on September 26th.

The Battle of the Somme proved to be one of the largest of all the battles during the War, besides being one of the bloodiest military operations ever undertaken. Over a million men were either wounded or killed, and the first day of the Battle saw the British Army suffer its worst day in its history with almost 60,000 casualties being sustained.

For the Welsh contingent, a massive loss of life occurred at Mametz Wood as it literally proved to be a baptism of fire for Britain's new volunteer armies with those who had received only a small amount of training being slaughtered in their thousands. Many of the Pals Battalions, comprising men from the same town who had enlisted to serve together, ended up dying together as the British suffered monumental losses, with the campaign itself, having a profound social impact.

Conditions in the trenches bordered on the inhumane, and an entry in his diary for July 1916 by John Thomas Cratchley, who served in the Sheffield City battalion, summed up the appalling conditions faced by those serving at Neuve Chapelle: 'There were scores of graves of unknown British and German soldiers, and rats like rabbits. One of our men one night while sleeping in a dug-out got part of his ear bitten off by one of these giant rats. The rats also bored down into the graves of these soldiers, which appeared to be like rabbit holes.'

By the time the battle ended, the British and French troops had moved just six miles into German territory, and were still three miles away from Bapaume, one of their major objectives. Today, the word Somme has become a byword for futile and indiscriminate slaughter, and General Haig's tactics still remain controversial.

Humphrey Bircham (Cardiff CC, Newport CC, Glamorgan and Monmouthshire)

Humphrey Bircham was one of the Welsh soldiers to die during the attacks near Pozières. Humphrey was typical of the gentlemen cricketers who played with success in country house matches during the late 1890s and 1900s, besides making occasional appearances in Minor County cricket. He made one appearance for Glamorgan in 1893, having also played the previous year for Monmouthshire.

Born in Brecon in 1875, he was the son of Francis Bircham, who himself had served in the Royal Horse Artillery, besides playing for both Breconshire and Monmouthshire. Humphrey was something of a schoolboy prodigy at Eton College, playing for the 1st XI before his 17th birthday, and holding a place in his final year at the College in 1893. Later that summer, the talented schoolboy appeared for Glamorgan in their trial match against a Cardiff and District XI, before accepting a place at Sandhurst and starting his military career.

Having opted for a military career, the talented batsman was never called up again by the Glamorgan selectors, despite some useful performances in club cricket for Cardiff CC and Newport CC, as well as for I Zingari, the MCC, the Royal Marines, Greenjackets and the United Services. His brother Bertie who was a captain in the Hampshire Regiment also played Minor County cricket for Monmouthshire as well as for the MCC.

Humphrey began his own military career with the King's Royal Rifle Corps in February 1896, rising to the rank of captain in 1901 and was twice mentioned in dispatches during the Boer War, during which he was wounded at Brakenlaatge in October 1901. Humphrey was elevated to the rank of Major in February 1914 and commanded the 2nd Battalion the King's Royal Rifle Corps during their service on the Western Front including at Ypres. Humphrey was mentioned several times in dispatches and his gallant actions in leading his men earned him the DSO.

In July 1916 Humphrey also took part in the Battle of the Somme, but his bravery was to cost him his life. His unit were deployed on the evening of July 23rd to mount an attack north of Mametz Wood on a newly dug 'switch' line to the north-east of the village of Pozières. The Rifles were supported to the left by the 2nd Battalion Royal Sussex Regiment and to the right by the 10th Battalion the Gloucestershire Regiment. Prior to their attack, there was an intense artillery barrage for around seven minutes, but this lit up the skyline and alerted the German troops to the presence of the Rifles poised to attack their trenches. To make matters worse the attacks to the left and right-hand flanks failed and the Germans counter-attacked on both flanks with hand grenades and shells. Humphrey was struck and fatally wounded during this ultimately futile operation and his unit withdrew back to their original position the following day.

Harry Fisher (Garth CC)

Harry Fisher, who lost his life fighting in the Battle of the Somme, was the son of Colonel Oakden Fisher, a member of an influential family in cricketing circles in the late Victorian and early Edwardian era in the Cardiff area. His grandfather was George Fisher, a Director of the Taff Vale Railway and Chairman of Cardiff Gaslight and Coke Company, whose son Oakden became a leading engineer with the Taff Vale Railway besides being a decent cricketer with the Cardiff club and playing for the Glamorganshire side between 1870 and 1872.

The Fishers mixed with the great and good of south Wales society and from the early 1880s lived at Tŷ Mynydd, an impressive mansion in the thriving suburb of Radyr. Their neighbours were coal magnate Sir Henry Lewis, and through the encouragement of Oakden, Lewis started to finance the creation of a cricket ground and pavilion in the southern part of his home at Tŷ Nant. Sir Henry subsequently presented the ground to the Garth club in 1893 which he and Oakden had formed, partly so that they could enjoy healthy recreation in their suburban retreat, but also so that they could enhance their political and social contacts, staging cricket matches against other teams such as Fairwater and Llanishen from some of the other well-to-do and fashionable parts of the suburban fringe that had rapidly developed around the coal metropolis.

To his father's delight young Harry showed prowess at cricket whilst attending Malvern School and during his summer holidays, the youngster featured in many of Garth's matches during the 1890s. Oakden had also been a Colonel in the Glamorgan Artillery Volunteers so he was delighted

Radyr CC with HO Fisher in the middle row, second left.

when Harry opted for a military career. Harry's military duties saw him move away from Radyr, and he became a regular officer, commissioned as a 2nd Lieutenant in the Wiltshire Regiment in 1899. He fought in the Boer War and was mentioned in dispatches, before returning to the UK and marrying Annabella Dansey of Richards Castle in Ludlow.

By the outbreak of the Great War, Harry had become a Lieutenant-Colonel in the Duke of Edinburgh's Wiltshire Regiment and he duly saw active service during 1915 and 1916 on the Western Front. Sadly it was to cost him his life, ironically after being temporarily attached as Commanding Officer of the 12th Battalion the York and Lancaster Regiment as they prepared for front-line duty in the autumn of 1916.

On October 2nd, 1916 Fisher and his Battalion were deployed to the Festubert area, and early the following morning he was undertaking a reconnaissance mission with other officers to assess the Regiment's next move, but at 3.45 a.m. he was shot through the head and killed instantly by a German sniper. His body was duly laid to rest at the Le Touret Cemetary. Oakden Fisher had died early the previous year, but the surviving members of his family were dealt a further loss when Harry's older brother Herbert, who was a Lieutenant-Colonel in the RFA, died in July 1919.

Charles Davies (Llandovery College and Glamorgan)

Charles Davies also died during events during the early part of the Battle of the Somme. Charles was the son of Daniel Davies, the owner of The Bear Hotel in Cowbridge, and like his elder brother Ewan, he was a talented all-round sportsman playing rugby for Cardiff, Swansea and Caerphilly, besides representing Glamorgan in their fund-raising friendly in August 1913 against an XI raised by Sir Harry Webb which included Gilbert Jessop and several other famous Gloucestershire cricketers as well as George Robey, the cricket-mad music hall entertainer.

At the time, the nineteen year-old Davies was regarded as one of the bright young prospects in cricket in south Wales having kept wicket with great aplomb for both Cowbridge School and Llandovery

Charles Davies.

College. Having secured a place at Brasenose College in Oxford for 1914, there were many who hoped that the young Welshman would press for a cricket Blue.

This was not to be, as in August 1915 he enlisted with the Royal Dublin Fusiliers and after basic training departed the following late spring for France to prepare for the Battle of the Somme. The Fusiliers subsequently made their base at Mailly Wood, but the weather conditions in June 1916 were atrocious, and as their official diary duly recorded: '8/6/16: Rain commenced – much work cleaning and draining trenches. 9/6/16: Weather still very bad and work held up in consequence.'

Given these grim conditions and adverse weather, the Fusiliers were eager to gain information on the precise whereabouts of enemy lines so on the evening of June 8th, Lieutenant Davies, plus three others, set out to reconnoitre the German lines. Only one of the party eventually made it back to the British trenches, with Davies being captured after suffering serious wounds. Indeed, the surviving member of the party recalled: 'The last I saw of Charlie was when he was struggling with a big German in one of their trenches. Charlie was a hard case and refused to believe he was going to die, although he had been badly wounded in five places and was heavily bleeding.'

Davies is believed to have died in captivity the following day although much mystery surrounds events following his capture, with the German authorities eventually confirming in September 1917 that Davies had died shortly after being taken prisoner.

Henry Gainey (Radyr CC)

Henry Gainey was a talented all-round sportsman who played both cricket and golf with distinction. He was one of seven children born to Samuel Gainey, a man who had risen up the social ladder during the late Victorian and early Edwardian era. Samuel started life as a labourer with the Taff Vale Railway, before becoming a crane driver at a quarry in the Radyr area. He subsequently became a publican and was mine host of 'The Old Post' in Bonvilston when Henry was born in 1889.

Despite moving to live in the Vale of Glamorgan Samuel appeared regularly for Radyr cricket club, and to his delight, Henry subsequently followed his father's footsteps by playing between 1908 and 1910 for the local club, besides becoming a publican himself shortly before the outbreak of War. By this time he was also the golf professional at Ton Pentre Golf Club

In August 1914 Henry became a member of Kitchener's New Army as he joined the 11th Battalion the Devonshire Regiment which had been formed at Exeter. He initially joined as a private and after promotion to Corporal was commissioned as 2nd Lieutenant in the 8th Devons. The recruits undertook training at Rushmoor Camp in Aldershot before moving to Farnham and preparing for embarkation to the Western Front.

In the summer of 1915 Henry and the rest of the Battalion sailed to Le Havre before moving towards the Somme where the Regiment were engaged in the bloody maneouvres in and around Mametz, some 6.5 kilometres east of the town of Albert. On July 1st Henry and his colleagues, together with those of the 9th Battalion successfully captured the village, although it was at a heavy human cost with over 160 soldiers being killed on the first day alone.

After consolidating their position, the 8th Battalion took part in a series of co-ordinated attacks to the east of Mametz Wood at Bazentin Ridge. The ground was taken but Henry was one of hundreds killed during the fighting on July 14th and his body was subsequently laid to rest in Flatiron Copse Cemetery.

Horace Thomas (Monmouth School)

Horace Wyndham Thomas, the Welsh rugby international and decent all-round sportsman was also killed on September 3rd, 1916 during the Battle of the Somme. Born in July 1890 to the Rector of Pentyrch, he initially attended Bridgend County School, before winning a scholarship in 1905 – at the princely sum of £40 per annum – to Monmouth School where he subsequently shone at both music and sport.

Indeed, Horace showed great prowess at rugby, athletics, hockey and cricket, with the youngster captaining the school's 1st XI in the latter two sports. His skills at hockey also affected his batting style as *The Monmouthian* commented how he 'played with a straight bat, but when trying to drive he was inclined to pivot on his left foot instead of following straight through. An alert and agile point with a safe pair of hands, he was also a reliable bowler with an awkward ball on the left stump.'

In 1908 his singing talents won him a choral scholarship – at £110 per annum – to King's College, Cambridge, where he was duly in residence from the autumn of 1909 until the summer of 1912. During this time, Horace read History besides continuing to shine in a number of sporting fields, representing the university in athletics, besides playing cricket for his college and the Cambridge Crusaders. His efforts whilst up at London also drew the attention of the Glamorgan selectors, but despite some excellent performances in the inter-college competition, he didn't win selection for the Welsh county.

However, His major sport was rugby, for which he won a Blue whilst at Cambridge. He was also selected for the Welsh side against the touring Springboks in 1912, despite an agreement which stated that no Welsh player could be chosen to represent the country if they played within the London area. However, eight selectors travelled to Queens Club, Kensington to watch Horace play in the Varsity match, which saw the Light Blues victorious for the first time in seven years, and his outstanding form duly saw his selection for the match against the South Africans.

He went on to play one further match for Wales, under the captaincy of Tommy Vile, in Wales' opening match of the 1913 Five Nations Championship against England, besides playing for Blackheath and the Barbarians. In mid-January 1913 he left Britain for India having secured a lucrative appointment working for Messrs Turner and Morrison as part of the Calcutta Harbour Defence Force. Whilst in Calcutta he also joined, and later became captain of the Calcutta Football Club besides playing cricket for Calcutta in domestic competitions.

Horace returned to Britain shortly before Christmas 1915 following the escalation in the War and joined the 16th Battalion the Rifle Brigade. He was soon to be in action on French soil as British troops advanced on the village of Guillemont which held a strategic importance in the area's transport network. In what proved to be his last letter home, Thomas wrote: 'Without wishing to be dramatic or boastful, I can say, truthfully that I am not afraid of death, my life has been a happy one – thanks to you all from the bottom of my heart.'

On September 3rd, at the age of 26, Horace was killed as his Battalion advanced north of the River Ancre, in an action which cost the lives of many British troops. According to the Battalion's official record Horace was 'hit by a shell, being blown to bits and killed outright ... I am afraid he will be posted as missing'. Horace Wyndham Thomas is commerated at the Thiepval memorial.

Frederick Turner (Cardiff CC)

The Battle of the Somme also claimed the life of Frederick William Robertson Turner, a 25 year-old lieutenant who, back at his family's home in Cardiff, had been starting to make a name for himself with the town's cricket club. Like his father James, Frederick was a skilled engineer and was just commencing an apprenticeship in his father's company when War broke out.

Born in July 1891, he had grown up in the leafy suburb of Lisvane, to the north of the Taff-side town, before attending Mill Hill School in north-west London from 1904. He thrived at his academic work, as well as at cricket, and by the time of the Great War, he was playing for Cardiff CC, having won a place in the 1st XI following some impressive innings for the junior sides, as well as for Mill Hill.

He was amongst the first batch of volunteers in 1914 serving initially as a Lieutenant in the Welsh Horse, before being swiftly promoted to the rank of Sergeant and receiving a commission with the Royal Engineers in 1915. Shortly afterwards, he departed for France and from July 1916 was involved in manoeuvres associated with the Battle of the Somme. Tragically he was killed on the morning of August 5th, 1916 with his Battalion Captain recording that 'he was a very able soldier, a splendid comrade, and one of those rare people who did everything well.'

David Roberts (Ferndale CC)

Private David John Roberts of Ferndale was typical of the rank and file soldiers, and a man of relatively modest means, to die in the skirmishes leading up to the Battle of the Somme. His background was, unlike many of his senior and commanding officers, who had been educated at a public school or university in Wales or England, as David had grown up in the mining community of the Rhondda Valley.

Indeed, Ferndale had been one of the first communities to be industrialized in the Rhondda Valley, with the first mine being sunk in 1857. It was also a community affected by two colliery disasters, which in 1867 and again in 1869, killed in excess of 230 miners. Recreational activities had begun in Ferndale during the 1880s with cricket and rugby taking place on the sloping playing fields at Darran Park. Within a decade, both teams were playing in the Glamorgan League, with crowds of around 3,000 watching Ferndale RFC play the likes of Neath, Llanelli, Bath and Pontypridd, besides being entertained at half-time by the Ferndale Prize Band. During the summer months the cricket team also drew a healthy crowd, especially against neighbours and rivals in the Rhondda or Glamorgan League.

David had been born in July 1889 to Richard Roberts – an engineman at the Ferndale Colliery – who together with his wife Catherine had moved from their native Pembrey in Carmarthenshire to the Rhondda in the late-nineteenth century. After leaving school, David joined his father at the Colliery where he worked underground as an electrical switchman, besides showing great prowess at cricket, as well as tennis and croquet. Following a series of fine performances for the Ferndale side, the young colliery worker was chosen to play for the Glamorgan League XI in 1913 and again in 1914. However, the latter year proved to be a very bitter-sweet one for David as his delight at playing for the representative League side was tempered by the death of his mother in July.

Like many who played for the clubs in the League, his cricketing skills had been largely self-taught and David had received little formal coaching whilst at school in Ferndale. His strength, developed by working underground and at the pit head, meant that he was a useful all-rounder, and he enjoyed the camaraderie with his fellow colleagues on Wednesday evenings and Saturday afternoons when they could play in the summer sun rather than undertaking their normal rotutine of heavy, manual labour.

Despite some match-winning innings and decent spells of seam bowling for Ferndale, there was no chance of David ever progressing to playing county cricket for Glamorgan. For a start, he was never going to give up his job in the colliery and play the game on a professional basis, especially as there were plenty of other professionals, including many veterans of English sides who were being hired by the leading clubs elsewhere in the Valleys and on the coastal plain. The rest of the county team was populated by amateurs, and the people who, unlike David, had the time to play the game as well as having the right social contacts.

But the Great War united men like David with these amateurs, and as hostilities increased in the lead-up to the Battle of the Somme the men, who had relished the chance of rolling up their sleeves and playing cricket on their half-day afternoons on the rough fields adjacent to the rows of terraced housing, fought – and died – alongside those who had worn the striped blazers and played in more rarified surroundings, far from the smoke and noise of the industrial valleys of south Wales.

In 1915 David enlisted with the 7th Battalion the King's Shropshire Light Infantry, and after training at Bournemouth, Romsey and Aldershot, he sailed with his colleagues on September 28th across the English Channel to Boulogne. He soon saw active service on the Western Front, and was involved in actions to the south of Ypres near the village of St.Eloi which was situated on the road towards Messines. German troops were situated on slightly higher ground to the south of the village which gave them a tactical advantage of having excellent observation of British positions.

Since the summer of 1915, the area had been the scene of mine warfare as British troops attempted to tunnel under and into German-held territory. David's skills, honed in the mines of the Rhondda Valley, came in very useful as the British slowly advanced on enemy lines. Constant shelling from German artillery had also produced a series of craters into which British troops had been able to advance and establish new positions as well as new mines. Their progress though was hampered by rainfall which filled many of the craters with water and mud, but by the spring of 1916 a series of six mines had been successfully dug.

On March 27th, the British troops, augmented by Canadian divisions, exploded the piles of dynamite they had placed in the many underground caverns which they had created by the tunnels. The explosions caused trenches on both sides to collapse, leaving seven large craters and many smaller ones, the occupation of which the Allied and German troops then fought over for three weeks. It proved to be a muddy and bloody battle as further storms turned the craters into quagmires, whilst the Canadians suffered over 1,300 casualties during thirteen days of quite confused fighting.

By early May, David and his Battalion had retreated to the positions they had occupied in late March when the assault had begun, but with plans afoot for the Battle of the Somme later in the year, there was a desperate need to quell the German resistance and to force them off the ridge, once and for all. A counter-attack with new mines was therefore planned, but tragically these plans were to cost David his life, as he was killed – at the age of 26 – in manoeuvres on May 10th trying to establish a new tunnel under German positions.

Dr. Gwyn Thomas (Neath CC and Glamorgan)

Gwyn Thomas was the eldest son of Dr. J.W. Thomas, a former Mayor of Neath, and he followed in his father's footsteps by becoming a leading personality in the sporting life of the West Glamorgan town besides winning the MC in November 1916 during the Battle of the Somme.

Gwyn attended Neath Grammar School before reading Medicine at Edinburgh University. Despite his studies, he still found plenty of time to represent Neath at both rugby and cricket. In particular, he was a bold striker of the ball, and was renowned for the way he freely scored against all types of bowling, often almost effortlessly lifting the ball out of the Gnoll ground, and into the gardens of adjoining houses.

His success in club cricket led to his selection in Glamorgan's Minor County game against Carmarthenshire at Swansea in 1910, but 'Dr. Gwyn' scored only five out of his side's mammoth total of 531-9 dec en route to a comfortable innings victory. He was chosen again in 1911 when the match with Buckinghamshire was staged at The Gnoll but the local man met with little success again as he was dismissed for a duck.

Despite these failures he was called up by the Glamorgan selectors on four occasions in 1912, besides appearing for the Gentlemen of Glamorgan against

Dr. Gwyn Thomas.

the Players. Yet again, he met modest success with the bat, but his outstanding from in club cricket led to further games for the Welsh county in 1913 and again in 1914 as the county's selectors hoped that Gwyn's good form for Neath would eventually rub off on his county appearances.

Following the outbreak of War, Gwyn enlisted as a medical corporal in the Brigade Field Ambulance section of Scottish Horse before forsaking his medical duties and transferring to the Northumberland Fusiliers where he rose to the rank of 2nd Lieutenant. Gwyn was in the 1st Battalion the Fusiliers when they were involved in the Battle of the Somme, and was awarded the Military Cross for his gallant actions in a raid on German lines. According to his citation, Gwyn 'advanced with a trench gun through a heavy artillery and machine gun barrage, before taking up his position with a company of another battalion, in conjunction with which he captured a battery of hostile trench mortars. Later in the day, he also advanced with the other company.'

After demobilisation in 1919, he returned to south Wales and resumed his sporting career, which also saw him captain Neath R.F.C. during the 1920-21 season, besides being chosen as a reserve in the Welsh side. As far as his cricketing was concerned, he continued to be a heavy scorer in club cricket for Neath, and again in 1920 represented the Gentlemen of Glamorgan against the Players, besides playing in the Welsh county's matches against Surrey 2nd XI, Cheshire, Devon, Wiltshire, Monmouthshire and Carmarthenshire.

As before the hostilities he failed to score a half-century in these games and after Glamorgan's elevation into the County Championship, he was viewed by some to be a little too loose in his strokeplay to succeed in first-class cricket. However, in 1922 he was called up for the match against Leicestershire at the Arms Park at the end of the 1922 season when other batsmen were not available. He duly scored 21 and 6 against the East Midlands attack in what proved to be his one and only first-class appearance.

He died in Neath on April 10th, 1932 after a short illness.

Phil Hornsby (Llandudno CC)

The son of the headmaster of Llandudno Church School, Phil Hornsby had been born in Menai Bridge in 1890 when his father John Edward held a position at a school in Anglesey. The family duly moved to Llandudno where Phil developed into a fine cricketer, playing with distinction for the town's cricket club and in one game taking 6-16 against an XI raised by Lord Mostyn who owned the ground where the town's cricket club became established.

On leaving school, Phil trained as a book-keeper and worked for a fishing company which sent out vessels from the resort town on a daily basis to catch fish for the local inhabitants and the thousands of tourists who flocked into the popular resort on the north Wales coast. His life, though, dramatically changed when he joined the South Wales Borderers in 1914, but after serving on the Western Front, he was sent back to Llandudno in December of that year after suffering from extreme frost bite.

Phil spent several months recovering at his parent's home in Morfa Road, before returning to France and serving as a Captain in the A Company of the 10th Battalion of the Borderers, but on September 2nd, 1918 he was killed during the Battle of the Somme. His body was laid to rest at the Sailly-Saillisel Cemetery.

David Cuthbert Thomas (Christ College, Brecon and the Gentlemen of Glamorgan)

Born on June 16th, 1895, David Cuthbert Thomas was the only son of Reverend Evan Thomas, the vicar of Llanedy near Ammanford, and between 1906 and 1914 he enjoyed a successful school career at Christ College, Brecon. From an early age 'Tommy' shone at cricket, rugby and hockey, besides showing rich promise in Classical Studies and editing the school magazine. His height served him well in the school's 1st XV where he dominated the lines-out whilst his good reach and unflappable temperament saw him play for the 1st XI for three seasons.

D.C. Thomas.

Tommy's abilities as a steady and technically correct batsman drew the attention of the Glamorgan selectors who were on the look-out for home-grown talent. In June 1914 he made a match-winning innings for Christ College as they defeated Builth Wells CC and, after a decent run of innings for the school, the nineteen year-old was chosen in their all-amateur XI – known as the Gentlemen of Glamorgan – for the match against their counterparts from Carmarthenshire at Llanelli on July 27th and 28th, 1914. It also happened to be the last week of the summer term with the youngster getting special permission from the Headmaster to play in the game.

His parents and girlfriend were delighted to travel the short distance from Ammanford to Stradey Park to watch the game, which very nearly

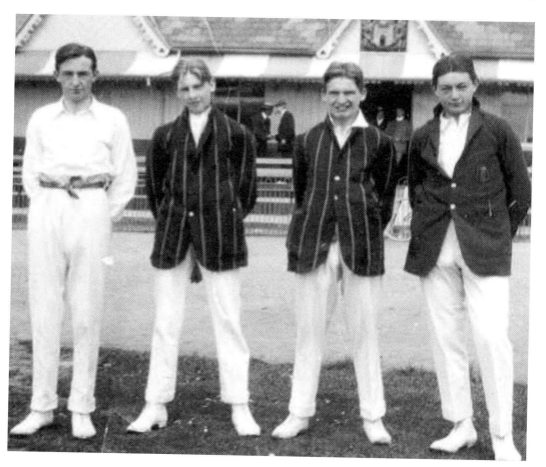

D.C. Thomas (second left) with a colleague and members of the Swansea Wednesday XI at St. Helen's in 1914.

saw the youngster play a match-winning role. Batting at number ten, Tommy only scored a single in the first innings before being bowled by Ernie Gee.

After a promising first innings, the Carmarthenshire Gentlemen set the Glamorgan side a target of 321 to win with Arthur O'Bree – a Colonel in the Territorial Army – scoring all around the wicket as he raced to his hundred. As O'Bree sailed past 150, it looked like the stockbroker might see the visitors to a thrilling victory, but a clatter of wickets occurred and young Tommy came to the wicket to continue the good work. O'Bree's wicket eventually fell for 199, and Tommy was caught off the bowling of Jack Bevan for seven. His replacement Archie Pritchard, the Swansea fast bowler, struck a couple lusty blows before departing as Carmarthenshire secured a narrow victory by five runs.

Despite the defeat, it had been a pleasant introduction to county cricket for the 19-year-old, and although he had scored just one and seven, his nimble and athletic fielding had impressed the watching officials who believed that he was someone to keep an eye on. However, the country was already on a War footing and rather than looking forward to his next county match, Tommy joined the Public Schools Battalion in August 1914 and trained at RMC Sandhurst, before securing a commission as a 2nd Lieutenant in the 3rd Battalion, Royal Welch Fusiliers.

He subsequently joined the 1st Battalion and was attached to the 7th Infantry Division. Also in the Regiment were the famous writers Robert Graves and Siegfried Sassoon, with whom Tommy became close friends. Each wrote poems about the young Welshman with the following being Sassoon's description of their first meeting in May 1915:

'He has unpacked and arranged his belongings, and was sitting on his camp-bed polishing a perfectly new pipe. He looked up at me. Twilight was falling and there was only one small window, but even in the half-light his face surprised me by its candor and freshness. He had obvious good looks which go with fair hair and firm features, but it was the radiant integrity of his expression which astonished me. While I was getting ready for dinner we exchanged a few remarks. His tone of voice was simple and reassuring, like his appearance. How does he manage to look like that? I thought; and for the moment I felt all my age. His was the bright countenance of truth; ignorant and undoubting; incapable of concealment but strong in reticence and in modesty.'

Early in 1916 the Battalion were involved in manoeuvres which were part of the Battle of the Somme, with Tommy and the others enduring bitterly cold temperatures whilst in the trenches. By early March, they were in the vicinity of Fricourt in Picardy and Tommy's mood must have been uplifted by the receipt of a food parcel from his former friends at Christ College. He duly wrote a letter of thanks back to the school, but tragically, it proved to be the last letter he wrote back to Brecon.

On the evening of March 18th, Tommy accompanied a party from C Company out into no-man's-land, near a building known as The Citadel, to check the barbed wire defences, to repair anything that was damaged and to strengthen any gaps where the Germans had been trying to cut through. This was routine work at night for the British, but it was fraught with danger as the Germans were also busy in the dark. If a flare went up the men would remain motionless – instinct was to duck or fall to the ground, but the slightest movement would draw fire from German snipers or from a machine-gun placement. Sometimes they would fire random shots into the darkness hoping to hit someone.

This was the case that fateful night for Tommy as at around 10.30pm a bullet struck him in the throat. He was able to make it back to the first-aid station unassisted and, initially, all seemed well as a dressing was applied by the regimental doctor who was a throat specialist in civilian life. "You'll be all right, only don't raise your head for a bit." said the medic. But the wound began to haemorrhage with Tommy taking a letter to his family and fiancée from his pocket and gave it to an orderly, saying "Post this!" They were the last words he would utter as shortly afterwards he started to choke. The doctor returned and desperately tried a tracheotomy, but it was too late and shortly afterwards, Tommy died.

His death deeply affected Graves and Sassoon, with the former writing the poem in Thomas' memory, besides devoting several lines to him in his autobiography , describing him as a popular and helpful chap with a smiling face and gentle personality. 'I felt David's death worse than any other since I had been in France' Graves later recalled, 'but it did not anger me as it did Siegfried. He was acting transport-officer and every evening, when he came up with the rations, he went out on patrol looking for Germans to kill. I just felt empty and lost.'

The following morning Sassoon, convulsed with grief, rode up to the nearby woods and wailed for his fallen companion. As he wrote, 'Today I knew what it means to find the soul washed pure with tears, and the load of death was lifted from my heart. So I wrote his name in chalk on the beech-tree stem, and left a garland of ivy there, and a yellow primrose for his yellow hair and kind grey eyes, my dear, my dear.'

Tommy also appears as 'Dick Tiltwood' in Sassoon's semi-autobiographical novel, in addition to several other poems as the writer became increasingly embittered and disenchanted with the War:

I thought of him, and knew that he was dead;
I thought of his dark hour, and laughter killed,
And the shroud hiding his dear, happy head --
And blood that heedless enemies have spilled --
His blood: I thought of rivers flowing red,
And crimson hands that laid him in his bed.

There were several moving tributes at Christ College, Brecon as well, with the school magazine containing the following anonymous tribute:

Since you were here two years have sped,
But you're remembered still;
Your memory has never fled,
Not yet it will.

You trod the muddy football-field
On many a hard-fought day;
'Twas then you learned to scorn to yield
In grim affray.

We've seen you batting, calm and cool,
When runs were coming fast;
In a greater game, for Country and for School,
You fall at last.

Rememb'ring what you were and did,
To you, who fighting fell, Breconians,
past and present, bid
A last farewell.

10

THE PALS BATTALIONS

"On the Somme, the Cardiff City Battalion died" – the words of William Joshua, a member of the 16th (Service) Battalion of the Welch Regiment, better known as the Cardiff City Battalion which suffered over 450 casualties, including over 150 deaths, at Mametz Wood.

The Battalion was like many other of the so-called Pals Battalions, formed in response to Lord Kitchener's rousing appeals, comprising men who had enlisted together in local recruiting drives, with the promise that they would be able to serve alongside their friends, neighbours, work colleagues and team-mates, rather than being arbitrarily allocated to other battalions.

At the outbreak of the War, Lord Kitchener believed that overwhelming manpower was the key to success and he set about looking for ways to encourage men of all classes to join. It was an approach which was in direct contrast to British military tradition which for hundreds of years had always relied on professional rather than conscripted soldiers, and had drawn its officers from the gentry with people of more humble means joining as enlisted men.

Across the country during 1914 a series of Pals Battalions were formed, with several in Wales being prompted by a speech on September 19th by Lloyd George at the Queen's Hall, London during which he called for the formation of a separate Welsh Army. Three weeks later, the War Office formally agreed that the National Executive Committee (NEC) should be responsible for the organisation of the Welsh Army Corps (WAC), and three battalions already forming under local initiatives were swiftly allocated to the WAC. On November 2nd, the NEC called on the Lord Mayor of Cardiff, Alderman J. T. Richards, to raise a battalion from the Cardiff area, tapping into the wave of patriotism with the new Battalion wearing the arms of the city.

On November 19th, the War Office authorised the creation of the Cardiff City Battalion, and four days later, the recruiting office was opened with Captain Frank Hill Gaskill appointed in command of the new battalion. Frank

JM Staniforth's cartoon from the Western Mail newspaper on September 5th, 1914.

had been recovering at his home in Llanishen, the popular suburb to the north of Cardiff, having been wounded in the face during early skirmishes whilst serving with 3rd Battalion the Welsh Regiment who were part of the the British Expeditionary Force in France. Born in Penarth in 1878, Frank was the son of Colonel Joseph Gaskell who lived initially in Windsor Road before moving to live at The Coldra in Newport and later New House in Llanishen. Educated at Llandaff Cathedral School, Frank followed his father into the military and served with distinction in the Boer War before returning to Cardiff and training as a barrister.

He was a useful sportsman, playing cricket for the Cathedral School, as well as for Llanishen plus the myriad of teams of gentlemen, and others from the legal world, which were assembled for matches during the late Edwardian era. Indeed, he was typical of many of the men who joined the Cardiff Pals, enjoying cricket as a form of social recreation, rather than actively seeking a place in the Cardiff 1st XI or hoping for selection in the Glamorgan squad for a Minor County match.

By the time the recruiting office opened, the War was over sixteen weeks old and the first rush of eager volunteers was well and truly over. With 1,000 men required, a vigorous campaign was undertaken throughout Cardiff and the surrounding area, with public meetings, concerts by military bands, grand military demonstrations, and appeals at soccer matches, places of work and music halls, with Gaskell and others using their network of contacts in the sporting and legal community to drum up further support. Cardiff Rugby Club was a particularly fruitful source of volunteers and amongst the Welsh rugby internationals to join up were John L. Williams, Bert Winfield and Clem Lewis. Others who played rugby for Cardiff 2nd XV or cricket for Cardiff 2nd XI or the other suburban teams in the coal metropolis dutifully signed up in a process of recruitment mirrored across other towns and cities in Wales as the sporting pals all joined up together – sadly, many were to die together as well.

After eight long weeks, the requisite number of men was raised, and the Cardiff Pals duly went into billets at Porthcawl before, in December 1914, heading by train to Colwyn Bay for further training, but only after breaking their journey with a parade through the streets of Cardiff to rousing cheers from the onlookers who, like so many others, thought the War would soon be over.

The Cardiff City Battalion duly spent eight months in North Wales, before moving to Winchester in August 1915 with the other units of the 38th (Welsh) Division. Whilst based at Hazeley Down Camp they undertook musketry training and after an inspection by Her Majesty the Queen on Salisbury Plain, they were deemed ready for active service. In late November, there was also an emotional final visit to Cardiff, which included a parade at the Arms Park, before the Battalion embarked from Southampton on December 4th on SS Margarette and sailed to Le Havre. The vessel was a paddle steamer and the majority of men were sea-sick by the time they reached French soil.

After a couple of days of recovery, they headed for the Western Front and were initially stationed in the Givenchy-Festubert-Laventie area, where around fifty men were killed, including Frank Gaskell himself, who as the Battalion's Commanding Officer was struck by a sniper's fire whilst inspecting the forward lines at Merville on the evening of May 15th. A bullet ignited his ammunition pouches, with Frank sustaining awful injuries. He never recovered and sadly died two days later.

Despite losing the man who had done so much for its creation, the Battalion regrouped and then moved south towards the Somme in June

1916. Like the other Battalions, it was to experience dreadful losses in the major battles which ensued, especially on the Somme in the attack on the Hammerhead at Mametz Wood, when the Battalion's right flank was brutally exposed to machine gun fire from Flatiron Copse and Sabot Copse. At the Battle of Mametz Wood, the Battalion, suffered terrible losses with over 150 dead including Welsh rugby internationals Dick Thomas and John L. Williams.

Arthur Solly-Wood (Crickhowell CC and the MCC)

One of the outcomes from the Battle of the Somme and the massive loss of life was the need for an improvement in the training of volunteers, especially the recruits in Kitchener's New Army who lacked both the experience and tactical awareness of the regular soldiers. After a review by Haig and others at General Headquarters, the task of overseeing these improvements fell to Arthur Solly-Flood, the son of Sir Frederick Solly-Flood, the former Commandant of RMC Sandhurst, who lived at Portmawr in Crickhowell.

Born in January 1871 and educated at Wellington College and Sandhurst, Solly-Flood had already enjoyed a distinguished military career, serving with the South Lancashire Regiment and fighting in the Boer War between 1899 and 1902 during which he was awarded the DSO. He later returned to the UK and served at the War Office from 1904 until 1908 alongside Haig.

Whilst back at home he was able to continue his cricketing career which had started whilst at school at Wellington. He rejoined Crickhowell CC, whom he captained in both 1905 and 1906, besides playing for the MCC. He was a useful batsman and medium pace bowler, and appeared for the MCC at Lord's in several matches in 1906 during which he shared a century stand with Pelham Warner against the Royal Engineers, besides opening the batting and scoring a century against the Household Regiment.

In 1909 Solly-Flood took up an appointment in the Middle East, but despite being many miles from home, he continued to play cricket and in 1912 oversaw the selection of a team called Egypt and the Sudan, who toured the UK and played a match at Lord's against the MCC. Following the outbreak of War, he became a Major in the 4th (Royal Irish) Dragoon Guards and was in charge of his Squadron during manoeuvres in France

Arthur Solly-Flood.

in 1914 whilst with the British Expeditionary Force. During this time he was wounded in action, besides being mentioned in despatches on seven occasions and being decorated with the Belgian Order of the Crown, the Belgian War Cross, and the French War Cross.

During the Battle of the Somme, Solly-Flood served as Brigadier-General of 35 Brigade, 12th Division, and after Haig's review into the Somme and its aftermath, Solly-Flood was appointed acting Commander of the Third Army School and together with a party of British officers, he investigated French methods at their Fourth Army training school at Chalons in November 1916. It was widely regarded that the French methods were superior and more effective, and on his return Solly-Flood compiled a report called 'Instructions for the Training of Platoons for Offensive Action', which became the most important tactical manual for the BEF of the rest of the War. In late January 1917 Haig appointed Solly-Flood to command the new Training Directorate at General Headquarters, and one of his first acts was to unify the training which had been carried out by the separate Army schools, and to abolish the divisional training schools.

After the cessation of the Great War, Solly-Flood became a Military Advisor to the North Irish government whilst continuing to advise about the training of recruits ready for military service. He died in Crickhowell in November 1940.

11

SHELL-SHOCK

The Battle of the Somme, as well as the other major battles of the Great War, saw thousands of men suffer from shell-shock – an adverse reaction to the trauma of battle, with the intensity of the bombardment and fighting producing a feeling of helplessness described variously as panic or an inability to reason, sleep, walk or talk. Indeed, many now regard shell-shock as the signature injury of the War, and at the end of the hostilities, there were so many officers and men suffering from shell-shock that nineteen British military hospitals were wholly devoted to the treatment of cases. Even in 1928, there were still 65,000 veterans who were receiving treatment.

In the early years of the War, this type of trauma was not fully understood by the medics, with some interpreting it as a lack of moral fibre, resulting in the court martial and even execution of troops. Its early treatment also varied widely according to the whims of the doctors involved, as well as other sundry factors such as the rank and social class of the patient.

Soldiers from the British Expeditionary Force had begun to report medical symptoms after combat, including tinnitus, amnesia, strong headaches, and dizziness as well as a hypersensitivity to noise. Indeed, it was estimated that by December 1914 as many as 10% of British officers and 4% of enlisted men were suffering from what medical staff described as 'nervous and mental shock'. The number of shell-shock cases steadily grew during the next two years, but it remained poorly understood by the medics and psychologists.

Some doctors held the view that it was a result of hidden physical damage to the brain, with the shock waves from bursting shells creating a cerebral lesion. Another explanation was that shell-shock resulted from poisoning by the carbon monoxide formed by explosions. An alternative view described shell-shock as an emotional, rather than a physical, injury, with evidence showing that an increasing proportion of men suffering shell-shock symptoms had not been exposed to artillery fire. Therefore, the British Army continued to try to differentiate those whose symptoms followed explosive exposure from others, and in 1915 the following instructions were issued:

'Shell-shock and shell concussion cases should have the letter 'W' prefixed to the report of the casualty, if it was due to the enemy; in that case the patient would be entitled to rank as 'wounded' and to wear on his arm a 'wound stripe'. If, however, the man's breakdown did not follow a shell explosion, it was not thought to be 'due to the enemy', and he was to [be] labelled 'Shell-shock' or 'S' (for sickness) and was not entitled to a wound stripe or a pension.'

Initially, the shell-shock casualties were rapidly evacuated from the front line, largely because of fears about their unpredictable and irrational behaviour. As the number of casualties increased, and manpower became in shorter supply, their treatment became a growing problem. Indeed, at the Battle of the Somme in 1916, as many as 40% of casualties were shell-shocked, resulting in concern about an epidemic of psychiatric casualties. Medics therefore suggested that if casualties were uninjured they could return to the front after a few days rest and continue fighting.

However, if symptoms persisted after a week or so at a local Casualty Clearing Station, which was often close enough to the frontline for everyone to hear the artillery fire, the casualty would be evacuated to one of the dedicated psychiatric centres which had been set up further behind the lines, and were labelled as 'NYDN – Not Yet Diagnosed Nervous', pending further investigation by medical specialists. At the Battle of Passchendaele a total of 5,346 shell-shock cases reached the Casualty Clearing Stations, equivalent to 1% of the British forces. However, around 75% of these men returned to active service without being referred to a hospital for specialist treatment.

Jack Mercer (Sussex and Glamorgan)

Jack Mercer was amongst the many thousands of soldiers to suffer from shell-shock, with the future Glamorgan cricketer suffering from a severe form of the illness compounded by having to lie injured in a shell crater during the Battle of the Somme in 1916. His story outlines the horrors of shell-shock, as well as the way playing cricket and getting out in the sun was used by medics as a form of therapy in the treatment of this horrible illness.

Jack had been born on April 22nd, 1893 in Southwick, a thriving suburb to the west of Brighton. His father Walt was a farrier, and a leading figure with the Southwick club. A decent batsman and a capable bowler in his own rights, Walt was the Southwick captain in the mid-1900s when Jack was old enough to play in senior games, and with Walt's words of encouragement, Jack's prowess for the local team and his school brought him to the attention of Sussex CCC.

At that time, however, Jack had no ambitions of being a professional sportsman so he did not actively pursue these early opportunities with the county club. On leaving school at the age of fourteen Jack initially secured a job as a postman, enjoying the chance to be out in the fresh air, and meeting people. At heart, Jack was a romantic and like so many living in coastal areas, he was curious about what lay beyond the seas which fringed his home. When walking along the seafront he often wondered – and probably fantasised – about the places from which the vessels had travelled. He was also fascinated by the origins and background of some of the well-dressed gentlemen of European origin who paraded, with their equally well-dressed ladies, along the sea-front promenades at Brighton and Hove.

Jack Mercer at Hove in 1921.

Jack was also intrigued by the tales told by the ostlers and stable lads when they brought their horses to his father's smithy, and in particular, he became fascinated about Russia, the Cossacks and their magnificent steeds. In 1913 he and a friend received an offer to become crew members of a sailing yacht which was heading to St. Petersburg. It seemed like a once in a lifetime opportunity to see what life was really like in Russia, so Jack accepted the offer, tendered his resignation as a postman and after telling his parents – who, no doubt, held a few misgivings – set sail on the yacht. It proved to be a highly enjoyable adventure with the pair enjoying their time in the St. Petersburg area where Jack met and became smitten with a ballerina. It meant, of course, that Jack had to teach himself Russian in order to communicate with his first love and, for a while, few of Jack's thoughts were about life back at home or playing cricket for Southwick.

Everything changed however following the declaration of War on August 4th, 1914. As the early battles began on France and Belgian soil, Jack's parents became increasingly concerned about his safety on the European mainland so Jack and his pal swiftly decided the time had come to return home. After their heady adventures overseas, and the brief romantic interlude, it was quite a shock for Jack to return home and to find the newspapers full of doom-laden stories about the War and the heavy loss of life in the early battles in the autumn of 1914. But, like other young men of the time, there was a job to be done for King and Country, and shortly after returning, Jack joined the Royal Sussex Regiment.

For the next few months, he took part in training at Witley Camp as a member of the 12th Battalion (2nd South Down), and together with the rest of the Battalion, remained on British soil throughout 1915, wondering when their time would come for active service. It duly arrived the following February as they travelled by train to Dover, from which they duly sailed across to Calais, arriving on French soil on March 5th, 1916. The Battalion then headed by train, lorry and then on foot towards Fleurbaix, which they eventually reached a fortnight later. After taking over a series of trenches on March 20th and establishing their headquarters in a series of nearby farmhouses, the Battalion remained at Fleurbaix for the next three months.

On arriving, the soldiers were given clean clothing, a chance to bathe and a series of inoculations against a host of real and imagined diseases that might affect them whilst they were in action. Their mission in northern France was to take part in the Battle of the Somme. Like other members of Lord Kitchener's newly-raised Army, they undertook more training activities whilst at Fleurbaix, with further instruction about going into combat, including route marches around the surrounding area, designed to get boots and feet in order. During the mornings Jack and his colleagues regularly took part in bayonet training as well as having training sessions with more advanced varieties of weapons and explosives. During the afternoons, the Battalion took part in physical exercise, including some rudimentary games of football, and occasionally cricket, Like the others, Jack revelled in the opportunity to enjoy some light relief, including games with other Battalions stationed locally, but everyone was brought back down to reality in early June when they were served with a notice that they should be ready to attack at short notice, and for the next few weeks regular briefings about the whereabouts of German troops replaced the afternoon recreation.

Throughout their time at Fleurbaix, there was plenty of decent food brought by the nightly convoy of trains from the northern ports, but it soon became clear that their excellent diet was part of a 'fattening-up' process prior to a phase of combat, Jack – who by now was a 2nd Lieutenant – was well aware that the time for fun and games was over, and after three weeks on standby, the time came for action as the Battalion took part in a series of assaults in the Richebourg and Ferme du Bois area. Their activities were part of a larger programme of diversionary activities prior to the Battle of the Somme, some twenty miles or so to the south which began in earnest the following day. At 3.05am on June 30th, the Battalion advanced on enemy lines whilst artillery bombarded their trenches, but after making a swift initial advance, the Battalion were soon facing superior German forces. Despite breaking through to the support line, there was a massive counter-attack by the German troops. As one of the historians of the Battalion later wrote: 'The Germans were ready for us, and many of the soldiers brought back a notice in English which read – 'Come on Sussex boys. We've been waiting for you for three days'!'

Besides being aware of the pending assault, the Germans had been unmolested since October 1914, so in the ensuing months constructed extensive lines of trenches as well as a myriad of defensive positions where machine guns could be sited. As the supply of ammunition gave out, the 12th Battalion had to hastily withdraw, and it was during this operation, moving back towards Ferme du Bois that Jack was wounded by an exploding shell, whose fragments struck him in the left arm, shoulder and chest, and whose defeaning noise caused him to lose hearing in his left ear. The soldier next to him was less fortunate as he was killed outright.

Jack Mercer.

Jack tumbled into the crater which the shell created, and he soon became covered by the debris from the explosion. As well as being defeaned, he was also disorientated and, at first, lay semi-conscious but increasingly aware that he had shrapnel in the upper part of his body. He steadily regained consciousness, but lay prone for the next 48 hours, listening through his undamaged right ear to the cries of anguish from other injured troops as well as the harrowing groans of those who were dying from their wounds. It was a truly appalling time, and with the Germans poised to advance, Jack was fearful of what would happen if he was taken prisoner: in those dark hours, he would be forgiven for wanting to be put out of his misery as he saw through the flying dirt and clouds of smoke, the shells fly overhead.

After a day of constant shelling and gunfire, the German counter-attack ceased as their attention switched to the south and the main battle which had started in earnest. Jack was forever grateful for this lull in activities as a couple of troops – largely sent out to gather the bodies of the dead – found him in the crater. The pair duly dug Jack out, before helping him limp his way back to where the medical units were based. Although being able to walk.

The Mercer family's home in Shoreham-by-Sea where Jack recuperated. The photograph shows his brothers Donald and Frank, standing with his sister Glory.

Jack had some nasty shrapnel wounds and after inhaling various types of gas, and still being deaf in his left ear, he was not in great shape. Like countless others, he also had a form of shell-shock and together with his wounds, it meant that when the regimental officer at Fleurbaix carried out his assessment, Jack's war was over.

He was duly sent to a casualty clearing station where his wounds were treated, before being despatched on a hospital train back to the Channel coast and later that summer he returned to Britain to recuperate at home in Shoreham. As his wounds eased, he gradually regained the use of his left arm, but his hearing never fully recovered. There were also some mental scars and, at first, Jack found it difficult to sleep at night, especially during the long, winter months as he had terrible flashbacks to his time in the crater. In an attempt to counteract this, he would pace around his home until sheer exhaustion meant he could sleep. As he gradually regained strength, he was able to reflect on being one of the lucky ones to survive the manoeuvres at Ferme du Bois. Together with the assault, and retreat at Richebourg, the 12th Battalion lost a total of 429 casualties including seventeen officers.

His brother Victor had also joined up with The Royal Fusiliers. He too was injured during 1917 but, unlike Jack, he was able to return to the front after a short period of rest back home. Jack was delighted to see his younger brother of whom he thought the world, and it uplifted his spirits to spend time with Victor who, after a week or so, went back to France. Tragically, it was the last that Jack and the rest of his family ever saw of the cheery 20-year-old as Victor was killed in November 1917 during the bloody Battle of Cambrai. News of his death shook Jack and the rest of the Mercer clan back home in Shoreham. His death put back Jack's recovery by many weeks and caused the return of dreadful nightmares. 1916 and 1917 were certainly the darkest years of Jack's life and ones that, quite understandably, he wanted to swiftly forget. Indeed, it may have been no coincidence that in subsequent years Jack always gave his age as two years less than it actually was.

By the spring of 1918 Jack was in greater physical as well as mental shape and, as life started to get back to normal, he secured a desk job in London with the Army. Jack was also encouraged to further his rehabilitation by taking part in healthy recreation, and it didn't take much persuasion for him to rejoin the Southwick club. His time out in the summer sun all helped him to forget those dark hours lying wounded in the shell hole, as well as helping to build back up his fitness.

His success as a bowler with the Southwick club once again brought him to the attention of the Sussex coaching staff. They had been aware of his talents as a bowler before the War, when Jack had appeared in a handful of Academy games against local clubs and had spent time as a net bowler. Whereas before the War, his involvement had all been very low key, the interest from Sussex was now much more formal and after further proof of his form and fitness he received an offer to join the Sussex groundstaff on a full-time basis. At 25, he was one of the oldest of the new faces to be approached but, with nothing else on the horizon and after the horrors of the War, Jack was only too delighted to get the chance of regularly playing cricket and to be paid for the privilege.

He knew that if he said no, he would not get a second chance of being a professional cricketer. Walt was also overjoyed as for many years he had hoped that Jack might get another chance with Sussex. Jack duly accepted the offer and during March 1919 he made his way to Hove to join the county's groundstaff and to start his life as a professional cricketer. One hundred per cent effort was expected from all of the youngsters, whilst the coaching staff, led by Head Coach Arthur Millward, spent hours and hours with the enthusiastic youngsters in the nets and at matches staged against decent local clubs. There were plenty of opportunities as well to bowl against the other professionals and those in the 1st XI. After the horrors of the War and those awful hours on the Somme, the chance to be out in the sunshine all day must have seemed heaven sent and, as the 1919 season got underway, Jack eagerly looked forward to the next chapter in his life.

His first-class debut for Sussex duly came on July 9th, 1919 when John Vincett was taken ill on the first morning of the Championship match at Northampton. It was, though, his sole appearance of the summer, and for the next few years he made further appearances without securing a regular berth in the side. The emergence of Arthur Gilligan and subsequently Maurice Tate further reduced his opportunities of regular Championship action. With Gilligan poised to accept the captaincy in 1922, it was clear to Jack that if he wanted to play regular county cricket, and have a secure position as a professional cricketer, he would have to look elsewhere.

He began talking with a couple of his fellow professionals who had been impressed by Glamorgan's victory over Sussex at the Arms Park in May 1921 in their inaugural Championship, and with the Welsh county on the lookout for fresh talent, he duly made contact with Glamorgan's officials and agreed terms. It was the biggest gamble he ever took but it was comfortably the best, despite the fact that the Welsh county had enjoyed a torrid time in their first couple of seasons in the County Championship, winning just four matches, as time and again, the Welsh batsmen struggled against the opposing attack. Their own bowlers, though spirited and enthusiastic, rarely produced match-winning performances, and Glamorgan were held in such low standing that teams would only book into hotels for two nights, rather than three, believing they would wrap up victory inside two days!

Yet despite their dreadful form, it was to Glamorgan that Jack headed in 1922, after receiving a decent offer from the Welsh county's officials who were desperate for a young bowler to spearhead their attack. At least, he reasoned, he was likely to get a regular place in the attack, and he couldn't do any worse than the souls who had already had a go! Any doubts however that he, or the Club, might have held, were dispelled as Jack became Glamorgan's opening bowler from 1924, and after increasing his pace and further developing his skills, he regularly was their leading wicket-taker during the next fifteen seasons

The Glamorgan side at Worcester in 1923 with Jack Mercer standing in the centre of the back row. Seated to the left on the bench is Norman Riches, next to Tom Whittington who is wearing the cardigan.

His finest hour came at New Road in 1936 when he became the first, and so far only, Glamorgan bowler to take all ten wickets in an innings as he took 10-51 against Worcestershire. His success was based on three factors – the priceless ability to swing the ball either way, seemingly boundless stamina and, once the shine had disappeared, some clever cutters as he cut down on his pace. These attributes helped him to amass 1,460 wickets for the Welsh county in first-class cricket. On six occasions, his seasonal tally topped the hundred mark, and his haul would have been much higher had his new employers secured the services of more athletic fielders and agile catchers. Many times, a greying and portly amateur would spill a catch close to the wicket but, unlike some modern bowlers, Jack rarely 'lost his rag' or descended into histrionics if things didn't go his way – instead he was a phlegmatic and jovial soul, saying "Bad luck and well stopped, Sir" to the red-faced fielder, before returning to his bowling mark.

At the same time, Jack was also superstitious and would frequently put a three-penny bit in his back pocket, believing that it brought him good luck. It led to a bit of leg pulling, but on one occasion at Swansea, it seemed to do the trick. Jack had bowled without any luck before lunch against the Gloucestershire batsmen, so he decided to put his lucky charm in his pocket for the afternoon session. Remarkably, Jack proceeded to take seven wickets, and he duly kept the coin in his pocket for the next few matches. Despite his fine haul, Jack's colleagues continued to pull his leg about the coin's powers. "I'm out of luck myself" said Arnold Dyson, the opening batsman, "so let's see what good it does for me," putting the coin into his trouser pocket before going out to bat. To Dyson's delight, he posted his first half century for several weeks and, on returning to the dressing room, he turned to the smiling Jack and said, "Thanks – I now believe in fairies as well!"

After retiring from playing at the end of the 1939 season, Jack joined Northamptonshire as their coach in 1947. In truth, he had been coaching for several years before that, passing on tips to the young Glamorgan bowlers during the 1930s and spending time with the county's coach Bill Hitch, as they groomed the next generation of bowlers. During the late 1930s, he was instrumental in recommending the bowling talents of Wilf Wooller to captain, Maurice Turnbull. During the winter months, he also coached in Australia and the West Indies. In particular, he spent several winters in Jamaica where he played a major part in the early career of one of the island's greatest cricketing sons – Alf Valentine, the left-arm spinner who became the first West Indian bowler to claim over a hundred Test wickets. Back in the winter of 1948-49, the tall, bespectacled youngster was a virtual unknown, living in a working-class suburb of Kingston. Jack was soon impressed by the amount of sharp spin Alf could impart from his long fingers. The pair duly spent many long hours in the nets, or on any patch of spare land in Kingston, with Jack helping the young spinner to perfect his skills and craft.

In 1963 Jack became Northamptonshire's 1st XI scorer – a position he filled until 1981 before spending a couple of seasons in a similar capacity with their 2nd XI. His new duties allowed him to retain close contact with cricketers young and old, as well as journalists with the scribes often

Jack Mercer coaching in Jamaica in 1949.

frequenting the same area on the ground as the scorers. If bad weather was interfering with play, the Press Box would come alive with stories of yesteryear as Jack delighted the hacks with his tales. It also gave Jack a new and eager audience for his card tricks, with his scoring colleagues – sometimes frustrated by his loss of mathematical accuracy – now left wide-eyed in amazement by one of Jack's special tricks.

Indeed, he was one of the most popular scorers on the circuit with a cry of "everything's approximate" as he answered a Pressman's enquiry. Of course, these were of the days when scorers only used books and pencils, rather than the laptops, printer and other electronic devices used by the current crop of county notchers. After lunch, Jack could doze off for a few overs – something that would be nigh impossible in this new digital era of scoring. But Jack's colleagues the length and breadth of the country were more than happy for him to quietly copy up a few overs after waking up from his nap. Instead of any ill feeling about his slumber, his fellow scorers were delighted to work with the 'grand old man of county cricket', and to be able to say that they had worked with someone who had first played before the Great War, and had survived the horrors of the Somme as well as the awful illness of shell-shock.

12

1916 – ADEN

Allied activity in South Arabia during the First World War witnessed a struggle for the control of the strategic port city of Aden, the British crown colony which was an important base for ships to and from Asia via the Suez Canal. The British Empire had declared war on the Ottoman Empire on November 5th, 1914, and in the course of the next few years, the Ottomans planned a series of invasions of Britain's Aden Protectorate in conjunction with the local Arab tribes.

In July 1915 an Ottoman force from North Yemen made their way across the frontier of the Aden hinterland and advanced towards Lahij, one of the most important towns in South Arabia and the capital of the Abdali Sultanate of Lahij. Situated at an oasis, and surrounded by a fertile plain, it was the centre of trade between Aden and its hinterland. During the years leading up to the outbreak of war, relations between Britain and Lahij had been cordial and friendly, and in 1915 the Sultan duly sent word to General Shaw, commanding the Aden Brigade, that the Ottomans were advancing from Mawiyah to attack him at Lahij, and asked for help as the British in the Sultan's capital found themselves faced by several thousand Ottoman troops, Fighting began on the evening of Sunday, July 4th, and sadly the Sultan was killed along with many of his men, well before British reinforcements could make their presence felt.

After their advance at Lahij, the Ottomans occupied Shaikh Othman, a town about two miles inland from the harbour of Aden, but on July 20th, 1915, troops from the Aden Brigade, the 28th (Frontier Force) Brigade, plus a battery of Royal Horse Artillery, surprised the Ottomans and drove them out of the place. Between fifty and sixty Ottoman soldiers were killed and wounded, and several hundred men, mostly Arab tribesmen, were made prisoners. This success was followed up in the following months by further attacks which kept the Ottomans at bay, although early in 1916 the Ottomans claimed that the British had been driven back on to Aden itself, and had retreated to within range of the covering fire of their warships

Many of the Ottoman claims proved to be grossly exaggerated, and some wholly false – one was that they scored a substantial victory in further heavy fighting around Shaikh Othman and Bir Ahmad. The eruption of the

British-sponsored Arab Revolt in the Hejaz diverted Ottoman attention from Aden during the summer of 1916. Those Ottoman troops who remained reverted to the defensive, allowing the British to construct an eleven-mile-long defensive perimeter around Aden and safely secure it for the duration of the War.

Joseph Townley (Crickhowell CC)

Joseph Swinburn Townley spent the majority of his working life in Crickhowell, serving as one of the town's doctors from 1906 and 1945, besides serving as Medical Officer of Health for Crickhowell Rural District Council and being a co-opted member of Breconshire County Council. A keen sportsman, he played cricket for Crickhowell prior to the Great War and was appointed the captain of the town's cricket club in 1909.

Born in Keswick in Cumberland in December 1877, he read Medicine at the University of Glasgow. After graduating in 1902 he became a house surgeon at Victoria Infirmary in Glasgow before opting to become a G.P, and moving with his wife Elizabeth to take up a position in Abergavenny in 1905, before the following year moving to Crickhowell. He threw himself into his work in the Breconshire town, and as befitted a decent sportsman, he played with distinction for Crickhowell's cricket club.

Dr. Townley joined the Royal Army Medical Corps shortly after the outbreak of war in 1914 and he accompanied the Crickhowell Volunteers who formed the 1st (Brecknockshire) Volunteer Battalion, The South Wales Borderers, duly serving alongside many of the men whose families and themselves he had tended from his practice in the town.

Now the 1st Brecknockshire Battalion The South Wales Borderers, the Battalion saw service in Aden and it was there in May 1915 when tragedy struck the Townley household back in Crickhowell, with his wife Elizabeth dying after a short illness. With three small infants at home, he applied to the Battalion's Commanding Officer for leave of absence, but owing to the gravity of the situation his allocation to return home was declined.

June 1916 saw the Battalion engaged in a series

Joseph Swinburn Townley.

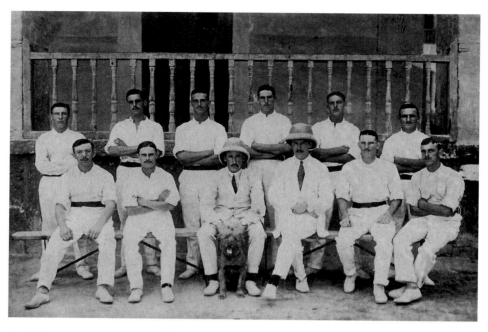

A cricket team representing the Welsh Regiment taken in Egypt during 1916.

of skirmishes with the Turks and during one engagement Dr. Townley was awarded the Military Cross for displaying great courage and disregard for his own safety whilst tending to the wounded, several of whom were good friends in Crickhowell. With his regiment being posted to India in August 1915, Townley appears to have transferred to a different unit as he later fought at Ypres in 1917 before returning to the Breconshire town and resuming his duties at his general practice. After retiring in 1945 he moved to Kinnersley in Herefordshire where he ran a poultry and dairy farm before passing away in June 1956.

13

1917 – ARRAS

The Battle of Arras was another operation on the Western Front, taking place between April 9th and May 16th, 1917 and witnessed British, Canadian, South African, New Zealand, and Australian troops attacking German defences near the French city of Arras. There were major gains on the first day, but the Battle overall resulted in around 160,000 British casualties.

The offensive was conceived as part of a plan to pierce the German line and to make inroads on the Western Front. It came at a time when politicians in both Paris and London were under massive pressure from the media, the people and their parliaments to bring the War to a victorious close. The loss of life from the battles of Gallipoli, the Somme and Verdun had been massive yet there was little prospect of victory in sight. The Battle also followed the United States declaring war on Germany. A long succession of U-boat attacks upon civilian shipping, starting with the sinking of RMS Lusitania in 1915 and culminating in the torpedoing of seven American merchantmen in early 1917 resulted in the United States Congress declaring war on Imperial Germany on April 6th, 1917.

The Battle was planned in conjunction with the French High Command, who were simultaneously embarking on a massive attack (the Nivelle Offensive) about eighty kilometres to the south. The military planners thought that, if successful, the offensive might bring a swift end to the War – sadly, this was not to be the case. The precise details were devised by General Allenby against the Sixth German Army led by 73-year-old General von Falkenhausen plus the Second Army under General von der Marwitz. The British plan was well developed, drawing on the lessons learned from manoeuvres on the Somme and Verdun, with the full weight of artillery being concentrated on a relatively narrow stretch of eleven miles, from Vimy Ridge in the north to Neuville Vitasse, four miles south of the River Scarpe.

The attack was planned to last about a week at all points on this line, with a much longer and heavier barrage at Vimy to weaken its strong defences. A series of tunnels were also dug by the Royal Engineers in the chalk-based topography with over 20 kilometres of tunnels being constructed which concealed around 24,000 men. Assault tunnels were also dug, stopping a few metres short of the German positions and ready to be blown open by explosives on Zero-Day. German military engineers also conducted their underground operations, seeking out Allied tunnels to assault and to counter-mine.

To keep German action to a minimum during the assault, a policy known as 'creeping barrage' was planned. This required a screen of high explosive and shrapnel shells to be laid down about one hundred metres in advance of the assaulting troops. It had not worked fully in other battles but on this occasion, it forced the Germans to remain in their trenches, and allowed Allied troops to advance without fear of machine gun fire.

After considerable bombardment, Canadian troops in the north were able to capture the strategically significant Vimy Ridge whilst British divisions in the centre made significant gains across the River Scarpe to the south, British and Australian forces made only minimal advances gains, and at a heavy cost, and by the time the battle officially ended, the Allied forces had moved forward, but had not been able to achieve a breakthrough.

Philip Hill (Llandaff Cathedral School and Crickhowell CC)

Philip Aubrey Hill followed his father Dr. Philip Edward Hill into the Crickhowell cricket team of the late 1890s. Sadly, he was to lose his life in the Battle of Arras on April 23rd, 1917 at the age of 43

Born in 1874 and educated at Llandaff Cathedral School, Uppingham School and Gonville and Caius College in Cambridge, Hill played for the Crickhowell club in the 1890s before entering the teaching profession and becoming a headmaster in Bromley in Kent. On October 24th, 1914, he became a Lieutenant in the Brecknockshire Battalion of the South Wales Borderers, which was a Territorial unit. He later became attached to the 2nd Battalion of the South Wales Borderers and after training at various camps in Britain, he travelled to France in mid-January as commander of 'A' Company of the Brecknockshire Battalion which at the time comprised around 30 officers and 500 in other ranks.

After several months on the Western Front, the Battalion were moved forward in mid-April to Arras where they were initially put into crowded billets before being moved to Schramm Barracks. On the evening of April 22nd they moved again into the front-line trenches to the east of the town of Monchy-le-Preux. At 4.45 a.m. on April 23rd the Battalion went over the top and successfully captured the first line of German troops, with both A and B Companies establishing strong points about 300 yards beyond the captured German positions.

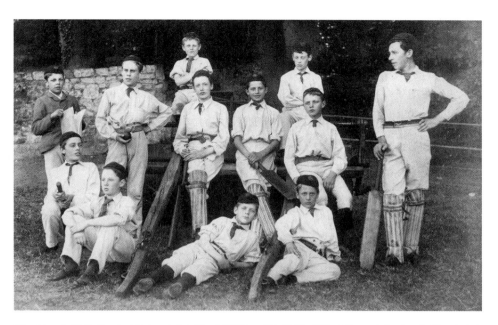

The Llandaff Cathedral School 1st XI of 1887, with Philip Hill sitting at the back (far right).

However, when making their advance, the covering fire from British positions was not as effective as planned and in securing these advanced positions, there was the loss of 228 troops from the 2nd Brecknockshire Battalion, with German snipers adding to the mayhem. Captain Philip Hill was one of several officers to lose his life during the advance on April 23rd, 1917 and having no known grave, he is commemorated on the Arras Memorial.

Crickhowell 1894 with Philip Hill (standing, second left) and C.P. Lewis (sitting, third from left).

14

1917 – PASSCHENDAELE

The Battle of Passchendaele, or Third Battle of Ypres, took place between June and November 1917, and proved to be another bloody battle as the German and Allied forces fought for control of a series of ridges to the south and east of the Belgian city of Ypres.

The strategy for the battle had been determined by the Allied commanders at conferences in November 1916 and again in May 1917 having identified Passchendaele, situated on the final ridge to the east of Ypres, as a vital part of the German Fourth Army's supply system. However, the attack on Passchendaele was hampered by stout resistance, unusually wet weather, the onset of winter and the diversion of British and French resources to Italy, following the victory by German and Austrian forces at the Battle of Caporetto in late October and early November. A few weeks before, a German retreat from Passchendaele had seemed inevitable, and it was not until the end of November that Allied troops, led by Canadian forces, eventually captured Passchendaele, but only after suffering over 245,000 casualties.

The whole campaign in Flanders during 1917 was highly controversial. The British Prime Minister, David Lloyd George opposed the offensive as did General Foch, the French Chief of the General Staff. The British commander Field-Marshal Sir Douglas Haig eventually received approval for the Flanders operation from the War Cabinet on July 25th but many doubted the wisdom of pursuing the offensive strategy ahead of the arrival of American troops in France. There were strong advocates for waiting a few more weeks whilst some questioned the choice of the attack compared with other areas further south, especially given the weather in Flanders and the likely effect that mud would have. Indeed, once the autumn rains came many felt that the offensive should be halted.

Preparations for the operations in Flanders had begun the previous year with the creation of new supply routes into the area as well as reconnaissance sorties on the likely area of attack. Consideration was initially given to the use of tanks, with a mass attack on the plateaux, but after intelligence gathering exercises, this plan was aborted in favour of continuing the wearing down process using foot soldiers, horses and heavy artillery

The first stage in the British plan was a preparatory attack using two dozen mines, starting on June 7th, on the German positions to the south of Ypres at Messines Ridge. These German positions dominated Ypres and unless neutralised, the Allied advance was likely to fail. Within a week, these aims had been achieved and a second attack began at the end of July on further German artillery on Pilckem Ridge, as well as the following month with advances at Langemarck, but poor weather frustrated the Entente troops as they strove to make further advances. Also in August and into September a second offensive battle took place at Verdun, at which an estimated 10,000 prisoners were taken, further draining German resources and their morale, which was further eroded by bouts of sickness and air attacks by the Royal Flying Corps.

After the success of these early assaults, British commanders started to plan their next advances, but the unusually wet weather, the poor visibility and heavy mud had slowed their earlier advances and a period of consolidation and reinforcement was therefore required before what the planners hoped would be the next and decisive salvo. The three week pause in British operations, whilst more artillery was moved into the area of the Gheluvelt plateau, also misled and agitated the Germans, who could not themselves rest, believing that day after day, the next assault would come.

At the end of September successful advances were made in better weather at the Menin Road Ridge and at Polygon Wood, but in early October the Gheluvelt Plateau and Broodseinde Ridge were occupied with the Germans suffering more heavy losses, and leading their commanders to consider a slow withdrawal from Ypres. The next part of the British plan was to advance in early October from Broodseinde Ridge towards Passchendaele, but the weather took a turn for the worse and the heavy rain and ever thickening mud slowed their progress

The first battle of Passchendaele began on October 12th, but with ground movements being difficult, little artillery could be used at the front. Allied troops were also exhausted after their earlier efforts and with flagging morale in their ranks, German counter-attacks successfully recovered most of the lost ground near Passchendaele. There were also around 13,000 Allied casualties, including 2,735 New Zealanders, 845 of whom were either dead or wounded and stranded in the mud of no-man's-land. This carnage led to Army commanders agreeing that the attacks would cease until the weather improved, and further artillery and ammunition had been brought forward for better support.

The second battle duly took place from October 26th until November

10th with British troops augmented by Canadian soldiers. Early manoeuvres were met with strong counter-attacks whilst a few communication failures occurred between the Canadian forces and Australian units to the south. On October 30th another Allied advance attempted to gain a base for the final assault on Passchendaele, but again it met with exceptional German resistance, and the planned objectives were not met. A seven-day pause then followed as well as a lull in the rain, before the final and decisive assault began on the morning of November 6th. Within three hours, the village of Passchendaele had been captured, but at a massive human cost of over 645,000 casualties of which 400,000 were Germans.

Amongst those British soldiers killed during the Battle of Passchendaele was the celebrated Welsh poet Hedd Wyn (meaning Blessed Peace) whose emotive works capture the feelings of frustrations and anger felt by many British troops during these long and bloody manoeuvres in Flanders, as shown in one of his most evocative poems, *Rhyfel* (War):

Gwae fi fy myw mewn oes mor ddreng	Why must I live in this grim age,
A Duw ar drai ar orwel pell;	When, to a far horizon, God
O'i ôl mae dyn, yn deyrn a gwreng,	Has ebbed away, and man, with rage,
Yn codi ei awdurdod hell.	Now wields the sceptre and the rod?
Pan deimlodd fyned ymaith Dduw	Man raised his sword, once God had gone,
Cyfododd gledd i ladd ei frawd;	To slay his brother, and the roar
Mae swn yr ymladd ar ein clyw,	Of battlefields now casts upon
A'i gysgod ar fythynnod tlawd.	Our homes the shadow of the war.
Mae'r hen delynau genid gynt	The harps to which we sang are hung,
Ynghrog ar gangau'r helyg draw,	On willow boughs, and their refrain
A gwaedd y bechgyn lond y gwynt,	Drowned by the anguish of the young
A'u gwaed yn gymysg efo'r glaw.	Whose blood is mingled with the rain.

Born Ellis Humphrey Evans, he had joined the 15th Battalion the Royal Welsh Fusiliers before travelling across to Flanders. He died of wounds from an artillery shell on July 31st, 1917, at Pilckem Ridge. Six weeks later, at the National Eisteddfod, Hedd Wyn was posthumously awarded the bardic chair for his poem *Yr Arwr* (The Hero).

Donald Boumphrey (Denbighshire and Wales)

Donald Boumphrey, the Cheshire and Denbighshire cricketer, was amongst those men to be involved in the Battle of Passchendale, winning the Military

Cross, and surviving the war to become an inspirational teacher and coach at Rydal School in Colwyn Bay.

Born in Birkenhead in October 1892, Boumphrey attended Shrewsbury School where he won a place in the school's cricket and rugby teams. One of his finest hours in the Shrewsbury XI came in 1910 when he made 76 against Uppingham. He continued in good form in club cricket in his native Cheshire and, during July 1914, won selection in their side to play Durham at South Moor CC in Stanley. Batting at number three, Boumphrey made a duck in his maiden innings but nevertheless was chosen again for the matches the following month against Staffordshire and Durham.

His fledgling career in county cricket was halted by the outbreak of war, with Boumphrey joining the Machine Gun Corps during October 1915 in response to the need for more effective use of machine guns on the Western Front, At the outbreak of war, the tactical use of machine guns was not fully appreciated by the British Military, with each infantry battalion and cavalry regiment containing a machine gun section of just two guns each. After a year on the Western Front, it became clear that to be fully effective, machine guns needed to be used in larger units and crewed by specially trained men. To this effect, the Machine Gun Corps was formed with Infantry, Cavalry and Motor branches.

Boumphrey's sporting talents and keen eye made him an ideal choice for the newly formed regiment and following initial training at Belton Park in Grantham, Lincolnshire, and at a base at Camiers in France, Boumphrey – who by now was a Temporary Lieutenant – made his way to Flanders where he saw action in tanks, as a machine gunner, during the Battle of the Somme, before being deployed the following year in the attacks on Passchendaele. It was during the latter battle that Boumphrey was awarded the Military Cross in 1917 for his nerve under heavy fire and bravery during a number of raids on enemy lines.

Boumphrey returned to the UK in the autumn of 1918 and the following summer resumed his sporting career as life slowly got back to normal. He soon met with success batting for Wallasey in the Liverpool and District competition, and 1919 he took a team representing the Merseyside city to Shrewsbury School. He duly made 94 against his former school, who included his younger brother Stuart in their ranks.

The following year he started to play regularly for Cheshire in the Minor County Championship, making 102 against Northumberland at Jesmond as well as 90 against the same opponents in the return game at Aigburth, besides posting a couple of fifties against Durham. These performances won him rave reviews, and no less a judge than Neville Cardus once described Donald Boumphrey as the best amateur batsman in England.

However, teaching was Boumphrey's chosen profession and after qualifying as a teacher of Latin and Maths, he moved to Colwyn Bay in 1922 to commence what proved to be the start of a long and distinguished career at Rydal School, the famous boys public school where he became Master in charge of cricket and rugby. Sport was on the up at Rydal at this time, following the creation of a new sports field and pavilion, with Boumphrey proving himself to be a gifted and inspiring coach to the young boys.

His move to the north Wales coast also led to his selection for both the North Wales side as well as Denbighshire in their friendlies against touring teams and the MCC, against whom he struck 73 at Marchwiel in 1925. But Boumphrey maintained his allegiance with Cheshire and continued to play for them in the Minor County Championship until July 1933. Indeed, he proved to be a successful top order batsman in the competition, making 109 against Lancashire 2nd XI at Macclesfield in an innings which included 23 fours.

In 1924 he also appeared for North Wales against the South African tourists at Llandudno whilst in 1928, at the same ground, he played his only first-class match representing Wales against the touring West Indians. Boumphrey opened the batting for Wales and made 6 and 4, dismissed in the second innings by the legendary Learie Constantine.

By this time, he had also become Housemaster of Glan Aber House at Rydal School and amongst his young charges was a fresh-faced youngster

An image of the home ground of Colwyn Bay CC in Rhos-on-Sea, taken in the 1920s, when Donald Boumphrey played at the ground for the club, Rydal Dolphins and the Denbighshire side.

called Wilf Wooller, who at the time had a great love of football. But the man who went on to become a Welsh rugby international as well as a legendary cricketer with Glamorgan came under the wing of Boumphrey and, by his own admission, 'soon forgot about football and quickly adapted to boarding life at the rugby-playing school. Boumphrey's paternal manner made me feel immediately at home and I can still remember how Boumphrey would often wander into our dormitory before lights out and talk at length about sport.'

It wasn't long before Wilf had transferred his skills from the round to the oval ball, and on both the rugby and cricketing fields of north Wales he tried to emulate the feats of the wartime hero. Youthful optimism sometimes got the better of young Wooller and the burly youngster often gave his wicket away trying a crude and brutal slog, much to the displeasure of Boumphrey who wrote in *The Rydalian*, 'a batsman's job is to make runs and if the bowling is too good to be hit for fours. He must be ready to accept every possible single run.' Important lessons were soon learnt and on Boumphrey's recommendation, Wooller played minor county cricket for Denbighshire, besides having a short trial with Lancashire 2nd XI.

Wilf also featured alongside his mentor in the Rydal Dolphins side which Boumphrey had created in 1927, comprising staff, old boys and other emerging players, in fixtures staged during the school holidays in July and August. The success of the Dolphins and their annual tours, as well as his successful time at Rydal all helped the master-in-charge of cricket to forget the horrors he had encountered on the fields of Flanders and at Passchendaele during the Great War.

Tom David (Cardiff CC and Glamorgan)

Tom David was one of thousands to fall during the fighting at Passchendaele in August 1917 and, whereas his elder brother Alex was decorated for bravery and returned home, he gave his life for King and Country during the fighting to the north of Ypres.

He had been born in Cardiff in August 1891, and was one of the eight children for George and Annie David. George was a well-to-do solicitor who hailed from Pwllheli in Caernarvonshire, and he ensured that his four sons had a decent education, with Tom following a similar educational path to his two elder brothers, being schooled first at Arnold College in Knutsford in Cheshire before studying Law at Keble College, Oxford. Whilst at Oxford Tom won his college colours for cricket and rugby, besides representing Keble at hockey and taking part in the various trials for the full university teams. He was unsuccessful in these but continued to play with distinction for Keble, before starting his solicitor's training in East Grinstead in Sussex, where he continued to play cricket and hockey,

In 1913 Tom returned to Cardiff and joined his father George's practice. Whilst back home, he also played cricket and rugby for the town club, frequently appearing alongside his elder brother. Indeed, the pair appeared together in July 1913 in the all-amateur match between Glamorgan and Carmarthenshire at Llanelli, with Tom taking a couple of catches off Alex's bowling. Tom himself took a wicket with his medium-pace deliveries, and from a position in the lower middle-order, he scored 1 and 24 in the contest which the home side comfortably won by 53 runs.

In 1914 he successfully opened the batting on several occasions for Cardiff when regular incumbent Norman Riches was absent on county duty, and as a result of his success against some of the best bowlers in club cricket, he harboured ambitions of further call-ups by Glamorgan. But the outbreak of the Great War swiftly ended these thoughts and in November 1914 he secured a commission in the 5th Battalion the Welsh Regiment. After undergoing his initially training in Pontypridd, Tom departed for France where by July 1917 he had risen to the rank of captain. For the next few months, he was involved in the fighting on and around the series of ridges to the south and east of the Belgian city of Ypres.

Tom David, standing second left with his colleagues in the Cardiff CC side during a match against Newport CC during 1914.

Now attached to the 15th Battalion Welsh Regiment, he was killed on August 27th, 1917 after a German aircraft – decked in British colours – had tricked its way over Allied lines adjacent to the Yser Canal and had flown low over the trenches before dropping a light close to where Tom and his brigade were situated. Having alerted the German artillery to the precise location of the Welsh soldiers, the German artillery then unleashed a fusillade of shells, one of which hit Tom and killed him instantly.

His body was subsequently laid to rest in the Bard Cottage Cemetery at Ypres, with news of Tom's passing arriving at the family's home at 199 Newport Road in Cardiff shortly after his father had suffered a heart attack. For several days, medics decided that news of Tom's death should not be given to George for fear of worsening his situation. His condition slightly improved, allowing him to be told the grievous news, but tragically within a month or so, George had suffered a second stroke from which he never recovered.

Ronald Robertson (Crickhowell CC)

Ronald Robertson had been an enthusiastic member of Crickhowell cricket club during the early 1900s. Born in Southend-on-Sea in August 1879, Ronald Hugh Wilson Robertson worked as a Land Agent's clerk in the Breconshire town, before emigrating to Canada in 1905 where he subsequently became an accountant in British Columbia.

In August 1915 he enlisted at Vernon, British Columbia and duly became a Lance Corporal in the 29th Battalion of the Canadian Infantry which became part of the Canadian Expeditionary Forces which travelled later that year to the UK to prepare for action on the Western Front.

Known as Tobin's Tigers after their Commanding Officer, Lt. Colonel JS Tobin, Ronald and his colleagues were involved as part of the 2nd Canadian Division in the Battle of Hill 70 which took place between August 15th until August 25th, 1917 between the Canadian troops and five divisions of the German Sixth Army.

The Battle took place on the outskirts of the industrial city of Lens in the Nord-Pas-de-Calais region of France, with the city and its adjoining coalfields having been under German control since October 1914. The primary objective of the assault was to inflict casualties and draw German troops away from the Third Battle of Ypres. To achieve this aim, the Canadian Corps were involved in an operation to firstly move into the suburbs of the city itself and secondly occupy the high ground at Hill 70, or Sallaumines Hill, a treeless expanse which had commanding views over the surrounding area and would provide excellent observation over the German lines, in preparation for any future offensives.

The Hill had already been the site of warfare in September 1915 when the British had over-run and secured it as part of the Battle of Loos. The actions almost two years later saw both sides suffer high casualty rates, whilst Lens remained under German control. The bloody battle which ensued also saw the extensive use of poison gas, including the newly introduced German Yellow Cross shell containing the blistering agent, sulphur mustard.

Bad weather led to the postponement of the attack on Hill 70, planned originally in late July until mid-August. During this delay, companies of the Royal Engineers fired regular salvos of gas drums and shells into the city. The weather had improved by August 15th when the attack began at 4.25 a.m. with the 1st and 2nd Canadian Divisions attacking on a front 3,700 metres wide, whilst Royal Engineers fired drums of burning oil into the suburb of Cité St. Élisabeth and at other selected targets in order to create a smoke-screen.

Within twenty minutes of the attack beginning, both Canadian Divisions had reached their first objective and by 06:00 Ronald and his colleagues in the Second Canadian Infantry Brigade had reached their second objective. It was after this that the Germans mounted localised counter-attacks aimed at wearing down the Canadian artillery resources through the use of poison gas, especially the Yellow Cross shells with many of the artillery becoming casualties after gas had fogged the goggles of their respirators, forcing them to remove their masks in order to set the fuses, lay their sights and maintain accurate fire.

The Germans mounted a major counter-attack on August 21st – a day which saw Robert Hill Hanna of the 29th Battalion win the coveted Victoria Cross for his brave actions at Hill 70. Sadly, it was the same day that Ronald Robertson lost his life in the battle and having no known grave. He is, however, commemorated at the Vimy Memorial overlooking Douai Plain, some 8km north of Arras.

William Odell (Cardiff CC and Glamorgan)

William Odell, the vastly experienced Leicestershire cricketer who spent time playing cricket in the Cardiff area shortly before the War, also lost his life during October 1917 at Passchendaele at the age of 35.

The son of the Rev Joseph Odell, a Primitive Methodist minister, William was born in November 1881 in Leicester and educated, along with his brothers, at the King Edward VI School for Boys in Camp Hill. He duly made his first-class debut for Leicestershire against London County on July 1901 at the age of nineteen and, much to his glee, he claimed his first wicket when Dr. W.G. Grace holed out on the long-on boundary. In the return match a fortnight later he produced a performance which led to further regular appearances for the East Midlands side, as he returned match figures of 9-73, and again removed the immortal doctor.

Between 1902 and 1908, the amateur was virtually an ever-present in the Leicestershire line-up and, on four occasions, he was the county's leading wicket-taker. He claimed over a hundred wickets in 1903, 1904, 1905 and 1907, with his haul of 112 wickets in 1904 proving to be the best of his county career and resulting in his selection the following summer for the Gentlemen against the Players. Twice during his career the accurate right-arm seamer claimed a hat-trick – the first came in 1904 whilst playing at Lord's for London County against the MCC's Club and Ground side, whilst the second in 1908 occurred during Leicestershire's County Championship contest with Northamptonshire.

Despite this success, Odell dropped out of regular county cricket in 1908 as he turned his attention to education and began working for an international correspondence school. He moved initially to Yardley in Warwickshire, but

The Odell family with William standing second right.

still made himself available to appear for Leicestershire during the school holidays in August. During the winter of 1912-13, he moved to Cardiff to oversee the management of a new branch of the business, and whilst in the city, he played for Cardiff CC, as well as making two appearances for Leicestershire in Championship cricket during mid-May. He also appeared in June 1913 in the two-day friendly at The Gnoll for the Gentlemen of Glamorgan against the Players of Glamorgan. Odell was in fine form, claiming eight wickets in the contest besides posting scores of 24 and 58, but his efforts could not seal a victory for the amateur side as the Players won by 40 runs.

Six weeks later, Odell played at the Arms Park against the Glamorgan side for Sir Harry Webb's XI in a two-day game arranged to boost the coffers of the Welsh county. Odell was one of the county stars, together with Gilbert Jessop, who were assembled by Sir Harry – a mining magnate and MP for the Forest of Dean who lived at Llwynarthen House to the east of Cardiff and was a passionate supporter of cricket. Odell made scores of 19 not out, 19, and claimed a brace of wickets in the drawn contest which proved to be his final appearance in a major match on Welsh soil as, soon afterwards, he moved to the Birmingham area with his wife Alice, and settled in Small Heath.

His return to the West Midlands also saw him return to first-class cricket, appearing in four Championship matches for Leicestershire during August 1914, with the 193rd and final first-class appearance of his career coming on September 1st when he played against Nottinghamshire. Shortly afterwards, he joined the 3rd Battalion the Sherwood Foresters (otherwise known as the Nottinghamshire and Derbyshire Regiment) before becoming a 2nd Lieutenant in the 9th Battalion in early December 1916 after the Battle of the Somme, which had ended the previous month. Within a fortnight, he was wounded during actions near St. Pierre Divion in Picardie, and for several weeks he was in a military hospital recovering from his wounds.

By the spring of 1917 he was able to return to the Western Front and he subsequently fought in the Battle of Messines in June before taking up positions at Ypres the following month. The Battalion subsequently came under very heavy shell-fire, as well as gas as German forces, aware of an imminent Allied attack, did their best to disrupt the advance and built-up of British troops. It was during these skirmishes that Odell won a Military Cross as he took out a patrol at a critical moment during the German assault, and bravely gained valuable information about where the enemy were massing, ahead of a planned counter-attack. Thanks to the information gathered by Odell and his group, the German troops were dispersed by artillery fire from the Sherwood Foresters, and his citation in the *London*

Gazette on September 17th, 1917 read that, 'throughout all operations he has consistently displayed the utmost courage and coolness.'

Tragically, he was killed early the following month during a further advance on the village of Poelcappelle, in what became known as the Battle of Broodseinde Ridge. The Sherwood Foresters met stiff resistance yet again from German troops, and during the first week of October, they lost fifteen officers, including Odell who was reported missing presumed dead, having probably gone out yet again on a reconnaissance mission, but unlike his previous scouting mission, this time he never returned. He has no known grave but is commemorated on the Tyne Cot Memorial near Passchendaele.

15

1917 – PALESTINE

In March 1916 the Egyptian Expeditionary Force, or EEF, was formed under the command of General Murray, amalgamating troops from the Mediterranean Expeditionary Force and soldiers already stationed in Egypt to protect the Middle East and, in particular, to secure the Mediterranean and its strategic shipping routes.

The EEF were also closely concerned with the security of Egypt and the Persian Gulf so an Allied advance into Palestine and the capture of Jerusalem, was seen as a major step to securing the region. The capture of Gaza, which dominated the coastal route from Egypt to Jaffa, was seen as a first step towards accomplishing these aims, but the EEF's initial battles at Gaza during March and April 1917 resulted in defeat, and by late June General Edmund Allenby replaced Murray and reorganised the Force and their strategies.

By mid October, Allenby's preparations for an attack on the key Ottoman garrison at Beersheba were nearly complete. Beersheba, located at the foot of the Judean Hills and on the eastern bank of the Wadi es Saba, was an ancient trading centre occupying a strategic location midway between the Mediterranean and the Dead Sea. Losing control of the town would be a major blow to the Ottomans whose strategic priorities at the time were to push the EEF back to the Suez Canal, and to retake Baghdad and Mesopotamia. With this in mind, their leader Enver Pasa activated the Yildirim Army Group commanded by the German General Erich von Falkenhayn, who formerly had been Prussian Minister of War as well as Chief of Staff of the German Field Armies, besides reinforcing it with surplus Ottoman units transferred from Galicia, Romania, and Thrace with an armoury of around 4,400 rifles, 60 machine guns, and 28 field guns.

Allenby recognised the need to attack Beersheba with 'resolution and vigour' in order to secure the town within 24 hours. Indeed, in this waterless country on the northern edge of the Negev Desert, if the town had not been secured within this time period, the attacking divisions would be forced to retire by the inhospitable and dry environment. The last week of October duly saw the Allied troops assemble whilst extensive reconnaissance operations took place to ascertain both the whereabouts as well as the strength of Ottoman resistance. With the benefit of a full moon, the infantry were in place by the end of October whilst their counterparts in the artillery were also in position so that they could be swiftly mobilised to support the attack.

The assault on Beersheba began at 5.55 a.m. on October 31st with an intense infantry bombardment before Allied troops stormed the Turkish trenches where hand-to-hand fighting took place, as well as Allied forces shooting or bayoneting the Turks. Two battalions of Royal Welsh Fusiliers met with stout resistance as the Ottomans fought to the last man and inflicted heavy casualties on the Welsh soldiers, with others suffering serious wounds from well-sited Ottoman machine guns.

By mid-afternoon, Ottoman reserves had been severely depleted and a mounted cavalry charge successfully captured the outskirts of Beersheba – something which military historians regard as amongst the last successful charges in the history of modern warfare. Around 4pm, Ismet Bey commanding the Beersheba Garrison, ordered a general retreat to a position about six miles to the north in the Judean Hills. At the same time, he instructed his engineers to destroy the Beersheba water supply but fortunately for the Allies, a thunderstorm on October 25th had left pools of water over a wide area and of sufficient depth from which the horses could be watered.

By dusk, units of the 12th Light Horse Regiment, part of the 4th Australian Light Horse Brigade, had moved further into the town and took the honour of securing Beersheba. Pockets of Ottoman resistance were successfully quelled whilst a couple of counter-attacks were rebuffed, including one by enemy aircraft but ground artillery hit the pilot causing the aircraft to crash into the hills. The day after securing the town, the Allied forces continued their onward assault along the road towards Jerusalem. Indeed, the assault on Beersheba proved to be an important and decisive victory in an offensive which saw the EEF capture Jerusalem six weeks later.

William Edwards (Swansea CC, Neath CC and Glamorgan)

William Armine Edwards was one of the Welsh soldiers to be killed whilst assaulting the western flank of Beersheba. Born in May 1892 in Sketty, he was the son of William Henry Edwards, a local JP who lived at The Hill. His sporting talents were nurtured initially at Harrow where he went on to win a place in the school's rugby XV and appeared against Eton in 1909. The Harrovian was also a talented wicket-keeper/batsman, having been coached as a youngster by Billy Bancroft and his father – the groundsmen-

William Edwards.

professionals at the St.Helen's ground – as well as important figures with the Swansea club. Edwards failed to win a place in the Harrow line-up, but the youngster won a place in the Swansea side before going up to Cambridge. He subsequently represented Trinity Hall at both rugby and cricket, but did not make the University teams besides leaving Cambridge without completing his degree.

After returning to south Wales, Edwards switched his allegiance to Neath CC, largely because Swansea had two other talented keepers in Jack Bancroft and Ernie Billings. With greater opportunities at the Neath club, he was able to display his talents with the gloves and in May 1913 when others were unavailable, Edwards was called up by the Glamorgan selectors to keep wicket in the Minor Counties Championship match against Surrey 2nd XI. He didn't let anyone down and during the Glamorgan second innings the youngster top-scored with 37 as Glamorgan hung on for a draw on 93-9.

The following month, he was chosen as the wicket-keeper in the Gentlemen of Glamorgan side which played the Players at Neath – confirmation of his standing as one of the best amateur keepers in south Wales. Later that summer, he was also chosen to play for Glamorgan in their return match with Surrey 2nd XI at the Arms Park, and again he kept wicket very capably.

1914 was a bitter-sweet year for Edwards. On a happy note, it was the year when he married his childhood sweetheart, Miss Aerona Sails, the younger daughter of a JP from Glan-yr-Onen in the Mumbles, a prominent figure in local politics in the Swansea area, and an influential supporter of the Suffragette Movement. In mid-July, Edwards was chosen once again to keep wicket for the Gentlemen of Glamorgan against their counterparts from Carmarthenshire at Swansea. The two teams met the following week at Stradey Park in Llanelli but this time he was chosen solely as a batsman and therefore had an opportunity to display his seam bowling. He duly claimed a couple of wickets, but tragically it proved to be the final county game in which he appeared.

Edwards duly joined up and became a 2nd Lieutenant in the Glamorganshire Yeomanry. After completing his basic training as a rifleman, Edwards and his colleagues briefly saw action in August 1915 at Suvla Bay in Gallipoli, before being withdrawn from the Dardanelles and after time back in the

UK and France as part of the Mediterranean Expeditionary Force, he was redeployed again into the Egyptian Expeditionary Force and departed in October 1916 to serve in the Middle East.

He subsequently became a member of the 4th Dismounted Brigade of riflemen, 24th Welsh Regiment, in the EEF, combining with comrades from Shropshire, Denbighshire, Cheshire, Pembrokeshire and Montgomeryshire. After a year in Palestine, Edwards and his colleagues were involved on the assault on Beersheba, with Edwards leading a platoon in an attack on the western flank on October 31st. Tragically, Edwards suffered a major shrapnel wound as his platoon approached the outskirts of the town where well-placed Ottoman artillery were positioned. He failed to recover and died during the early hours of the following day, and was buried at Beersheba War Cemetery.

James Maxwell (Swansea CC and Glamorgan)

James Maxwell was another Glamorgan cricketer who saw active service in the Middle East, with the all-rounder serving with the Mountain Battery of the Royal Garrison Artillery.

The Taunton-born professional had made his debut for his native county against Warwickshire in May 1906, but despite some promising spells with his fast-medium bowling the West Country side did not offer him terms for 1907 and he moved instead to south Wales where he joined the Swansea club. He soon made an impact with in local cricket and his success for the St. Helen's club won him selection in the Players of Glamorgan side which met the county's Gentlemen, as well as a brief recall the following summer by Somerset, with Maxwell appearing in the away matches with Lancashire and Yorkshire. Despite taking 5-63 against the Red Rose county, the West Country side showed no further interest in him. With his playing career taking off in south Wales he also agreed to play for

James Maxwell.

Glamorgan whilst the qualified draper, also opened a sports outfitters in Swansea.

James made his Glamorgan debut in June 1909, taking 4-28 and during an impressive season, he also returned the remarkable figures of 6-6 from 5.5 overs in the game against Devon as well as 7-43 against Wiltshire. These performances duly won him a place in the South Wales attack for the game against the 1909 Australians at the Arms Park. James had also played some forthright innings in club cricket and 1910 saw him make 90 against Carmarthenshire as well as 108 against Surrey 2nd XI as he moved up Glamorgan's batting order and became a forceful middle-order striker.

1911 saw him continue to enjoy much success with the ball, with a haul of 6-29 against Monmouthshire, as well as match hauls of 13-64 against Carmarthenshire and 13-139 against Buckinghamshire. However his greatest all-round performance came against Kent 2nd XI at Bromley in 1913 where he made an unbeaten 113 and returned match figures of 10-94 as Glamorgan recorded a comprehensive nine-wicket victory.

Whilst he continued to enjoy success with the bat and ball in 1914, it proved to be a difficult season off the field for the all-rounder. Despite taking 6-72 against Monmouthshire and scoring 102 in the game with Essex 2nd XI, it was a summer to forget as his sports outfitters met hard times and he had to close the business. As a result, he returned to Somerset shortly after the declaration of war, before enlisting with the Royal Garrison Artillery.

The all-rounder had previously been a member of the West Somerset Yeomanry, so after a brief refresher course he served at a number of positions with a Mountain Battery, including postings in Cyprus, Salonika, Egypt and Palestine. However, during the latter he was wounded in the arm and leg and was forced to return home. His wounds duly recovered but after being discharged in March 1920, James was unable to resume his cricketing career. However, he returned to Swansea and restarted his drapery business. He met with more success, but his premises were destroyed by German bombing in 1943.

16

1917 – CAMBRAI

The Battle of Cambrai, November 20th to December 7th 1917, was the first time tanks were deployed *en masse* by the Allies, resulted in the Hindenburg Line being breached, and proved to be a precursor to the subsequent Hundred Days Offensive when Allied forces successfully penetrated German defences.

Cambrai, in the department of Nord-Pas-de-Calais, was a key supply point for the German troops. The battle began at dawn on November 20th, with a carefully prepared barrage by over a thousand guns on German defences. Despite efforts to preserve secrecy, the Germans had received intelligence that an attack was imminent. The attack on Havrincourt was anticipated, as was the use by the British of tanks, but their troops made significant advances of up to five miles, prompting German authorities to call up reinforcements for the following day. Consequently, the rate of the British advance on the 21st was much slower, with the villages of Flesquières and Cantaing captured as the British consolidated their position.

However, the subsequent advance was less straightforward with some fierce fighting around Bourlon and Anneux, whilst German counter-attacks forced British troops out of Moeuvres and Fontaine. The strategic point of Bourlon Ridge was eventually taken, but it came at a cost of more than 4,000 casualties in just three days. British reserves, both in terms of men and weapons, were rapidly depleted during the assault whilst more and more German reinforcements arrived.

British commanders stopped the offensive on November 28th and their troops were ordered to lay wire and dig in. The Germans, though, did not let up in their artillery attack on the new British positions, and more than 16,000 rounds were fired on that day alone. This was a prelude to their counter-attack on the morning of November 30th, which saw the Germans employ new tactics of short and intense periods of shelling followed by the so-called Stormtrooper manoeuvre adopted by General Hutier against the Russians whereby pockets of soldiers attacked in small groups rather than the traditional method of advancing in longer lines or waves.

The German attack began at 7 a.m. on November 30th and met with much opposition from the British, especially around Bourlon Ridge, with one group of eight British machine guns firing over 70,000 rounds in their efforts to thwart the German advance. By concentrating their defensive efforts near the ridge, it meant that the Germans could breach other areas, but the arrival of British tanks and the fall of night allowed the line to be held. By the following day, the impetus of the German advance had been lost, but even so, on December 3rd, they captured La Vacquerie and prompted a British withdrawal to the east of the St Quentin canal. Later that day, Field Marshall Haig ordered a retreat from the Bourlon Ridge and by December 7th all of the territory gained had been abandoned except for a portion of the Hindenburg line around Havrincourt, Ribécourt and Flesquières.

It had been a costly battle with casualties of around 45,000 for each side. In addition, 11,000 Germans and 9,000 British troops were taken prisoner, but it had shown to the British policy-makers that trench defences could be overcome by a surprise artillery and infantry attack, if supported by tanks. The success of the German counter-attack boosted their morale, but the fact that further attacks could occur meant that they diverted their resources to anti-tank defences and weapons, thereby stretching their reserves even further.

Alexander David (Cardiff CC and Glamorgan)

Alexander David was another amateur cricketer who was decorated for extreme bravery during the closing years of the War when, during a skirmish in the Battle of Cambrai, he single-handedly extinguished an ammunition dump which had been set alight.

Born in Cardiff in November 1889, Alexander was educated at Arnold

Alexander David.

College as well as Keble College, Oxford, he showed great prowess as an all-round sportsman representing Keble at cricket, football, hockey, athletics and rugby. After graduating in Law, he began his solicitor's training in Cardiff, besides finding time to play rugby for the town's rugby club as well as for their cricket club.

His prowess with bat and ball for Cardiff CC led to his call-up for Glamorgan during August 1911 as he played for the county side against Monmouthshire at Rodney Parade. It was, though, very much a watching brief as he did not bat or bowl in either innings as Glamorgan won by an innings. A couple of weeks later, he also played for Glamorgan against Staffordshire at Stoke-on-Trent and made 11 in his first innings for the Welsh county.

In 1913 he was chosen again for Glamorgan for their Minor Counties Championship match against Monmouthshire at the Arms Park. Once again, Alexander played a minor role making just eight runs in Glamorgan's first innings before they went on to record a seven-wicket victory. Later in the month he was rather more active in the all-amateur match between Glamorgan and Carmarthenshire at Llanelli, taking three wickets with his seam bowling, but scoring just 3 and 5 as Carmarthenshire completed a victory.

He did not play for Glamorgan in 1914 as his legal training took priority, but the outbreak of war brought a change to everything as he joined the Royal Field Artillery and secured a place with the 113th Brigade Ammunition Column. His role as a 2nd Lieutenant was to help oversee the supply of ammunition to the front line, and from 1915 he saw active service on the Western Front.

By August 1917 Alexander had become an Acting Captain in the 113th Brigade and, in early December, he won the Military Cross for his actions in putting out a fire at one of the Brigade's ammunition dumps which supplied material for the Battle of Cambrai. With the German counter-attack in full swing, he knew how important it was to prevent the loss of valuable ammunition and, as his citation read, 'when the ammunition dump had been struck and set alight by hostile shell fire, he ordered all the men except one NCO to take over and at great personal risk left his post and extinguished the fire. His presence of mind and quick decision undoubtedly saved many casualties and prevented the fire from destroying the battery position with all its ammunition.'

This was his finest hour on the Western Front, despite being involved in further – and thankfully less dramatic – advances during the Hundred Days Offensive. He duly returned to south Wales during the autumn of 1918, and resumed his duties as a solicitor, working in Cardiff and Cowbridge between 1919 and 1923, before moving to Montgomeryshire and working in the Newtown and Welshpool area between 1923 and 1944. Indeed, shortly after his move to the county, he won a place in the Montgomeryshire hockey team and gained a place in the final Welsh trial.

Glynne Yorath (Cardiff CC)

Not so fortunate, in the Battle of Cambrai, was Glynne Lougher Yorath, a 23-year-old who lost his life whilst serving with the South Wales Borderers at Bourlon Wood. He was a member of the respected Yorath family of Cardiff,

William Yorath.

with his grandfather having established a successful brewery and his father William, being one of the best-known faces in the legal world of the town, besides acting as a Conservative councillor as well as being Coroner for Cardiff for over fifteen years.

William Yorath had also been a talented cricketer and after leaving Bedford School, he played with distinction for Cardiff CC and the South Wales CC. He also played rugby for the town club and was a leading member of Radyr Golf Club. In 1888 William Yorath also agreed to assist J.T.D. Llewelyn and other leading members of the cricketing world of south Wales in creating Glamorgan CCC. Indeed, William was present on the evening of July 6th at The Angel Hotel in Cardiff when the county club was formally created, with William agreeing to act as secretary for the fledgling club.

Given this outstanding sporting pedigree, it was no surprise that Glynne proudly followed in his father's footsteps and whilst attending university he mixed his studies, training to be a solicitor, with playing rugby and cricket for Cardiff. The onset of the Great War brought an abrupt end to this, and in November 1915 Glynne gained a commission as a Temporary Lieutenant in the 12th Battalion the South Wales Borderers.

For the next two years, he saw active service on the Western Front and was engaged from the late autumn of 1917 in the actions at Bourlon Wood, which on November 23rd were to cost him his life as the Borderers attempted to seize control of the strategically-located ridge. A few days later his grief-stricken father received the dreadful news confirming Glynne's death, contained in a letter from his Company Commander, in which was written, 'We placed the greatest trust in his abilities and the men had great confidence in him. His loss is very keenly felt by all ranks, to all of whom he endeared himself by his consideration and kindly nature. On behalf of his brother officers, myself and the men, I tender you my sincerest sympathy.'

The loss of his cherished son, deeply affected William Yorath and his wife and, in truth, neither never really recovered, with William dying of heart failure in 1924.

17

THE ROYAL FLYING CORPS

Aerial supremacy has become a vital ingredient of modern warfare, and during the Great War, the actions of the Royal Flying Corps greatly assisted the Allies in securing a number of decisive victories.

At the start of the War, the RFC had a mere five squadrons and around 2,000 personnel who supported the British Army by assisting in artillery bombardments and undertaking photographic reconnaissance, as well as manning and operating a number of observation balloons on the Western Front.

As the warfare unfolded, the work of the RFC soon diversified into aerial engagements with enemy pilots, bombing raids and other assaults on German troops and military airfields, as well as dropping off spies behind enemy lines. Following a report by the South African General Jan Smuts in 1917, the RFC was expanded and during April 1918 the RFC was amalgamated with the Royal Naval Air Service to form the Royal Air Force which by 1919 had 4,000 combat aircraft and 114,000 personnel in around 150 squadrons.

The early work of the RFC was fraught with danger, not least given that many of the aircraft were quite flimsy and had not been designed to carry heavy military equipment. As a result, early missions over enemy lines in 1914 saw the aircraft carry just a pilot, rather than a pilot and observer. Consequently, many machines and their brave pilots were lost, but the value of the RFC was highlighted on August 24th when a pilot saw the First German Army's

A pilot from the Royal Flying Corps seen in Belgium during August 1917.

advance towards the flank of the British Expeditionary Force. This allowed information to be passed to their Commander-in-Chief Field Marshal Sir John French, allowing him to realign his troops and save many of his men during the advance on Mons.

Sir John duly reported back to the military authorities in Whitehall and stressed, 'the admirable work done by the Royal Flying Corps ... Their skill, energy, and perseverance has been beyond all praise. They have furnished me with most complete and accurate information, which has been of incalculable value in the conduct of operations. Fired at constantly by friend and foe, and not hesitating to fly in every kind of weather, they have remained undaunted throughout.'

As a result, new machines were swiftly ordered and a host of new pilots were recruited, including men currently serving on the ground as well as many dashing young men, fresh from the universities and public schools, who had learnt to fly with the various Officer Training Corps and Combined Cadet Forces run at these educational establishments.

Freddie Mathias (Cardiff CC and Glamorgan)

"I flew like a bird during the War." The words of Freddie Mathias, the Glamorgan cricketer when returning home from the Great War and speaking to his friends about his duties with the Royal Flying Corps. His abilities aboard the bi-planes won him the Military Cross besides being the reason why the talented amateur batsman was subsequently known to one and all as 'Birdie'.

Born in Abercynon, Freddie was the great-grandson of Richard Mathias, an itinerant builder who had moved to the Gelligaer area from Tenby in Pembrokeshire. His grandfather William Henry Mathias had been a railway entrepreneur and mining magnate who owned many collieries in the Rhondda Valley, having shrewdly acquired the mineral rights of many areas of farmland in the valley and amongst others, owned the Princess and Albion Steam Coal Companies. At the time of Freddie's birth, William had become a County Alderman, Urban District Councillor and Magistrate, who lived in the splendour of Tŷ'n y Cymmer Hall in Porth.

Freddie's father, James Henry Thomas Mathias had become the Manager of the mining enterprise, as William diversified his interests and during 1901 went into a partnership with the Windsor Steam Coal company with George Insole, a Cardiff-based grandee whose business interests included collieries in the Rhondda and whose sporting interests included hunting and cricket, with the Insoles being leading figures in Fairwater CC – a gentlemen's side whose members included Jack Brain, the captain of Glamorgan CCC.

A few years later, the Mathias clan also became involved in a milling business in Cardiff with the thriving operation run by Spillers, as well as overseeing the operation of various quarries in the Vale of Glamorgan. William also served on Rhondda Urban District Council and later Glamorgan County Council, in addition to becoming a major shareholder in companies supplying electricity to the thriving industrial settlements in south Wales. He also bought several farms and other substantial properties in the Rhondda and the Vale, further adding to the family's already quite diverse portfolio of business interests.

William had lived initially at 'The Hollies' in Nelson, near Caerphilly, before moving to Tŷ'n y Cymmer Hall, whilst James lived at Brynteg in Radyr, a popular suburb to the north-west of Cardiff, where his good friend Oakden Fisher also had a substantial property, and was a kindly patron to the local cricket team, allowing them to play on

Freddie Mathias, standing in front of a bi-plane at Hendon in 1916.

his land, besides being a Vice-President of Glamorgan CCC following the Club's formation in July 1888. The Mathias family therefore mixed with the great and good in both the business and cricketing world of south Wales, and it must have therefore delighted both William and James to see Freddie show from a young age such a keen interest in sport.

Freddie was one of five children born to James Mathias and his wife Eveline. James himself had attended Christ College, Brecon and had shown great promise as a rugby player, so he was keen that his son should also have a good education so he was sent initially to board at Cowbridge Grammar School before passing the entrance exams to Clifton College in Bristol. To the delight of his father, he soon showed great promise on the sports fields, excelling in both rugby and cricket.

In 1915 and 1916 Freddie won a place in the school's 1st XI as a spin bowler and lower-order batsman. Many thought that the youngster would win a place in the Glamorgan side, but unlike many other Welsh sportsmen who had attended the famous school, his mind was on matters of more

The Cowbridge Grammar School 1st XI of 1911 with Freddie Mathias standing third left.

grave national importance rather than thinking about a place at university, more opportunities to play cricket, and a place in the county side. Indeed, during the summer of 1915, Freddie and a group of his pals from Clifton had undertaken voluntary work for the War Effort by helping to staff a YMCA canteen at Willingdon Army Camp near Eastbourne.

On leaving Clifton College during the summer of 1916 Freddie immediately joined the RFC as a 2nd Lieutenant. He was one of many recruits straight from school as the RFC swelled their ranks, and like his fresh-faced colleagues he had shown great prowess in flying gliders at Filton Airfield whilst serving with the Training Corps at the famous public school in Bristol. He swiftly passed his flying exams with the RFC at the Beatty Flying School at Hendon in January 1917 flying the Caudron biplanes, and local legend had it that shortly after qualifying he crashed the last surviving training plane, much to the glee of other trainees who had found it such a devil to fly!

He briefly returned home to see his family in south Wales, where his grandfather William had arranged for Clydach Court to be let free of charge as a holding base for Belgian refugees and others displaced by the War. But it was just a brief respite as soon afterwards Freddie was sent on active service to the Western Front with C Flight of 34 Squadron. The natural aptitude of the eighteen year-old for flying the Sopwith Camels and Sopwith Pups – as much as his fearless attitude – saw him quickly rise to the rank of Temporary Captain, although the loss of several colleagues over

A bi-plane at Hendon in 1916.

enemy lines and in training accidents sadly also played a role in his swift promotion. He himself also encountered a few hairy moments, including one mission during June 1917 when he had to land his plane without one of its wheels which had been shot off in an attack on German forces.

Freddie Mathias sat second left with his Royal Flying Corps colleagues in June 1916.

The two-seater bi-planes were equipped with a machine gun, housed above the heads of the airmen. It was usually operated by the navigator which in Freddie's case, was the job usually undertaken by another Welsh lad called Sylvester. But it could be quite a precarious operation for the pair if the Germans attacked from behind, requiring the navigator to swiftly rotate the guns through 180 degrees before unleashing a salvo of bullets at the approaching planes. Apparently, Sylvester was very eager to do his bit for King and Country and on several occasions Freddie had to yell to his trigger-happy colleague: "For heaven's sake, don't shoot off the bloody tail!"

However, the pair were very successful and whilst many of the new recruits to 34 Squadron lost their lives, the pair enjoyed a series of successful sorties against the Imperial German Army Air Service which included Manfred von Richthofen, the notorious Red Baron. Whilst there are no records of Freddie engaging fire with the notorious German airman, the law of averages suggests that he was probably one of several planes which were engaged in actions against the famous flyer and his colleagues in the Jagdgeschwader 1.

During 1918 Freddie actually came face to face with one of the German pilots who had to make an emergency landing near the 34 Squadron's base. As the German scrambled out of his machine and dusted himself down after his landing behind Allied lines, Freddie was in a small group of British airmen who had been summoned by the Brigadier on duty to go and capture the German pilot. The Brigadier himself accompanied the party, each armed with guns and ready to use the weapons if the pilot resisted capture. But Freddie and his colleagues could have been no more surprised when the Brigadier, after ordering the German to remove his helmet and goggles, said, "Good God, it's Fritz – we were at Cambridge together!"

As the two men cordially shook hands, and exchanged pleasantries, Freddie quietly walked up and removed the luger pistol which was in the German's possession. The old pals duly walked back chatting away merrily with each other to the British airfield where the German pilot duly remained for several weeks. As far as the gun was concerned, it subsequently remained in Freddie's possession for many years, although fearing the mickey-taking and leg-pulling about the incident, he was loathe to actually recount the precise events associated with his disarming of a German airman!

There was nothing humorous though about one of Freddie's other sorties a few months later when he was tasked with the job of flying an RE 8 bi-plane down to Italian forces based in Verona. After the spats with the Red Baron and his colleagues, Freddie jumped at the chance of flying the plane to Italy and the prospect of enjoying some rest and recuperation as he headed back by train to the Western Front. A few days in the sun at Asiago, and the chance of some hearty Italian hospitality seemed too good an offer to turn down, but in fact it was a mission that nearly cost Freddie his life as Italian troops, not recognising the unmarked plane, started firing on him from their positions in the trenches.

Thankfully he made a safe, if understandably hurried, landing at Verona before giving the Italian gunners a piece of his mind. The bullets though had rendered the plane unusable and with more than a touch of anger, Freddie instructed Italian troops to remove one of the wooden propellers from the damaged fuselage. He duly returned back to the 34 Squadron's headquarters with another, somewhat larger, item to add to his cache of weaponry and sundry prizes of War.

Fred Mathias wearing his RFC uniform with his sister Dorothy.

However, in September 1918, Freddie was able to add something far more valuable to his collection as, at the age of just 20, he won the Military Cross for his gallantry in completing many hours of successful reconnaissance flights. These took place above positions in Italy, as well as over the trenches in France and Belgium where he and Sylvester – who subsequently went into the hotel trade in the Paddington area of London – often had to fly without any air cover. The camera had replaced the machine gun in front of Sylvester, and whilst taking off and flying toward enemy lines, they had an armed escort, but often when taking the photographs over the combat zone the only protection the intrepid pair had was from a rifle which Sylvester had taken onboard.

From their base in Northern France, the pair duly took a superb series of images of the German lines allowing the Allied forces to know exactly where to attack, and given the presence of dummy soldiers and decoy lines, where not to go. His citation for the Military Cross duly paid tribute to his 'conspicuous devotion to duty having carried out several successful shoots which did considerable damage to the enemy. He also successfully took a large number of photographs and obtained much valuable information.' He subsequently was presented with the prized medal by King George V, and joined a list of relatively few airmen who won this award, as many others won the Distinguished Flying Cross instead.

Given the fact that the life expectation for pilots on the Western Front was only about eight weeks, Freddie did very well to return home unscathed. Indeed, the only direct attack on his person, as opposed to his plane, had come from a woman who had struck him with an umbrella whilst on the London Underground during a Zeppelin raid. At the time, Freddie was training at Croydon Airfield and was wearing his pilot's uniform, but the lady was in no doubt about what he should have been doing instead, and after striking him with her brolly, she yelled, "You should be up there young man, fighting the Hun!"

At the end of the War, he was offered a job training pilots in India, but despite being very keen to head to the sub-continent, his grandfather contacted the War Office and scuppered Freddie's hopes of continuing to

The Glamorgan side at Worcester in 1924 with Freddie Mathias (standing, third left) and Frank Ryan (standing, fourth left), who also flew biplanes in the Royal Flying Corps during the Great War.

fly planes by rejecting the offer. Instead, Freddie went up to Cambridge University and read Geography at Gonville and Caius College, where he continued to show great promise as a right-handed batsman and leg-spin bowler, besides representing the College at rugby and football as well as winning a place in the rugby club's rowing eight. Although he did well on the cricket fields for the College, he failed to make the Light Blues XI, but during the university vacations he met with further success playing for Cardiff as well as playing rugby for Glamorgan Wanderers.

Indeed, it was during one match for the Wanderers against the Clifton Club that Freddie also travelled back home to south Wales by train sat on the roof of a carriage! His feat – either very daring or extremely foolhardy depending on your outlook – was sufficient for the youngster to gain entry to Cambridge's notorious Narkover Club whose membership required the undertaking of a daft deed. After surviving the spats with the Red Baron and other German pilots, to say nothing of his other sorties over German lines, riding on the roof from Severn Tunnel Junction to Newport must have been a dream ride.

Freddie also owned a Harley-Davidson motorbike whilst at Cambridge and loved to ride it on various trips into the East Anglian countryside with fellow student motorbike enthusiasts. But, by his own admission, his greatest moment whilst at Cambridge came in mid-November 1921 when together with fifty other students from Gonville and Caius he took part in a daring prank which 'acquired' a mounted gun from the Great War which had been placed in front of Jesus, a rival college. Great planning and subterfuge took place with the gun carriage being towed by the students through the town at dead of night before, to the great glee of the raiding party, being safely tethered at its new home.

It was during his days as an undergraduate that Freddie was first called into the Glamorgan team, for the match in July 1922 at the Arms Park against Nottinghamshire. Freddie was chosen at number four in the batting order but it proved to be an inauspicious debut as he made 9 and 0, as the visitors from the East Midlands eased to a comfortable victory by an innings and 125 runs. 1922 proved to be a year of highs and lows for Freddie as his grandfather passed away after a short illness. The cricket season, though, ended on a high, as during September he joined Glamorgan colleagues Johnnie Clay and wicket-keeper Mervyn Hill on the MCC tour to Denmark, which comprised three matches in Copenhagen. Freddie thoroughly enjoyed the tour and in the second match, against a Combined Copenhagen XI he made 53 as the MCC secured an innings victory.

After coming down from Cambridge he became a stockbroker based in Westgate Street – a very convenient location given his sporting interests –

and his close proximity to the Arms Park and willingness to turn out, almost at the drop of a hat, if Glamorgan found themselves short if somebody pulled out on the morning of a game. He continued to play occasionally for Glamorgan until 1930, and fully enjoyed the camaraderie of life as an amateur on the county circuit, especially the socialising with other amateurs.

In the case of the rain-affected match with Lancashire at the Arms Park in May 1927, this led to a bit of a spat with Ted McDonald, the Tasmanian fast bowler who was playing for the Red Rose county. Only a couple of overs in the Glamorgan first innings were possible on the opening day of the contest, and shortly after the umpires had called play off for the day, Freddie and Johnnie Clay took a group of the visiting cricketers out to Cowbridge where they had several drinks in the market town's pleasant hostelries. But as the evening wore on, the conversation between Freddie and the fast bowler become less and less convivial, to the extent that after Freddie had told the Australian he wouldn't get him out the following day, the Lancastrian replied amidst other fiery oaths, that he would knock his block off the next day when play resumed.

Freddie was largely undeterred by the threats and when his turn came to bat the following afternoon, McDonald was true to his word as he unleashed a series of short balls against the Glamorgan number eight, who politely smiled back every time the ball whistled over his shoulder. With steam almost coming out of his ears, McDonald unleashed another thunderbolt which Freddie hooked for four, with the local journalists writing that 'he almost played the ball off his eyebrows.' The Australian's response went unrecorded, but shortly afterwards, it started to rain again, washing out the rest of the day's play and with rain still falling the following morning, the umpires abandoned the game, although at least one member of the Glamorgan dressing room was keen to have another go at the Lancashire attack!

Another incident came during the match against Hampshire at Southampton in 1923, when the opposition captain The Hon. Lionel Tennyson took exception to the grubby pads which Freddie wore as he made his way out to bat. The reason for their dirtiness was that Freddie had been in a purple patch of form in club cricket, with a string of good innings to his name for Cardiff and, as quite a superstitious man, he didn't want to inadvertently do anything that might halt his run of good luck.

But the Hampshire skipper was so incensed by the state of Freddie's pads that he instructed his bowlers not to deliver another ball until the Glamorgan man had gone back to the pavilion to clean them. With something of a smirk on his face, Freddie duly went back and found a tub of whitener which he duly daubed onto the offending grubby marks before resuming his place in the middle. Many of his colleagues – both amateur and professional – also had smiles on their faces, including left-arm spinner Frank Ryan who had previously played for Hampshire and was one of many to have been been irked by Tennyson's petty attitude.

Like Freddie, Frank had also been a pilot in the Royal Flying Corps and although in a different Squadron, had flown many sorties over enemy lines as well as trading gunfire with German pilots. No doubt the spinner mumbled something like, "Doesn't he realise that there's more to life than worrying about a little bit of dirt?" as Freddie applied the white paint onto his pads on the steps of the pavilion at the Northlands Road ground. His luck – as he feared – duly ran out as he was dismissed for 14 with Hampshire going on to win the contest by ten wickets.

Freddie Mathias at Chesterfield in 1926 with his Glamorgan colleagues Johnnie Clay, Norman Riches and Trevor Arnott.

Freddie also played for Wales against Ireland at the Ormeau ground in Belfast in June 1926, where he amassed a career-best 65, besides sharing in a productive stand with Cardiff and Glamorgan club-mate Norman Riches who posted an unbeaten 239 in the drawn game. The following September, Freddie also appeared for the Welsh Cygnets in a two-day game against the 1927 New Zealanders at Llandudno with the contest against the emerging nation from the Southern Hemisphere at the end of their long and arduous tour of the United Kingdom designed to showcase the emerging talent in Wales. The tourists however adopted a more serious-minded approach with Freddie subjected to a torrent of caustic comments from the Kiwi captain Tom Lowry. "This fellow can't bat" was the politest thing which Lowry uttered as Freddie made an unbeaten 30 and ensured that after half-centuries from Norman Riches and Cyril Walters, the Welsh side were able to declare on 250-6. Freddie was also able to have the last laugh as Sam Jagger, the Denbighshire-born seam bowler who had previously played for Worcestershire, took five wickets on the second day as the tourists were dismissed for 195.

July 1929 saw Freddie appear against Derbyshire at the Arms Park in what turned out to be his final County Championship match for Glamorgan. It was, though, something of an inglorious finale as he was run out in each innings by Eddie Bates. In the first innings, he had made six when the grizzled Yorkshireman sent him back after Freddie had called for what appeared to be a straightforward single. Second time around, the pair were batting again with Freddie on 22 when Bates called for an impossible single, leaving Freddie – who as an amateur was honour bound to respond to the professional's call – left hopelessly stranded for the second time in the game.

Freddie had continued to play rugby after coming down from Cambridge, and he regularly turned out for Glamorgan Wanderers – as well as briefly for the Cardiff club – with his priceless ability to kick off both feet, allied by his speed and low centre of gravity, making him a more than useful full-back. Some suggested that he be given a Welsh trial, whilst he was offered the captaincy of the 'Rags' – the Cardiff 2nd XV – but he preferred to stay instead with the Wanderers.

His final cricket match of note came in April 1936 when he played for Pat Brain's XI in their annual match against Glamorgan at the Arms Park as the county prepared for the forthcoming season. He claimed two wickets and, batting at number three, made 16 before being bowled by his old friend Johnnie Clay. After the Second World War, and following an evening at the Ty Nant pub in Morganstown, Freddie agreed to turn out for Radyr CC the following day. He regretted his decision, but his wife insisted that he kept his promise. A huge crowd, though, had gathered in the afternoon to watch the former county cricketer in action, but Freddie was clean bowled first ball!

Throughout the 1920s and 1930s, Freddie had been a well-known figure in social circles in Cardiff and amongst the variety of guests to his home, initially at Ty Mawr in Marshfield and later at Brynteg in Radyr, were members of the Tiller Girls plus a number of actors from shows in Cardiff's theatres, as well as flying ace Guy Gibson. Indeed, Freddie maintained his links with the flying world and besides playing golf, he retained his pilot's licence and was an active member of Cardiff Aeroplane Club. He owned a Tiger Moth and, on more than one occasion, had flown to away matches in his bi-plane when called up at relatively short notice by Glamorgan's selectors. According to family legend, Freddie also wooed Eileen Davies

Freddie Mathias on his wedding day with his bride, best man and a bridesmaid.

– the daughter of W.E. Davies of Cranmore House in Radyr and another coal magnate – by flying over the hills and valleys of south Wales, as well as out over the Severn Estuary, although their first flight together had ended up with a forced landing owing to fog in the grounds of a country house.

Indeed, when the Second World War broke out, Freddie was excited at the thought of going back into action against Germany and flying either Spitfires or Hurricanes with the Royal Air Force. He duly contacted the relevant personnel, but despite his distinguished record in the Great War, he was turned down. Undeterred, Freddie duly joined the Lisvane Home Guard and took delight in manning the machine-gun positions and other gun batteries, before moving from Llanishen to Radyr where he continued to live until his death in April 1955.

Many tributes were duly paid to Freddie following his early death at the age of 57. In the words of one writer, 'F was for Freddie as well as for Fun. He was endowed with whimsical humour, an impish nature and a loveable character.' J.B.G. Thomas, his good friend and sporting journalist also commented how 'his Peter Pan qualities have delighted so many who do not remember him on the field of play, and his courage and whimsy – even in his last illness – will never be forgotten.' Tregelles Edwards, the Chairman of the Cardiff Stock Exchange, wrote: 'A friendly soul, generous to a degree, charitable in his judgements to everyone, never in my long association with Freddie did I hear him utter an unkind word of anyone. This world would be a happier place if we all possessed the natural instincts of Freddie Mathias.'

Victor Lowrie (Radyr CC)

Victor William Valette Lowrie was a school friend of Freddie Mathias, with the pair both attending Clifton College, and having connections with the Radyr area.

The son of a timber merchant who had made his money supplying the material for mine props and other constructions, Victor was born in Radyr in July 1899 and initially attended Llandaff Cathedral School before winning a place at Clifton College. Like his good friend, the youngster was a talented young sportsman representing the College as well as Radyr cricket club, alongside his brothers, before becoming the racquets champion at the famous public school.

Together with Freddie and other Cliftonians, he learnt to fly gliders at Filton Airfield before training at Edgware and winning, in record time his wings on January 6th, 1918. He was then posted to the newly-opened Hooton Park training base on the Wirral, where the 18-year-old was appointed a 2nd Lieutenant with specific responsibilities for being a pilot instructor with a number of American and Canadian youngsters who were training to be pilots with the RFC.

Sadly, he was never to emulate the achievements of his friend in the RFC, as on Saturday morning, April 27th, 1918 Victor was fatally injured whilst flying a Sopwith Pup B1742, one of 150 aircraft built by the Standard Motor Company as the military authorities looked to boost their resources and gain aerial supremacy ahead of the last big push on the Western Front. Tragically, he hit an air pocket and spun into the ground. Badly wounded, Victor was rushed to the Chester War hospital where he later died of shock and the injuries he sustained in the crash. His body was subsequently buried at St. John's Church in Radyr.

Alan Boswell (Cardiff Alpha CC and Glamorgan)

Alan Boswell had played for the all-amateur Glamorgan side in the 'last hurrah' match in August 1914 at Weston-super-Mare. Tragically, it was the nearest that the talented young sportsman came to playing for the Welsh county and within a fortnight of the game in the Somerset resort he had enlisted in Cardiff before joining the Grenadier Guards.

Born in Kent in May 1890 and raised in Cardiff, Alan had shown great prowess in a number of sports whilst a pupil at Cardiff High School, and then subsequently whilst studying chemistry at University College, Cardiff. He was an outstanding footballer with Cardiff Corries FC and shortly after graduating he won the first of three amateur soccer caps for Wales besides also leading the Cardiff Corries to win the Welsh Amateur Cup.

He was also a talented hockey player and won a place in the Whitchurch side, whilst as far as summer pastimes were concerned he soon became a leading light with the Cardiff Alpha club who were based in Canton. Some decent batting performances for the Alpha club led Boswell to come to the attention of the Glamorgan selectors, and in August 1914 he was invited to play in the all-amateur side which met a Weston and District XI at Clarence Park.

Alan initially had trained as a teacher at University College Cardiff, before becoming a science teacher at Canton High School, but in October 1914 he joined the Grenadier Guards and after training at various camps in the UK he embarked from Southampton in September 1915 to Le Havre, before being redeployed to Marseilles and subsequently serving with the Mediterranean Expeditionary Force in Salonika.

In May 1916 Alan returned to the UK and was transferred to the Machine Gun School before joining the Royal Flying Corps and trained to become a pilot. He undertook a number of courses on flying the Sopwith Camels and the other biplanes belonging to the Royal Flying Corps before heading to the Western Front. In September 1917 he duly became a 2nd Lieutenant in 108 Squadron and undertook a number of successful sorties over enemy lines but sadly, on October 2nd, 1918 he disappeared whilst flying over Dunkirk. Nothing was seen or heard of him after his aircraft disappeared into a cloud, and it is believed he was shot down, and subsequently killed. He is commemorated at the Arras Flying Services Memorial.

Trevor Akrill-Jones (Christ College, Brecon)

Trevor Akrill-Jones was another of the 'bright young things' to lose their life whilst training as a pilot with the Royal Flying Corps, with the former pupil of Christ College, Brecon being killed in an accident during a flight over Norfolk on March 18th, 1918 at the tender age of just 19.

A successful future had been predicted for the son of the Rev. David

Akrill-Jones, who had lived initially at Bolsover Vicarage near Derby before moving to a similar position in Porthcawl. Having been an Old Boy of the Brecon school, the Rev. Akrill-Jones made the necessary arrangements for his second son to attend the college. Trevor, known as 'The Babe' because of his slight physique and bright eyes when first arriving at the school, duly shone at rugby, hockey and cricket, besides showing rich academic promise, and during the summer of 1914 started to contemplate reading Modern History at Cambridge.

However, with war looming, he was desperate to enlist and as his obituary in the school's magazine outlined, 'He was only 16 but ... He couldn't bear to think he was out of it, while two of his friends had just joined up.' During 1914 and 1915, whilst waiting to turn 17 and thus being old enough to enlist, he was selected for Christ College's 1st XI and, in the latter season struck a handsome 33 to top-score in the College's first innings of their two-day game against a Masters XI.

Despite the plaudits for his cricketing and academic promise, Trevor's 17th birthday fell mid-way through the summer term of 1915, at which point he immediately enlisted as a volunteer with the Sherwood Foresters. He swiftly rose to the rank of Lieutenant in the 4th Battalion of the Notts and Derby Sherwood Foresters, but was wounded in an attack near Thiepaul in 1916 and was forced to return home to rehabilitate, as he explained in a letter to the school: 'I got a piece of shell in the top of my right calf, which kindly came out eight inches lower down, thus avoiding complications of any sort.'

During his period of recovery in the military convalescent home, Trevor decided to join the Royal Flying Corps and, after being given a clean bill of health, he commenced his pilot's training and got his wings. Tragically, in mid-March 1918 he died whilst taking off at Harling Road Aerodrome at Thetford in Norfolk. At the Court of Inquiry which followed, a witness reported: "As he was taking off, he allowed the machine to swing badly to the right and after leaving the ground, reaching a height of about ten feet, the machine slipped into the ground and cart wheeled twice before smashing into pieces and catching fire."

18

1918 – THE SPRING OFFENSIVE

The spring and early summer of 1918 witnessed an abortive attempt by German forces on the Western Front to repel the weary British forces back to the Channel ports and potentially out of the War. The Battle of the Lys, and the Battle of Moreuil Wood were two of the skirmishes which took place as part of this Spring Offensive – each ended in failure for the German troops, and also saw a heavy loss of life.

The Lys Offensive was part of a plan to capture the town of Ypres, and involved the German Fourth and Sixth Armies who had been re-inforced by newly trained volunteers against a line held by the Belgian Army in the far north, together with the British First and Second Armies. The battle opened on the evening of April 7th, with a heavy German artillery barrage against the southern part of the Allied line. It continued until dawn on April 9th before the Sixth Army attacked with eight divisions and made further headway through sporadic defence.

The attacks by the German forces worried Douglas Haig especially as American troops were yet to arrive to swell Allied resources. On April 11th the Commander-in-Chief of the British Army duly issued his famous 'backs to the wall', special order of the day, fearing that if German forces broke through to the Channel ports and cut off supplies, it could potentially knock the British out of the war.

Haig's special order of the day read as follows: 'Three weeks ago today the enemy began his terrific attacks against us on a fifty-mile front. His objects are to separate us from the French, to take the Channel Ports and destroy the British Army. In spite of throwing already 106 Divisions into the battle and enduring the most reckless sacrifice of human life, he has yet made little progress towards his goals. We owe this to the determined fighting and self-sacrifice of our troops. Words fail me to express the admiration which I feel for the splendid resistance offered by all ranks of our Army under the most trying circumstances.

'Many amongst us are now tired. To those I would say that victory will belong to the side that holds out longest. The French Army is moving rapidly and in great force to our support. There is no other course of action open to us but to fight it out. Every position must be held to the last man; there must be no retirement. With our backs to the wall and believing in the justice of our cause each one of us must fight on to the end. The safety of our homes and the freedom of mankind alike depend upon the conduct of each one of us at this critical moment.'

Following his rallying cry, the Allied troops defended stoutly, repelling German assaults at Bailleul, Kemmelberg and Bethune. After several weeks of skirmishes, a final German attack on April 29th captured the Scherpenberg, a hill to the northwest of the Kemmelberg, but the headway made by German troops, was soon countered by considerable French reinforcements. The overall cost of the offensive was estimated at around 120,000 men and on April 29th the German High Command called off their assault and retreated.

The Battle of Moreuil Wood was another part of the abortive German Spring Offensive, with heavy fighting in the areas adjacent to the Arve River in France, as they tried to capitalise on the weariness of Allied forces. The major part of the Battle took place on March 30th, but fighting continued in the area for many months, and it was not until August that German forces were completely cleared from the area

Moreuil Wood had a commanding position over the flood plain of the Arve as well as much of the surrounding area, which included the Amiens to Paris railway line, and as such, it was a most strategic location for either side. Fighting in the area began on March 21st at 4 a.m. when a heavy artillery barrage by the 2nd, 17th and 18th German Armies attempted to break the lines held by the Allied Third and Fifth Armies. The latter occupied a 40 kilometre stretch of poorly prepared trenches which had recently been taken over from French forces, and an order to withdraw was made. Two days later the Germans had reached the village of Ham, and with supply lines being threatened reinforcements were summoned by Allied forces with two hundred men from the Canadian Cavalry Brigade being sent to the nearby village of Bouchoire.

However, the German advance continued and by the morning of March 30th, the German 23rd Saxon Division had occupied Moreuil Woods. An Allied counter-attack duly began at 8.30 a.m. with the Canadian Cavalry entering the wood from the north-west and driving German troops towards the east where another platoon of Allied troops awaited them. After being driven back from their first assault by heavy machine gun fire, the cavalry units dismounted and proceeded to attack a second time with fixed bayonets. There were also instances of hand-to-hand fighting with swords and pistols being used as Allied forces fought with the German 101st Grenadiers.

Shortly after the initial assault by the Canadian forces, further Allied troops crossed the river as reinforcements and approached the high ground and wood, whilst overhead, aircraft from the Royal Flying Corps dropped 109 bombs and fired around 17,000 bullets on the German positions and by the end of the day the wood was in Allied hands. A German counter-attack took place the following morning and further instances of hand-to-hand combat took place, as well as heavy artillery bombardment as the Germans regained the wood, but it was at a massive cost. There were over 250,000 German casualties during the bloody exchanges, whilst the Allies suffered 240,000 killed or injured.

The German offensive had captured 1,930 square kilometres of territory, but the massive loss of life badly affected their forces and unable to swiftly summon reinforcements, German commanders halted the offensive in this area on April 5th. In contrast, Lloyd George agreed to send reinforcements to Haig, with the number of American soldiers in the area rising from 162,000 to 318,000. This, together with the dwindling morale of the German forces, allowed the Allies to launch a series of successful counter-offensives during July, and having successfully captured Amiens, a few miles to the north, the Allies – further swelled by French and Canadian forces – were able to recapture Moreuil Wood in August.

Trevor Sanby Thomas (Pontypridd CC)

Trevor Thomas was one of the bright young things of club cricket in south Wales to lose his life during the Battle of the Lys. A Lieutenant in the 5th Battalion the Welsh Regiment, he died during the early skirmishes on 7th April, 1918. He was the third son of James Sanby Thomas, Esq., a bank manager from Pontypridd, and had attended King's Worcester, initially on a choral scholarship. He also proved to be a hugely talented schoolboy sportsman representing the Worcester school at cricket and rugby, besides showing decent ability as a rower and representing the 2nd IV in 1913, in addition to representing Pontypridd CC in the Glamorgan County League.

He left the Worcester school in 1913 and through his father's contacts secured a post with the National Provincial Bank at Cardiff Docks. Everything appeared rosy in his garden, as he enjoyed much success with Pontypridd in the Glamorgan County League during 1913 and 1914, and appeared in their representative side, besides playing on his Wednesday half-days for various teams from the dockland's business community on both the Arms Park and other recreation grounds in the Splott and Grangetown area.

In 1915 he enlisted with the Welsh Regiment and joined training exercises in the UK with the 5th Battalion. The following year he went to France with the Manchester Regiment, and after various engagements on the Western Front, he took temporary charge of D Company in late March

1918 as they occupied positions near Ypres. Tragically, on April 7th he was fatally wounded during the German bombardment which signalled the start of the Battle of the Lys, and in the letter sent back home to his parents in Pontypridd, his Commanding Officer wrote how Trevor had been, 'not only a dear friend, but a splendid officer. He was always the same – cheery, unselfish and loyal.'

This was the second piece of tragic news which James Sanby Thomas received during 1918, as his eldest son, David Cecil, had also been killed on February 16th in Egypt whilst serving as a flying instructor with 57 Training Squadron of the Royal Flying Corps. Like Trevor, he also attended King's School, Worcester whom he represented at rugby and cricket. David also played cricket for Pontypridd before joining the Welsh Regiment and subsequently served in Gallipoli and Egypt. In 1917 he transferred to the RFC but died in a training exercise in the Middle East.

Bert Tayler (Cardiff CC and Glamorgan)

Bert Tayler survived the bloody battles associated with the Battle of Moreuil Wood, and for his brave efforts on July 23rd, 1918 he was subsequently decorated with the DCM and the French *Médaille Militaire*. Born in

Aldsworth, Gloucestershire, Bert hailed from a farming family who also dabbled in brewing. He was educated, along with his cousin Fred Tayler – who played county cricket for Warwickshire and Gloucestershire – at Burford School and then subsequently Wellingborough School, where both won a place in the cricket XI.

After leaving school, he worked in the family's brewery at Northleach, and in August 1914, after some outstanding batting performances for the local club, he was called up by Gloucestershire to play against Sussex and Surrey in the Championship matches which were part of the historic Festival at the Cheltenham College ground. He marked his first-class debut by making 13 and 43* batting at number seven in the draw against Sussex, before making 23 and 5 against Surrey, but the latter match ended in an innings defeat and a loss inside two days for the West Country side, and he was not called up for Gloucestershire's remaining two fixtures of the season at Bristol and The Oval.

Bert Tayler seen at Cheltenham in 1914.

Shortly afterwards, Bert enlisted with the Royal Artillery and subsequently undertook training with the Tank Corps where he duly rose to the rank of Sergeant as his unit undertook several successful missions on the Western Front. However, his finest hour came in mid-July 1918, when his unit were summoned to the Amiens area as part of the manoeuvres to regain Moreuil Wood and to further quell the German Spring Offensive. On July 23rd he took part in an assault on German positions, and after losing his commander, Bert seized the initiative himself and led his tank in a successful raid on a machine-gun nest, before moving into a position where he was able to protect the advancing Allied troops and help them regain an important section of the Wood.

His fearless actions won Bert both the DCM and the French *Médaille Militaire*, with his citation stating: 'in the absence of the tank commander, Sergeant Tayler commanded the tank throughout the action with conspicuous success, and showed great skill and gallantry in destroying upwards of a dozen machine-gun nests, as well as bringing in several guns complete with spare parts. On his own initiative, Sergeant Tayler advanced through our protective barrage and patrolled far in advance of the infantry, thereby rendering great assistance. By his cheerfulness, personal control and gallantry, Sergeant Tayler set a splendid example to his crew.'

After being demobilised, Tayler moved to south Wales where he joined his maternal uncle, Percy Cadle who ran a tobacco manufacturing and retail business in Cardiff. His decision to settle in south Wales was also influenced by the prospect of playing further county cricket and qualifying as an amateur for Glamorgan. He duly played for the Cardiff club and made his Glamorgan debut during 1920 in their friendly against Captain Pat Brain's XI at the Arms Park. In June 1921 Bert made his Championship debut for the Welsh county at the Arms Park against Northamptonshire, but it proved to be an inauspicious first appearance as he was dismissed for a duck.

He re-appeared in four matches for Glamorgan during 1923, and struck 31 in their match against his former colleagues from Gloucestershire. The amateur, who continued to enjoy much success in club

Bert Tayler wearing his military uniform.

cricket, also played against Yorkshire in May 1924, plus three matches in June and July 1926, during which he made an assertive 44 against the powerful Nottinghamshire side. After his bravery on the Western Front, the fiery bowling of the visiting attack certainly did not ruffle his feathers, but his business commitments prevented him from playing for Glamorgan on a regular basis and he made only one further Championship appearance, in June 1927 when he scored 42 against Derbyshire.

Ben Nicholls (Christ College, Brecon)

Born in Swansea in mid-February 1892, Ben Nicholls attended Christ College, Brecon where he won honours in the school's rugby team and, in 1908, appeared regularly for the 1st XI, displaying a cool and level-headed approach to batting. These qualities were to serve 'Inky' – as he was known to one and all at the school because of his jet black hair – very well during the course of the next few years after he emigrated to become a farmer in Toronto. He returned to fight with Canadian Forces during the Great War and proceeded to win not one, but two Military Crosses, before losing his life in April 1918 after being struck by a shell whilst supervising operations in a trench near Bellacourt.

His father, Frederick, had been a well-known baker in Swansea, but had died when Ben was five years of age. Six months later, his mother Emma remarried John Viner Leader, a prominent solicitor in the town, and it was his step-father who arranged for the youngster to attend the boarding school at Brecon. It gave him an excellent grounding but after leaving school and having by now also lost his mother, he looked to establish a new life for himself and emigrated to Canada.

In November 1914 Ben joined the Canadian Expeditionary Force and became a Sergeant in B Company of the 20th Battalion, known as the Ontario Regiment. After initial training in the Toronto region, Ben and his colleagues sailed across the Atlantic on the SS Meganic before undertaking further training near Folkestone. On September 14th, 1915 the Battalion headed across the English Channel and within a few weeks were at the front line.

In January 1916 the Battalion were involved in fighting at Ypres during which Ben was wounded whilst carrying rations from a nearby farmhouse to the trenches. Struck in his right shoulder, the bullet broke his clavicle bone before exiting his body just below his neck. He was duly transferred to a field ambulance station before returning to the UK to convalesce at the Canadian Red Cross Hospital which had been set up at Cliveden, near Taplow in Berkshire. He was discharged four months later and, after further physical training in Kent, he re-joined the Battalion in France at the end of October, 1916.

The following April, Ben was mentioned in despatches during the Battle of Vimy Ridge when the 20th Battalion was stationed near Roclincourt and involved in a series of skirmishes with German troops. By this time, he had been promoted to Acting Captain and on August 9th, 1917 he won the first of two Military Crosses when he was involved with two platoons on a raid on German positions in Maroc. No less than 49 out of the 72 men were either wounded or killed and, in broad daylight, Ben led a mission to recover the bodies and wounded. He returned that night with a bearer party into no-man's-land where they recovered a further fourteen injured colleagues and seven bodies.

Ben 'Inky' Nicholls.

A week later, he won a second Military Cross as the battalion carried out a major assault on German trenches near the village of St. Eduard. It was a successful mission, but only after Ben shrugged off a bullet wound to lead a raid on one of the remaining German machine-gun positions. Two guns were captured and Ben shot four German troops as the emplacement was put out of action.

During the autumn of 1917 he was temporarily transferred to the First Army School in France and served as an instructor to the next batch of Allied troops who were preparing for the Spring Offensive. In late February 1918 Ben returned to the front line and took charge of D Company which had about a quarter of the 20th Battalion's manpower. By early May, the Battalion had reached Mercatel, some five miles to the south of Arras. It was here on April 8th that his good fortune finally ran out, when he was struck by a shell around 8.15pm as he was supervising the consolidation of the Battalion's position. Ben was killed instantly and three others were badly wounded. A measure of his popularity can be gauged by the fact that the entire Battalion was present for his funeral a few days later.

19

1918 – THE ITALIAN FRONT

Italy was a member of the Triple Alliance with Austria-Hungary and Germany, yet it did not declare war in August 1914, as the nation's leaders believed that the Alliance was largely defensive in nature and, as such, Austria-Hungary's aggression did not oblige Italy to take part. Allied diplomats subsequently courted Italian offficials, and following the 1915 Treaty of London, engineered by the British Foreign Secretary Sir Edward Grey, plus the Italian Foreign Minister Sidney Sonnino and the French Foreign Minister Jules Cambon, Italy sided with the Allies and on May 23rd,1915 they declared war on Austria-Hungary.

Italian troops duly began their involvement in the Great War by participating in a series of offensives in the north-east of the country which their leaders hoped would secure a position for an onward advance towards the towns of Trieste, Fiume, Kranj and Ljubljana. At the beginning of the offensive, Italian forces outnumbered the Austrians by three-to-one, but they failed to penetrate their strong defensive lines along the Julian Alps and were also found to be both severely undertrained.

Further battles took place during 1916 and 1917 which largely resulted in no significant gains for either side, whilst one major engagement in the Dolomites on December 13th, 1916 known as 'White Friday', ended with the death of 10,000 soldiers as a result of a series of avalanches. During this time, Austrian troops were also augmented by reinforcements from the German Army, aided by the withdrawl of Russia from the War. The involvement of German troops also saw some changes to the tactics, and after using the Hutier tactics for infiltration, the Austrian troops made further headway into Italian territory, whilst mutinies and plummeting morale crippled the Italian forces.

The Italians had been pushed back to defensive lines near Venice on the Piave River, and with around 600,000 casualties to date, they were bolstered from November 1917, by contingents of British and French troops. Believing that the Italian Front was relatively safe, German commanders switched their troops in February 1918 for use in supporting the upcoming Spring Offensive on the Western Front. In contrast further reinforcements were made to Italian forces by British and French troops, and a major turning point came in mid-June 1918 following the success of Allied forces in the Battle of the Piave River, although the Italian Army suffered sizeable losses.

As a result, the Italians had to re-gather and augment their forces and, by October 1918, they had sufficient resources to mount another successful offensive which secured the town of Vittorio Veneto. On November 3rd, 1918, 300,000 Austrian troops surrendered, sending a flag of truce to the Italian Commander to ask for an armistice and terms of peace. Terms were duly arranged by telegraph with Allied authorities in Paris, and then communicated to the Austrian Commander who signed the Armistice in the Villa Giusti, near Padua.

John Bell (Cardiff CC and Glamorgan)

John Bell was one of the British servicemen from the Royal Artillery who augmented Allied forces in Italy, and his brave actions saw the Yorkshireman mentioned in dispatches.

Born in Batley in June 1895, John grew up in the Yeadon area and shortly before the War he showed much promise as a batsman in the Airedale and Wharfdale League. In November 1915 the 20-year-old enlisted at Ripon with the Royal Artillery and after training at Catterick Camp he went in May 1916 to the Western Front. However in August 1917 he contracted trench fever and returned to the U.K where he was treated at South Camp, Ripon.

John had recovered sufficiently by July 1918 to return to active service and he was amongst a battery of Artillerymen to assist the Italian forces in their assault on Vittorio Veneto. It was during these actions that John was mentioned in dispatches, with his commanding officer noting how, 'during a four hour bombardment, he continually visited each gun-pit, and supervised the fitting of new springs under heavy fire. It was largely through his untiring efforts that the guns of this battery were all kept in action. Later in the day, when ammunition was running short, he took charge of a party and carried ammunition for two hours along a heavily shelled track.'

After being demobilised, he returned to the UK and resumed his cricket-playing career. His rich promise as a batsman led to him joining the

John Bell.

Yorkshire groundstaff in 1920, and the following May he made his first-class debut, playing against Hampshire and Leicestershire. He re-appeared in five matches during the middle of the 1923 season, but despite some steady performances, his limitations in the field were exposed, and at the end of the season, he was released from the Yorkshire staff.

John knew of the success of fellow Tyke Eddie Bates from playing in their Championship side from 1921, so in 1924 John accepted an offer from Cardiff CC and spent the summer qualifying for the Welsh county. The qualification rules prevented him from playing in Championship cricket in 1924 and 1925, but he showed great promise on his Glamorgan debut against the 1924 South Africans, as well as in other friendly matches, plus some of Wales' first-class matches.

In 1926 he became Bates' regular opening partner and responded to his new role by recording centuries against Warwickshire, Northamptonshire and Somerset. It was a landmark summer both for him and the Glamorgan club as during the season he became their first-ever batsman to score a double-hundred in County Championship cricket. His feat came at Dudley where he made 225 against Warwickshire – initially, he adopted a quite watchful approach, but he increasingly played with greater freedom and shared a rapid partnership of 177 in just 70 minutes with Trevor Arnott.

It was a turning point in John's career as in the course of the next few seasons he played further long and steady innings, including 209 for Wales against the MCC, as well as two further Championship hundreds in 1928 during Glamorgan's games with Leicestershire and Nottinghamshire. 1929 saw John add two more to his tally – against Lancashire and Derbyshire – besides making a majestic 157 for Wales against Sussex.

1930, though, was a quiet year for him, with just one Championship hundred to his name, against Warwickshire at St. Helen's, and with only one more hundred coming his way in 1931, the Glamorgan committee decided to release both John Bell and Eddie Bates from their playing staff at the end of the summer. It was a difficult decision for Maurice Turnbull and the Glamorgan hierarchy to make as each had enjoyed some productive times following their move from Yorkshire. But with their financial reserves being paper thin, plus a desire to recruit and promote home grown talent, they simply could not gamble on John re-discovering his form of 1926. He duly returned to Northern England and re-joined Yeadon CC.

After the Second World War, John returned to county cricket as he stood as a first-class umpire between 1948 and 1951, before becoming a male nurse at Menston Hospital.

20

1918 – THE HUNDRED DAYS OFFENSIVE

By July 1918 the offensives started by the Germans during the spring on the Western Front had petered out. In contrast, the Allied Supreme Commander Ferdinand Foch decided that the time was ripe for a counter-attack, now known as the Hundred Days Offensive.

His thinking was based on the fact that there was a large number of American troops now in France, whilst the British Army had been strengthened by large numbers of replacements previously held back by David Lloyd George as well as large numbers of troops who had returned from campaigns in Palestine and Italy including members of the Glamorgan Yeomanry who had merged with the dismounted members of the Pembroke Regiment to form the 24th Battalion Welsh Regiment.

A number of proposals were considered for the offensive, with Foch agreeing to a proposal by Field Marshal Douglas Haig, for an initial strike, starting on August 19th, on the Somme to the east of Amiens, and to the southwest of the battlefield which had witnessed the bloody battle in 1916. The aim was to force German troops away from the strategic railway line from Amiens to Paris, and to the delight of Haig and the Allied leaders it proved to be successful, pushing the German Second Army back over 34 miles, besides capturing the town of Albert. To the south, the French Tenth Army captured the town of Noyon, whilst to the north the British First Army also made headway in what was known as the Second Battle of Arras.

With the front line broken, Foch planned a further series of attacks on German lines with the aim of severing their means of communications and supply lines, making the efficient maintenance of the German forces on the front well nigh impossible. His plans also included breaching the Hindenburg Line, a series of defensive fortifications stretching from Cerny on the Aisne River to Arras. The offensive, which began on September 29th, involved attacking over difficult terrain, and it witnessed advances by British, Australian, American and Canadian troops and on October 8th they broke through the Hindenburg Line at the Battle of Cambrai.

The Allies then made swift headway as the German troops swiftly retreated and abandoned increasingly large amounts of heavy equipment and supplies. Their hasty retreat and the swift advance by the Allies forced the German High Command to accept that the War had to be ended. The original plan by the Allies had been to mount a decisive attack in 1919 in order to bring hostilities to a close, but ailing German morale swiftly convinced the Allied commanders, as well as the politicians back home that the War could be ended in 1918.

Geoffrey Byass (Bridgend Town CC and Glamorgan)

Geoffrey Byass, the son of steel magnate Sir Sidney Byass, was one of the troops in the 24th Battalion Welsh Regiment to successfully take part in the Hundred Days Offensive and to return home from these battles on the Western Front in the closing years of the War.

Born at Craigafon, Port Talbot in September 1895, Geoffrey had been educated at Winchester where he showed great promise as a sportsman.

Geoffrey Byass.

After attending Sandhurst he joined the Glamorgan Yeomanry and swiftly rose to the rank of Lieutenant in April 1915 before being promoted to the rank of Captain in February 1917. This followed a successful campaign with the Yeomanry in Palestine, before the regiment was redeployed to France for the Hundred Days Offensive.

Geoffrey and his colleagues arrived at Marseilles in May 1918 before heading north and taking part in the Second Battle of the Somme as well as the advance on the Hindenburg Line. Captain Byass subsequently took part in a final advance into Flanders and was at the small town of Ath in Belgium when hostilities finally ceased on November 11th, 1918.

He subsequently returned to south Wales and to his family's new home at Llandough Castle – a rebuilt and fortified manor house, dating back to the 14th century which in the early 1800s had several castellated effects added to the main building. The house had a great cricketing pedigree, as during the second half of the 19th century it was the home of the Stacey family who were highly influential in cricket in south Wales, whilst from the 1890s onwards it had been the home of Harry Ebsworth, a wealthy businessman and cricket fanatic who oversaw the creation of a ground for Cowbridge and personally financed the acquisition of a professional.

Given the Byass family's social standing and great cricketing pedigree, Llandough Castle was a fitting new home. In September 1919 Geoffrey married Marian Bruce, the daughter of Sir Gerald Trevor Bruce of St.Hilary and sister of Clarence Bruce, the Middlesex and Wales cricketer. Indeed, it may well have been at a match staged by the MCC, of which both gentlemen were playing members, that Geoffrey first met Marian. Geoffrey was a very talented all-rounder, playing with distinction for Bridgend Town CC, as well as for the South Wales Hunts and for Glamorgan in 1920 against Carmarthenshire at Swansea.

Had the Great War not taken place, Geoffrey might well have played for Glamorgan on a regular basis. As it was, the match at the St. Helen's ground was his sole game in the county's colours, with Geoffrey opening the bowling. He went wicket-less in the first innings, but did claim one wicket a second time around whilst, at the other end, Frank Pinch took nine wickets. 1920 also saw Geoffrey play for the MCC against Glamorgan, again at Swansea, where he made 0 and 15 against the county professionals.

Geoffrey's cricketing credentials, as well as his social contacts, saw him subsequently play against Glamorgan in the mid 1920s for Capt. Pat Brain's XI in their annual pre-season matches at Cardiff Arms Park as the county players prepared for the new season. Several other members of the South Wales Hunts also played for Pat Brain's side and in 1926 his younger brother Rupert also appeared in the side which met Glamorgan. His father Sidney was also a fervent supporter of Glamorgan CCC and for a short while acted as the club's Chairman, besides providing them with a £1,000 loan in 1921 to assist with their arrangements as they made their bow as a first-class county.

Geoffrey maintained his military links by serving with the Territorial Army during the 1920s before going, in 1924, into local politics, serving on the local council in Port Talbot as well as learning about the management of his father's business. Sidney died in February 1929 and Geoffrey, as the eldest son, duly became Second Baronet Byass and inherited his late father's steel and tinplate business. During the 1930s he oversaw the operation of the Margam and Port Talbot works, besides serving as Mayor of Port Talbot in 1937-38. The following year however, he sold the Margam complex to Richard Thomas and Baldwins.

Geoffrey had five children, and in 1949, on the marriage of his daughter Daphne, he became father-in-law of Guy Mathews, an Army captain who, like Geoffrey, was a talented cricketer and member of the South Wales Hunts, who played for Glamorgan in friendly matches during their Championship-winning summer of 1948. Geoffrey Byass died in Surrey in November 1976 after a busy life in the military, business and cricketing world.

Horace Beasley (Pontypridd CC, Cardiff CC and Glamorgan)

Horace Beasley, the son of the General Manager of the Taff Vale Railway was another gentleman cricketer who was involved in the Hundred Days Offensive. The Beasleys hailed from the Chiswick area, with young Horace attending Westminster School where he showed promise as a cricketer and footballer.

He subsequently went up to Cambridge to read Law, and whilst in residence at Jesus College, won football Blues between 1896 and 1899, and led the Cambridge XI in his final two years. On coming down, he opted not to follow his father into the railway world, and trained instead to be a barrister.

He subsequently became a leading figure in Conservative politics in south Wales, and this – together with his close allegiance to the Taff Vale company – soon won him many friends within Glamorgan's hierarchy. It was these contacts, as much as his prowess on the cricket field for Pontypridd CC and Cardiff CC, that prompted his selection for three of the county's fixtures in 1899, including the away matches in the Minor County Championship against Cornwall at Truro and Wiltshire at Trowbridge.

Beasley made little impact in these matches and soon after, he concentrated his efforts on his legal career, working initially in south Wales. After hostilities began in 1914, Beasley became a Major in the British Army and led a brigade in the Labour Corps in the Hundred Days Offensive, and after his distinguished service, and fearless approach, he was awarded the OBE in the New Years Honours List in January 1919.

After the Great War was over, Beasley emigrated to Burma where he became a High Court Judge. In 1929 he moved to India, where he served as Honourable Chief Justice of Madras until 1937. He was knighted in 1930, before returning to the UK in the late 1930s, and subsequently being awarded a CBE after acting as President of the Pensions Appeal Tribunals Board between 1943 and 1958.

William Carrington (Glamorgan)

A less happy fate however befell William Carrington who, nine days after his sixteenth birthday, had made his debut for Glamorgan in their match against Surrey Club and Ground at The Oval in late May 1896. Carrington was a member of the Surrey groundstaff and, when one of the Welsh county's squad was injured on the morning of the match, Carrington was drafted in as a very late replacement.

He duly scored 10, batting at number nine in the order, besides taking a catch, but the drawn game proved to be his only cricket match of note, and despite having represented London Schools, he did not play any further representative cricket and participated instead in club cricket in the London area.

Carrington was residing in Tottenham when the War broke out. He duly joined the 1st Battalion the Leicestershire Regiment, and underwent basic training in Cambridge before crossing the Channel on September 10th, 1914. He and his battalion duly became veterans of various actions on the Western Front, including the action at Hooge in 1915, the Battles of Flers-Courcelette and Le Transloy in 1916, as well as the Battle of Hill 70 in 1917.

They subsequently were involved in The Hundred Days Offensive, but sadly on April 28th, 1918 Carrington lost his life during a skirmish in Flanders as the British Army attempted to make further inroads into German-held territory.

Jack Bevan (Neath CC, Llanelli CC and Glamorgan)

Jack Bevan, the son of an industrialist from Llanelli, played in one match for Glamorgan in 1920, besides making several appearances for his native Carmarthenshire before the Great War.

Educated at Clifton College and Cambridge University, Jack inherited his father Isaiah's love of ball-games. Isaiah had been a popular captain of Llanelli CC in the 1880s, besides being a founding member of the town's rugby club. Tragically, in January 1893, Isaiah was crushed, and instantly killed by falling dockside machinery at Briton Ferry.

After completing his education, Jack Bevan stepped into his late father's shoes and oversaw the management of the family's steelworks at Briton Ferry and Llanelli. He still found plenty of time to play in club cricket for Neath and Llanelli, as well as for Carmarthenshire from 1909 onwards. He made his Minor County debut aged 22 for the West Wales side against Glamorgan at Stradey Park and the young all-rounder batted at number 11 in the order on his first county appearance, besides

Jack Bevan.

going wicketless. His maiden wicket for Carmarthenshire came during the match a few weeks later against Cornwall at Camborne. In July 1911, Jack appeared again for Carmarthenshire in their Minor Counties Championship match with Glamorgan at Swansea, and his haul of 4-51 included the wicket of Tom Whittington, the opposition captain, who posted a fine 176.

His finest hour in Carmarthenshire ranks came at Stradey Park in July 1914 when he struck an unbeaten 108 against an all-amateur Glamorgan side, before taking 5-59 and lead his team off the Llanelli ground after they had recorded a thrilling victory by five runs, By this time, other things were on Jack's mind, especially ensuring the output of steel from his factories would be sufficient to meet the military demands and after ensuring that all was well at his family's works, he joined the Royal Field Artillery and went off to serve King and Country.

He soon rose to the rank of Colonel with the Royal Field Artillery whose units were responsible for the medium caliber guns, larger howitzers and trench mortars which were deployed close to the front line. In September 1918 during the advance on the Hindenburg, Colonel Bevan was awarded the Military Cross as Allied troops crossed the Somme River and broke German lines near the town of Mont Saint-Quentin. His citation duly stated that it was awarded for 'conspicuous gallantry and devotion to duty throughout sixteen days of operations. On one occasion he voluntarily carried a message under heavy, hostile machine-gun fire at about 300 yards range.'

Once hostilities ceased, Jack returned to the world of cricket and business in south Wales as he continued to manage the family's steelworks in Llanelli. His high standing in cricketing circles in south Wales is evidenced by the fact that in June 1920 he was chosen in the Gentlemen of Glamorgan team which met the Players of Glamorgan in a two-day contest at The Gnoll in Neath. A couple of weeks later he made his one and only appearance for Glamorgan against Monmouthshire at Ebbw Vale.

After the Great War, Jack was largely a specialist batsman and went in to bat at number five for Glamorgan against Monmouthshire. It was a role he fulfilled as well for Carmarthenshire in their all-

Jack Bevan, alongside one of the artillery's guns.

amateur games with Glamorgan at Llanelli and Swansea in 1920, although in the match at Stradey Park he did service for a while as wicket-keeper following an injury to the regular gloveman and also opened the bowling when Glamorgan batted for a second time.

The 1920s also saw Jack commence various roles off the field with Glamorgan CCC, as he joined the club's committee in 1923 and oversaw the introduction of various Carmarthenshire players into the Glamorgan side including Dai and Emrys Davies. Indeed, Jack's devotion to the west Wales county as well as recognition of his high social standing can be gauged from the fact that in 1929 he was appointed High Sheriff of Carmarthenshire.

During the 1930s he was overjoyed when Glamorgan staged County Championship matches at the Stradey Park ground, with the inaugural game against Worcestershire in 1934 drawing a bumper crowd. When the Second World War broke out, he agreed to act as Chairman of the Emergency committee which oversaw the club's affairs during the wartime years, and when hostilities were over, he remained in the position of Chairman. Indeed, after his lifetime of service to cricket and the sporting community in west Wales, there was no more delighted person than Jack Bevan who, as the Glamorgan Chairman in 1948, could celebrate when the Welsh county won the County Championship title for the first time.

Joe Hills (Barry CC and Glamorgan)

Born in Plumstead in Kent in 1897, Joe Hills had shown great promise as a schoolboy sportsman but on leaving school in 1915 he initially trained to be an electrician before enlisting with the Royal Engineers in mid-May 1916. The eighteen year-old then spent time at Hitchin Signals Depot before going to France on January 7th 1917, with the Cable Section of the Royal Engineers. He soon saw active service on the Western Front, ensuring that cabling and other wiring from Brigade HQ reached the forward positions.

During the summer of 1918 he was involved in manoeuvres associated with the Hundred Days Offensive and on August 27th, 1918, during heavy shelling and gunfire during the Battle of Amiens, he showed great bravery in ensuring that the communication links were maintained between Brigade HQ and the forward lines in what proved to be a decisive passage of warfare. His efforts did not go unnoticed and he duly received the Military Medal for his brave deeds.

He subsequently returned to civilian life in Kent

Joe Hills.

and continued to show rich promise in both football and cricket, before securing a place on the Kent groundstaff, besides having trials as a goalkeeper with various Football League clubs. During the mid-1920s, he secured a professional contract with Cardiff City, and on New Years Day 1925 he made his debut for the 'Bluebirds' against Sunderland.

Following his move to south Wales, he also secured a professional post with Barry CC, and his fluent strokeplay, classical cover drives and neat wicket-keeping attracted the attention of Glamorgan's officials who were looking for a young and agile person behind the stumps. Terms were agreed for the 1926 season, and Joe soon proved to be a useful acquisition for Glamorgan, recording his maiden hundred against Nottinghamshire on a quite lively Trent Bridge wicket.

As befitted someone who had been decorated for gallantry, this was one of many brave and gutsy innings that Joe played, and he took part in several stubborn lower order partnerships, adding 202 for the eighth wicket with Dai Davies against Sussex at Eastbourne in 1928, as well as an unbroken 203 with Johnnie Clay for the ninth wicket against Worcestershire at Swansea in 1929 which still stands as a Club record.

In 1926-27 Joe had a spell as goalkeeper with Swansea Town, before joining Fulham as their reserve goalkeeper, but in September, he broke his forearm and ruptured elbow ligaments in a reserve team game. Although he was able to return to action later in the season, he was increasingly handicapped by the injury, so he retired from football, and concentrated on cricket. The injury also meant that he had to give up keeping wicket, and he played as a specialist batsman for the next few seasons.

By the early 1930s, Glamorgan's finances were in a sorry state, and with ever increasing costs, they regrettably had to save money by releasing various professionals, and Joe was one of the players released at the end of 1931 as an economy measure. Joe returned to club cricket, but he missed the *bonhomie* of the county circuit, and in the mid-1930s he started umpiring, standing in Minor County games in 1936, before officiating in first-class games from 1937.

In 1947 he stood in the Fourth Test of England's series against South Africa. Joe remained on the umpire's list until 1956, during which time he earned a reputation as a cheerful and popular official, and perhaps drawing on his grim experiences in the trenches, he was always ready to pass on a word of encouragement to a young player who was down on his luck.

Joe retired from umpiring in 1956 after standing in 273 first-class matches. He died in Bournemouth on September 21st, 1969, just a few weeks after his former county had become county champions for the second time in their history.

21

DEALING WITH GRIEF

The Great War, with a death toll of around nine million is regarded as one of the greatest acts of barbarity and futility. It was viewed initially as a soldiers' conflict, with hundreds of men mobilised to fight overseas, but as hostilities increased, the death toll rose and Zeppelin raids took place on London. It soon became everybody's war, with the entire population and the nation's resources being harnessed to the War Effort.

On the front line, the soldiers knew that King and Country expected them to fight to the death. Indeed, such was the expectation of the political and military leaders, their peers and even their loved ones that there was no question that if mortal danger came, they should face it like men and fight to the bitter end. It was, from this standpoint, the only way for good to triumph over evil.

Ladies taking part in a fund-raising football match held at the Arms Park in Cardiff in 1916, in aid of various War charities. In the back row are several wounded servicemen.

But as the years passed, such was the scale of the human loss of life that not even the most seasoned military veteran was prepared for the scale of carnage and bloodshed which occurred. One of the greatest social effects was a feeling of disillusionment. Many of the Tommies who had gone off to War in the summer of 1914 had believed in heroism and nobility, whilst others readily signed up as they agreed in the benefits of working together for a common goal, as typified by the Pals Battalions.

The reality was so very different and the brutality of trench warfare, the use of poison gas, and the loss of friends and colleagues steadily transformed these feelings towards disbelief. There was also anger, expressed so eloquently by the soldier-poets, directed towards those who had sent them to the War, rather than the enemy, and the futility of some of the manoeuvres during which only small gains in ground were achieved. These changes to the young soldiers' outlook is most famously shown in the writings of Wilfred Owen, who died on the Western Front in 1918, having been transformed from a happy romantic into a bitter and powerful denouncer of those who had sent young men off to war.

Many questioned the tactics, and the competence of officers, often situated a safe distance from the trenches, the military top-brass situated at an even safer distance from the fighting as well as government officials and ministers who were situated in a totally different country. At the time, the principal strategy was to send troops over the top of the trenches to walk across the bleak and blitzed no-man's-land with the target of reaching the enemy's trenches and then shooting or bayoneting them.

But in reality, no-man's-land was often without cover following the blasting by the artillery, whilst the bad weather in the winter months meant that the ground, already littered with body parts, plus the remains of shells, was knee deep in mud. Moreover, when a British soldier did reach the German or Turkish trenches, they would often only be able to kill a couple of enemy troops before being shot themselves.

The immense loss of life on the Western Front and at Gallipoli also had very deep and psychological effects, as young men watched their friends and fellows literally being blown apart or dreadfully wounded by flying shrapnel. The sight of so many maimed bodies, plus the carcasses of dead animals would have fuelled a thousand nightmares, and for some, it led to thoughts of desertion. But it wasn't just in the trenches or battlefields where the horror unfolded and one can only wonder at the impact on families and local society in general in south Wales where news was received on a daily basis about the death of so many young men, and the loss of a generation.

In modern times, information is much more immediate, and visible on the rolling 24-hour news channels with images from the front line, plus other content from social media bringing events into everyone's homes and workplaces. In contrast, during the Great War there was limited information in the newspapers, with families reliant on basic telegrams or the dreaded knock on the door from representatives of the Regiment for news of the death or injury of their loved ones.

Morgan Lindsay (Ystrad Mynach CC)

The experiences of the family of Colonel Morgan Lindsay – one of the most prominent sporting country gentlemen in south Wales in the late nineteenth century – was an example of the massive effect the War had on families throughout the UK, with the Colonel and his wife losing three of their four sons during the hostilities, including two in the space of one week in March 1918.

Born at Tredegar Park in February 1857, Henry Edzell Morgan Lindsay was the eldest son of Lieutenant-Colonel Henry Gore Lindsay of Glasnevin House, County Dublin, and the Hon. Ellen Sarah Morgan, the daughter of Lord Tredegar. Married in May 1856 Morgan Lindsay was their first son with the youngster attending the Royal Academy in Gosport and growing up at the family's home, Woodlands in the attractive village of Leckwith to the south-west of Cardiff. His father had enjoyed a distinguished Army career, serving in the Crimea and in the Indian Mutiny before becoming Chief Constable of Glamorgan. As the grandson of Lord Tredegar – a generous patron to sporting activities – it was not surprising that the military and sport therefore loomed large in the life of young Morgan as after leaving school he joined the Royal Engineers, besides being invited to play in various country house matches which were in vogue at the time.

In fact, in 1870 Henry Lindsay formed a cricket team called Woodlands to give his sons and their well-connected friends some suitable recreation during their school holidays.

Whilst in his teens Morgan Lindsay was also invited by Hugo Pearson, a captain in the Royal Navy who lived in Monmouth to play in his team of aspiring young gentlemen against the Glamorganshire side in a two-day match at Cardiff Arms Park in June 1872. Lindsay batted at number ten and did not bowl in either innings but his agile and alert fielding was a great asset. The following summer he also appeared for the Breconshire side against Glamorganshire at the Arms Park and from his position at number eleven it would appear that the schoolboy's nimble fielding was the principal factor in his selection for the so-called county side.

In September 1874 Henry Lindsay also raised an XI which challenged his father-in-law's side at Tredegar Park, with Morgan opening the batting for his father's side in what was quite a light-hearted game which involved many members of Lord Tredegar's household, as well as his brothers and Henry himself.

In 1876 Morgan Lindsay commenced his military training with the Royal Engineers at Gillingham, and whilst in Kent he found plenty of time to still play cricket. Indeed, in July 1877 he struck a fine 77 against the Quidnuncs, besides taking five wickets with his useful seam bowling. During August that year he also picked up five wickets against the Royal Marines and I Zingari, and the following summer he played in his first major matches after accepting an invitation to play for the South Wales CC on their London tour. It was quite a modest debut, though, amongst the ranks of some of the top cricketing gentlemen of the region as he made just 1 and 2 against Surrey Club and Ground at The Oval, before claiming two wickets in the match against the MCC on the hallowed turf at Lord's.

Cricket was, however, just one of Morgan's sporting loves as he also showed great prowess at association football and during the 1877-78

Morgan Lindsay (right) seen on his return from serving in the Boer War.

season he won a regular place as a forward in the Royal Engineers side. It proved to be an extremely successful season for the military side as they progressed to the final of the FA Cup with Lindsay being a member of the side which lost 1-3 in the final to the Wanderers at The Oval, where four months later he made 1 and 2 on his debut for the South Wales CC. His footballing prowess also earned him selection for the South of England against the North of England in 1879-80.

For the next couple of years, Morgan continued to represent the Royal Engineers at both football and cricket, although a football injury meant that he concentrated more on his batting and did less seam bowling, besides turning his hand instead to wicket-keeping. Indeed, the summers of 1879 and 1880 saw him appear as a top-order batsman and wicket-keeper against some decent opposition in club and military cricket, including the Royal Artillery, Harlequins, Cobham, The Mote and the Band of Brothers.

Soon afterwards, Lindsay commenced his military service overseas and was posted to South Africa in the early months of 1881 after Transvaal had formally declared independence from the United Kingdom. The so-called war had begun on December 16th, 1880 with shots fired by Transvaal Boers at Potchefstroom. This resulted in action at Bronkhorstspruit on December 20th where the Boers ambushed and destroyed a British Army convoy. From December 22nd until January 6th, British Army garrisons all over the Transvaal were besieged, with Morgan and his colleagues in the Royal Engineers summoned to the Cape as British troops sought to regain the upper hand.

The fiercely independent Boers had no regular army, and relied instead on a civilian militia, but they inflicted heavy losses on the British side. The initial skirmish at Bronkhorstspruit, and the subsequent uprising had caught British troops by surprise, and further heavy losses were sustained in late January at Laing's Nek and in early February at Schuinshoogte.

Morgan Lindsay was part of the reinforcements which arrived shortly afterwards, with the grandson of Lord Tredegar surviving the bloody battle of Majuba Hill after military leaders had led a brigade during late February to a position which overlooked the main Boer position. Early one morning, the Boers counter-attacked, with many of Lindsay's colleagues being killed or wounded with some falling to their deaths down the mountainside. A truce followed in

Morgan Lindsay at Ruperra Castle in 1904.

early March, with the British government under William Gladstone adopting a conciliatory stance as it realised that any further action would require substantial troop reinforcements, whilst a full-scale war could be extremely expensive. Sir Evelyn Wood duly signed a peace treaty at O'Neil's Cottage on March 6th, with the Pretoria Convention subsequently being negotiated by a three-man Royal Commission, as the British agreed to complete Boer self-government in the Transvaal.

Lindsay returned home later during 1881 but three years later he was in action again during the Suakin Expedition in Central Africa, as two military expeditions were led by Major-General Sir Gerald Graham to Sudan with the intention of destroying the power of Osman Digna, the first in February 1884 and the second in March 1885. The first expedition, in February 1884, led to several notable British victories including the Battles of El Teb and the Battle of Tamai, with Morgan Lindsay and his colleagues fighting the 10,000 strong Mahdist Sudanese, largely comprising men from the Hadendoa tribe who were known to the British troops as 'Fuzzy Wuzzies' because of their distinctive hairstyle.

Following the fall of Khartoum, Morgan Lindsay was in action again in March 1885 as a second expedition was undertaken under the leadership of General Gerald Graham and General John McNeil, against Mahdist forces in the deserts of eastern Sudan. On March 22nd, 1885, the British troops marched eight miles towards Tamai with the goal of building three fortified bases known as zaribas.

Whilst the Engineers were engaged in the construction work, they were heavily attacked upon by Arabs of the Hadendoa tribe, and severe fighting took place. In the space of twenty minutes around 1,500 Sudanese were bayoneted and after severe fighting, the enemy were driven off. Although it was also successful in the subsequent Battle of Hasheen, these actions failed to change the military situation with the result that Lindsay and his colleagues were withdrawn. The completion of the Suakin Campaign marked the end of Morgan Lindsay's commission with the Royal Engineers and he duly returned to his home at Woodlands, and transferred his military allegiances to the Monmouthshire Royal Engineers Militia.

With his footballing days having finished, Lindsay's main sporting activities became hunting and shooting during the winter, and playing cricket in the summer. As far as the latter was concerned, he accepted invitations to appear in various gentlemen's teams and for other scratch elevens, including a side assembled by WJG Cartwight of Newport CC which met a Monmouthshire side at Rodney Parade in August 1886.

Playing alongside him in the scratch XI was Jack Brain of Oxford University and Gloucestershire who subsequently moved to Cardiff to manage the family's brewery, besides playing a massive role in the affairs of Glamorgan CCC and their elevation into the Minor Counties Championship. Also playing in Mr. Cartwright's side was Frizzie Bush, the Gloucestershire wicket-keeper and a great friend of Dr. W.G. Grace. Lindsay certainly did not disgrace himself in this august company and top-scored with 60 in his team's first innings.

Lindsay also played regularly for the MCC and I Zingari, and in August 1888 was chosen in the I Zingari side which toured Ireland, with Lindsay appearing in the principal fixture against an Irish national side at Phoenix Park in Dublin. These were also important years from a personal point of view for Lindsay as he met and fell in love with Ellen Katherine Thomas who lived at Thames Bank House in Whitchurch, a prosperous and well-to-do suburb to the north-west of Cardiff

Ellen was the daughter of George Thomas, an Oxford-educated barrister and a prominent member of South Walian society, who had served as High Sheriff of Glamorgan. Thomas was a keen and enthusiastic sportsman who had played cricket for Glamorganshire in 1875, besides being a member of the South Wales CC, and a very prominent figure in point-to-point circles and hunting. George Thomas had lived initially at Coedriglan to the west of Cardiff before moving in the early 1870s with his young family to The Heath, a large manor house and estate to the north of the town which had stables and areas of exercise for his horses. Ellen herself was a keen horsewoman, and Morgan Lindsay's subsequent interest in horse-racing is said to have stemmed from his wife's passion for all things equestrian.

Through marriage to the daughter of a member of the Crawshay family of Merthyr Tydfil, Thomas had inherited Ystrad Fawr (or Ystrad House) in Ystrad Mynach, some eighteen miles to the north-east of Cardiff. The Thomas family also had business interests in coal mining, canals and railway lines, besides the supply of gas and water to Llanbradach, Ystrad Mynach and Tredomen, as well as Pencarrig in Breconshire and other parishes in Monmouthshire and Radnorshire. George

Ystrad Fawr House, the home of the Lindsay family, seen in 1898.

Thomas was also a leading figure in the world of steeple-chasing, and when living at The Heath in Cardiff he organised races on his land, besides training a series of decent point-to-pointers from his own stables. Ellen inherited her father's love of horses, and as a result, Morgan too became something of an expert in hunting and equine matters in general.

George Thomas had died in 1885 so when Ellen married Morgan Lindsay on July 24th, 1889, it was her elder brother, Edward who had inherited the family's estate at Ystrad Mynach, who gave her away. But the following year, Edward also died, so it was Ellen and Morgan Lindsay who made Ystrad Fawr their family home in the late Victorian era. During the next eight years, the couple had three sons and two daughters – George Walter Thomas (born January 1891), Claud Frederic Thomas (born January 1892), Ellen Blanche (born December 1893), Archibald Thurston Thomas (born June 1897) and Nesta Jessie (born May 1898).

Besides overseeing the running of his wife's estate, Lindsay also emerged as the archetypal sporting country gentleman, riding with the Glamorgan Hunt in the winter months and taking part in local point-to-points, besides serving from 1890 as both President and Chairman of the South Wales Football Association. He also supported Glamorgan CCC and served on the county's committee at a time when the club were stepping up into the world of Minor County cricket.

Lindsay also created a cricket ground close to Ystrad Fawr and, besides being used by the local village team which had been formed in 1884, the ground was used for annual matches between the Glamorgan Militia and the Monmouthshire Militia, he raised his own side for matches against leading clubs and other scratch XIs. He had many friends and contacts within the sporting and political world and amongst the talented sportsmen who guested for his side were Welsh rugby internationals, Ralph Sweet-Escott and Selwyn Biggs, Joseph Stratton, a successful batsman in the Monmouthshire side, and Viscount Southwell

Indeed, by this time, Lindsay had became quite active in local politics, having joined the Caerphilly Urban District Council in 1892, before being elected onto the Glamorgan County Council, and rising to the position of Chairman of Caerphilly UDC in 1914. In 1900 Lindsay was also nominated in the General Election by the Conservative Party for the East Glamorgan Parliamentary Division. He held strong views against Disestablishment and Disendowment, besides being a strong advocate of the colonial system, believing in a closer union between the UK and her colonies and dependencies, especially for purposes of mutual defence.

At the time of the election, quite fittingly, Lindsay was on active service once again following the outbreak of the Boer War, so it was his wife who oversaw his election campaign. His opponent was Alfred Thomas, the Chairman of the Welsh Liberal Parliamentary Party, who had held the seat since 1885, and went on to once again secure a majority in the election.

Lindsay served in the Cape with Number 8 Company of the Monmouthshire Royal Engineers until 1901, during which he was mentioned in dispatches, before returning home aboard the SS Victorian to Southampton in October 1901 to be met by his wife and eldest son. For the next few years, Lindsay devoted his energies to his family – both at Ystrad Fawr and at Glanmor, their holiday home at Southerndown, as well as continuing to serve in local politics. He maintained his interests in sport, actively supporting – and playing for – the Ystrad Mynach cricket team, besides following the fortunes of Glamorgan CCC and generously supporting their fund-raising campaigns as they strove to raise their financial reserves in a bid to enter the world of first-class cricket. During the winter months he continued to serve with the South Wales Football Association, besides riding in point-to-points and, together with his wife, becoming involved in the breeding of thoroughbreds from his stables at Ystrad Fawr.

Given his long and distinguished military record, it was fitting that he should join up again with the Glamorganshire Yeomanry on the outbreak of the Great War in August 1914, and briefly spent time in France with the British Expeditionary Force before retreating back to the UK following the Battle of Mons. He also encouraged his three sons, all of whom had been educated at Wellington College, to join up. In fact, they didn't take much persuasion having inherited their father's love of sport with all three winning a place in the Wellington 1st XI both

George Lindsay.

George and Claud had also become cadets at the Royal Military Academy at Woolwich, with Capt and Mrs. Lindsay sitting proudly in the audience when George passed out from one of the world's foremost military college in 1911. Little could the proud parents have known that within half a dozen years, their eldest son would be killed in a tragic accident whilst testing planes near Bristol.

Like his father, George had been amongst the first wave of British troops to depart for foreign field in August 1914, sailing to France in 1914 with the Royal Field Artillery. In November he was wounded during the Battle of Ypres and briefly returned to his family home to recover, before heading back to the European mainland and commanding a battery at Salonika during 1915.

In November 1916 George joined the Royal Flying Corps and after flying a series of successful sorties over enemy lines in France and Belgium, he was deployed back in Britain during the summer of 1917 to test a series of newly-built and repaired aircraft from the Rolls-Royce factory adjacent to Filton Airport in Bristol. With events on the Western Front poised to move into a decisive stage, his new duties for the War Effort were important in ensuring a decent supply of fit-for-purpose planes. Tragically, his work – ironically well away from enemy fire – was to cost him his life, as he was killed, together with an air mechanic who was aboard the plane, when it crashed near Chipping Sodbury on June 25th, 1917.

It was a grievous blow for Lindsay and his wife, as well as their children living at Ystrad Mynach House, who now included young David Edzell Thomas who had been born in February 1910 and was at the House alongside his younger sister Nesta. But within nine months, the Lindsay family were dealt two further blows both Archie and Claud were killed within a week of each other on the Western Front.

Archie had followed his father in a career in the Royal Engineers and was serving as a Lieutenant in the 7th Army Troops Company, Royal Monmouthshire Engineers, when they were caught up in skirmishes in the Pas-de-Calais area in March 1918. Archie lost his life on March 26th, with news of his death coming as a second hammer blow for the family of Captain Lindsay who had just about come to terms with the loss of George in the tragic accident near Bristol. Yet later that week, a third piece of dreadful news arrived

Archie Lindsay.

at Ystrad Mynach House with confirmation that Claud had also been killed in action on the Western Front.

He had enjoyed a glittering career at both Wellington College and RMA Woolwich and by the summer of 1918 the 26-year-old had risen to the rank of Acting Major in the 33rd Battery Royal Field Artillery. In June 1915, during a short spell back at home, Claud had also married Dorothy Forde, and in early March 1918, prior to the advance on the Western Front, he had briefly returned home to see his wife and family. Tragically, it was the last they saw of him, as he was killed in action on Easter Day, March 31st during an Allied offensive on the Somme.

The tragic loss of their two sons within a week of each other was tempered by news a few weeks later that Dorothy was pregnant and on November 16th, 1918, she gave birth to a boy, named George Morgan Thomas who, tragically, like so many other babies born at that time, never knew his father.

The birth of the little grandson was a modicum of comfort for Capt. Lindsay and his wife, and one can only wonder at how they coped with such personal tragedy. As a devout Christian, Lindsay took great solace in his faith, believing that his sons had died for the greater good, and in the years that followed he threw himself more and more into the world of sport, possibly as a way of forgetting what had happened during those grim and dark days in 1917 and 1918 when they had received news of the death of George, Archie and Claud.

With the support of his wife, Capt. Lindsay became very active in the racing world after the Great War and trained several very useful horses from his stables at Ystrad Fawr, having many winners in point-to-points in south Wales as well as those held by the Beaufort Hunt in Gloucestershire, close to where his brother lived in Burford.

Claud Lindsay.

He also obtained a training permit to run horses in races organised by the Jockey Club and, either side of the War, he was also a member of the National Hunt committee, besides being a familiar face at races in south Wales and the West of England.

The highlights of Lindsay's career in the horse-racing world came during the 1920s when his horse, Miss Balscadden – named after a parish in Ireland close to his mother's home – won the Welsh Grand National in 1926 and 1928 at Ely Racecourse in Cardiff. The mare was ridden in 1926 by her owner David Thomas, an amateur jockey from Pyle, and began the 12-runner race as an 8-1 chance. After other more fancied horses had fallen, Morgan Lindsay's charge joined the favourite Postino, which had been fourth in the Cheltenham Gold Cup, approaching the final fence and through the urgings of her jockey she won by a head, thanks also in no small part by being in receipt of almost two and a half stone

Two years later Miss Balscadden won the Welsh Grand National again, this time in receipt of just a stone from the second placed horse, to defy a starting price of 20-1 in the 15-runner event during which professional jockey George Bowden – one of a select band to have ridden in both the

Morgan Lindsay with his team of boys which he assembled for games against club sides during the summer holidays. The photo was taken at St.Fagans in 1924.

Derby and the Grand National – opted to take up the running a mile or so from home.

None of the other horses could match her stamina as Morgan Lindsay's brave mare came home virtually unopposed, much to the delight of her new owner Sir David Llewellyn, who had purchased her from David Thomas for £1,000. Llewellyn – who was the father of Harry Llewellyn of Foxhunter fame – had several horses in the care of Morgan Lindsay at his Ystrad Mynach stables, and he built up a great rapport with the Colonel, whose eye for a promising racehorse had been as sharp as his assessment of a decent cricketer some thirty or so years before.

Probably the best horse that Lindsay trained was a steeplechaser called Ego. A winner of the National Hunt Chase at the Cheltenham Festival, it also finished third in the Welsh Grand National run at Cardiff's Ely racecourse during April 1935, and it was the last big winner which the enthusiastic Lindsay and his supportive wife trained from their hillside establishment at Ystrad Fawr.

Sadly, Morgan Lindsay enjoyed poor health during the summer of 1935 and he died, after a short illness on November 1st at his home, with his funeral being attended by the great and the good of society from south Wales including the Marquess of Bute and the Earl of Plymouth. A memorial service was also held a fortnight later, at which the Bishop of Llandaff gave the address, describing Lindsay as "a great gentleman, a great Christian and a great Churchman."

22

THE ARMISTICE AND THE AFTERMATH

'It's Over' – so proclaimed the newspaper billboards on Monday, November 11th, 1918 following the signing of the Armistice, and the ceasing of hostilities at 11am that morning. Rumours had abounded at the end of the previous week that the German High Command had already signed but these proved to be premature until the Monday morning.

Shortly after lunch all work ceased as the news was confirmed. Lessons were halted at schools, church bells rang out and factory sirens were hooted in celebration, whilst within an hour or so, the streets of the main towns across south Wales were full of joyous men, women and children, many of whom were waiving flags in sheer delight that the bloody conflict was, at long last, over. Drapers stores freely gave out flags for all the Allied nations whilst impromptu speeches were made at civic gatherings across the country.

The *Western Mail* reported how, in Abertillery, railwaymen let off detonators in celebration of the glad news whilst, in Blaina, cannons were fired throughout the afternoon. In Penarth Docks, the steamboats greeted the news by a series of tout-touts from their sirens, whilst according to the newspaper, 'in Blackwood women wept out of sheer joy and children were heard saying, "Daddy will soon be home"...' The newspaper's editor also summed up the nation's mood the following day, writing in his editorial how there was 'a feeling of devout thankfulness at the cessation of hostilities. The stress, the strain, the anxieties of four years and more – a period of peril and strife without precedence in our history – have given place to sensations of relief and joy equally without parallel. From the monarch to the lowliest peasant, the sensation is the same: as we have been united in combat and deprivation, so we are united in rejoicing.'

Alongside these patriotic words was an equally heartfelt message from David Lloyd George to the people of Wales – 'What can I say now more than that the cause of righteousness has triumphed, and the freedom of the small nations of the world has been won and established forever. I am proud to think that my own little nation of Wales has borne its full share of the task of winning this great triumph.'

A special thanksgiving week was organised by civic authorities in Cardiff, with the festivities including a special rugby match at the Arms Park between Cardiff and Tredegar. Amongst the decent-sized crowd were over 500 American sailors who had been given special permission to attend after the military authorities, who were still in charge of the recreation ground, had given their blessing to the game taking place. It was the first tangible sign that life would soon, albeit very slowly, be getting back to normal.

Lists of the dead and injured continued to be published for many weeks as either side of Christmas, British troops arrived back on home soil, many with grim and ghastly tales of the War and the final hours of the conflict. Interred Germans were also repatriated, whilst British servicemen held as Prisoners of War in German camps were also released and to the sheer joy of their loved-ones at home, they were reunited with their family and friends.

After the horrors in the trenches and seeing the mass killing of friends and foe alike, adjusting back into civilian life was arguably the greatest challenge faced by those who returned home after the end of the War. As hard as many tried, there were countless numbers who were unable to adjust back to a normal life on 'Civvy Street'.

Dyson Bransby Williams (Killay House CC, Public School Nondescripts and Glamorgan)

Dyson Bransby Williams was one of thousands of souls who were broken either physically or mentally – or both – by the horrors of war.

Born in October 1877, he was the third son of civil engineer Morgan Bransby Williams of Killay House – a comfortable house with spacious grounds to the west of the town of Swansea. Cricket was in the Bransby Williams' blood with matches taking place in the grounds of his home, whilst his eldest son George created during the late 1880s a team called the Public School Nondescripts as the Bransby Williams boys, together with their well-heeled friends from other well-to-do families in the area played matches against the leading club sides and other scratch XIs.

Dyson Williams.

Dyson attended Malvern College where he represented the school at both cricket and association football before going up to Trinity College, Oxford where he read History. After graduating in 1900 he dabbled in various occupations before training to be a solicitor and qualified in 1911. By this time, he was well known in the cricketing world of south Wales having graduated from club cricket for Killay in the Swansea and District League plus country house games in the grounds of his home to the Glamorgan side which played in the Minor Counties Championship.

He made his debut for the county in June 1901, playing against Monmouthshire at Rodney Parade, and duly became the first player from the Swansea and District League to win honours at county level. However, he did not re-appear for Glamorgan for eleven years as his legal training and establishing his practice in Swansea took priority.

1912 was a red letter year for Williams as he captained Swansea CC and returned to the Glamorgan side, finishing in fourth place in their batting averages and posted a career-best unbeaten 43 against Kent 2nd XI. In May 1912 Williams also changed his middle name by deed poll to Brock. Through his friendship with Tom Whittington, the Neath-born solicitor who was Glamorgan's captain, Williams also agreed to succeed Hugh Ingledew, the Welsh rugby international, as Glamorgan's Treasurer as the decision-making powerhouse of Glamorgan CCC shifted west and away from the coal metropolis.

Whilst very proud of his achievements in securing a place in the Glamorgan side, Williams was happiest playing in the more relaxed and convivial world of cricket at Killay House, especially playing for the Public School Nondescripts. As historian Jack Morgan later recalled, 'Dyson Williams, with his panama covering his baldness, was a familiar figure on the cricket field in those days We were engaged in amateur theatricals together and this led to many invitations to play cricket at Killay House, and there is no better way of enjoying the game. Something went out of cricket when those house parties became a diminishing feature in the sporting life of south Wales.'

He was also well known locally as an amateur singer, and poet, and briefly after the War, appeared as Florian in a production of Princess Ida at Swansea's Grand Theatre. As the *South Wales Daily Post* noted at the time of his tragic death, he participated in these theatricals as wholeheartedly as he did his cricket – 'His was a particularly ambitious mind, never content with the ordinary accomplishments in sport or in art. His chief characteristic was his amiability. He was a man of generous instincts, and when he gave his services, he gave them fully and enthusiastically.'

Given these traits of character, Williams became a fine soldier and a popular officer. He also took part in the recruitment, and training at the St. Helen's Cricket Ground of the 14th Battalion (Swansea) The Welsh Regiment, and to Williams went much of the credit for its initial formation under Colonel Benson on September 16th, 1914, with Williams himself acting as Captain and Adjutant.

It was no surprise either that Williams swiftly rose to the rank of Major in France, and was to be second-in-command of the Swansea Battalion throughout the War, apart from a six-week period in the autumn of 1918 when he commanded a brigade of the Royal Welsh Fusiliers.

1916 saw Williams and the Swansea Battalion travel to France where they were thrown into the attack on Mametz Wood in which so many Welshmen lost their lives. Williams, himself, was severely wounded advancing up the slope leading to the wood and it was feared that he would die in the ambulance train. For a long period 'he lay between life and death', and his actions won him the Military Cross, but this was of little comfort to Williams as so many of his comrades and friends lost their lives.

He returned to the Battalion in 1917, and subsequently showed outstanding leadership at Ypres, with his Regiment going over the top at Pilckem Ridge and routing the crack Prussian 'Cockchafers'. It was an action which deservedly earned him the DSO. In the same year his 'Swanseas' also won high honours in an attack on the salient known as Caesar's Nose, and subsequently figured in the Ancre crossing and the engagements at Auveley Wood and the River Selle.

During the peace negotiations in 1918, Lieutenant Colonel Williams was chosen to act as a guide to Prime Minister Lloyd George across the battlefields of the Somme. It was no surprise therefore that in December he succeeded Colonel Brooke to the command of the Swansea Battalion. But the War had taken its toll and, if truth be known, he never fully recovered from the bloody horrors, with the man who marched through Swansea at the head of his battalion in June 1919 to present the colours to the Mayor being a very different fellow to the happy and jolly man who had marched off to War five years before.

In July 1919 he was invalided out of the Army, largely as a result of the injury to a lung, sustained whilst on the Somme and he returned to live with his mother and brothers at Killay House. He did not, however, return to the legal profession, and in the following year had his name removed from the rolls to engage in a stock and share business. This failed, as did the Welsh Aviation Company in which he had speculated. He continued to play a bit of cricket and continued to serve as Glamorgan's Treasurer, although his heart was not really in the club's affairs and he only agreed to carry on to help out his old friend Tom Whittington who was now actively seeking assurances and support from English counties to support Glamorgan's campaign for first-class status

Whittington was fortunate enough in the autumn of 1920 to secure the minimum of eight home and away fixtures with existing first-class counties, and there was great celebration when the MCC endorsed Glamorgan's application to join the County Championship in 1921. By this time, Williams' best years were behind him but he still managed to make an appearance in first-class cricket, at the ripe old age of 44, as he appeared in the last match of Glamorgan's first County Championship season of 1921, against Hampshire at Cardiff. He duly made 5 and 9 as Glamorgan, dismissed for 37 and 114, lost by an innings inside two days.

But Williams' mind lay elsewhere – his great friend Tom Whittington observed how his friend's character had been completely shattered by his wartime experiences – and in 1921 he left Swansea to try his luck in London and elsewhere. In particular, he went to live with an old Army comrade, Major Arnold Wilson, who had become a boxing promoter, at his house at Maidenhead. Williams duly became a close friend of the world light-heavyweight champion, Georges Carpentier, with whom he wrote a song with the music penned by Williams under the pseudonym Florian Brock, to the words by Carpentier himself, called *Vagabond Philosophy*.

It was sub-titled *It'll Be Alright*, and it poignantly included the following lines:

> 'And so in life you'll get
> A regular knockout blow.
> Don't lie and grouse, but try to smile
> And have the pluck to cry.
> The mud and dust will soon rub off.
> I'll be all right, by and by.'

But Williams' optimism proved to be misplaced and, shortly before the publication of *Vagabond Philosophy*, he was declared bankrupt. He vanished for a while after the bankruptcy hearings, with his brother Morgan finding him "in a rather down and out state", and he took him to his home in Maidenhead where he stayed for a while. Whilst with his brother, he spoke about his financial problems, attributing the situation to an inadequate Army pay, coupled with the cost of maintaining his law firm during the War. But in truth his betting and gambling, in addition to taking out loans at a heavy interest, had had a crippling effect on his personal situation and these were the real reasons for his predicament.

In late February his world collapsed when his mother died. Unmarried, he told a friend he felt "desolate", and soon afterwards went to Belgium to play the casinos. His behaviour relapsed again as cheques started to bounce, including one to the value of £200 he'd cashed with a local bar owner. His debts to Wilson also mounted, but he was able to write to Wilson saying: 'I have at last struck a bit of luck, just when apparently things were hopeless. I shall be able to pay you back what you have let me have.' Wilson had that letter on April 19th. Tragically, the day before, the charlady had gone to clean Wilson's offices in St. Martin's Court in London. She found the room full of gas, with Williams slumped to the floor. The gas stove had two taps fully turned on. The 45-year-old solicitor–soldier–cricketer had become yet another, if belated, victim of the War, with the coroner duly recording a verdict of 'suicide while of unsound mind'.

After hearing the news about his friend's demise, Major Wilson said "He was highly strung with a nervous temperament, and the war used him up more than it did men of a quieter disposition." Warm tributes were also paid to him by friends in south Wales, whilst the following appreciation, which appeared in the local newspaper in Swansea at the time of his tragic death, illustrated the high regard and esteem in which he had been held by his men:

'It was whilst serving with the 14th Battalion, the Welch Regiment, that I came into touch with the late Lt. Col. Dyson Brock Williams. I formed one of a draft who joined the 'Swansea's' on the Ypres Salient. The major was pointed out to me by one of the men who had accompanied the battalion overseas. I was impressed at the time by his studious manner and military appearance ... and I was struck by the kind manner in which the men always referred to him, but to those who served under him the reason for this did not require much seeking. It is left to the men who are spared and who served under him and came in personal contact with him to remember all that he did for their amusement and comfort under most trying circumstances and conditions. At his own personal expense he organised the Battalion Concert Party (known as 'The Swans'), promoted the sports, in which he joined in the Boxing, ably assisted by Major Arnold Wilson), and provided the bugles and subsequently the cornets for the Battalion band.

'In one of the villages through which the battalion passed he bought a piano, which was used in connection with the concert party. On the occasion when the battalion was out on rest, or was staying a night or two after being on the march, the men were given the opportunity of attending the concerts. The idea of this was conceived Williams thus showing his kindly thought for the men. I remember how distressed he was when the news came through of the death of a very popular officer of the battalion. His sympathy was alike for brother officer or man. The last time I saw him in

France must have been in July or August 1918. He had done his share of the 'gruelling', and for the time being had come back for a rest; he looked tired and worn, but after a day or two he was working preparing to give the men a 'show' when they came out again.

'I saw him a week or two ago in London. I had an opportunity of watching him before he recognised me. I observed a great change in him, particularly his nervous pacing to and fro. I spoke to him and after a while he remembered who I was, and we had a few minutes conversation, referring, amongst other things, to the happenings 'over there', but he seemed particularly sad, and his laughter lacked that heartiness which I had often heard when a particular member of the concert party was giving a turn. I shall always remember him as a sportsman, an officer, and a gentleman, and, as I have said before, one who took a keen delight in giving the men amusement under difficult circumstances. His reward was the appreciation of the men amongst whom I had the honour of serving.'

Maurice Griffiths (Llancarfan)

Maurice Griffiths was no different to many other young men in Wales, born during the closing years of the nineteenth century and growing up in the early twentieth century with much to look forward to in life. In Maurice's case, he grew up in the Vale of Glamorgan, and during the 1900s and early 1910s he and his friends played informal games of cricket around the small village of Llancarfan. From this quiet, picturesque and loving place, Maurice and his friends went off into the unknown, answering the calls of Lord Kitchener and others that 'Your Country Needs You'– several did not return as they paid the ultimate price for their deeds or returned disabled, whilst those that did miraculously return still physically in one piece, like Maurice, came home mentally scarred and disillusioned.

Born in 1895, Maurice had led a blissful life with his friends in the village of Llancarfan, and during the summer months, he and the other adolescents played cricket in the fields around the pretty village. For them, helping out at harvest time and hoping that the Llancarfan cricket team would defeat local rivals Cowbridge were amongst the most important things in their lives. For Maurice and his young friends, being able to visit the market town, and having the chance to hold the bragging rights on cricketing matters was something that they fervently cherished.

This sense of camaraderie, kinship and community spirit was evident during the summer of 1914 as Maurice, his close friend David Rhys Davies, and the other Llancarfan pals all answered Lord Kitchener's call and went off to fight for King and Country. Maurice and David joined the 2nd Battalion the Rifle Brigade, and after weeks of training, headed across the Channel.

His letters home to his family were at first quite upbeat, with one in April 1915 saying, 'I have no doubt you are disappointed that I am not coming home on leave, but as you know things are very uncertain these days; it's no use grumbling – just got to put up with it and get on with the job.' On another occasion he apologises for not having sent his sister's birthday card and writing with further updates – 'we only came out of the trenches a day or so ago and until just now I have been so busy I hardly knew what to do.'

The pair duly fought together on the Somme, and at Passchendaele, where they avoided the enemy bullets as well as the terrible mud. But near Armentieres, David Rhys Davies was less fortunate and during an attack, running forward alongside his friend Maurice, he was shot dead. It was an experience from which Maurice never really recovered, although he did fight with distinction at Guillemont and Villers-Bretonneux, near Amiens where his brigade joined up with Australian Forces in mounting an assault on German positions.

Maurice Griffiths

Indeed, at Villiers-Bretonneux he was commended by the General Officer in Command for his bravery during the fighting between April 21st and 28th. His citation read, 'Lance-Corporal Griffiths displayed great gallantry and devotion to duty. When the telephone wires were cut, he repeatedly went out under heavy shell and machine gun fire to mend them. He showed utter disregard for personal safety and was to a great extent responsible for such communication as was kept up.'

After the death of David, his letters back home became so much more gloomy – 'I have given up on the idea of a commission. I have a decent job and am going to hang on to it,' he wrote in one letter back home to his mother, whilst in another he wrote, 'I'm getting so fed up with the cry of "Be British, Be British", which the officers shout when men go over the top.'

In 1917 Maurice and the other surviving members of his Battalion were taken prisoner at Berry-au-Bac. After having their boots removed, a

THE RIFLE BRIGADE
PRISONERS OF WAR HELP FUND.

President:

His Royal Highness Field Marshal The DUKE OF CONNAUGHT, K.G., Colonel-in-Chief.

Vice-Presidents:

Colonels Commandant

Major-Gen. Sir LEOPOLD SWAINE, K.C.B.   Gen. Rt. Honble. Sir NEVILLE LYTTLETON, G.C.B.
Major-Gen. Sir FRANCIS HOWARD, K.C.B.   Major-Gen. C. RICE H. NICHOLL

Hon. Secretary 1st, 2nd, 3rd & 4th Batts.
   Mrs. JOHN BURNETT-STUART,
     Selborne Lodge, Winchester.

Hon. Secretary 10th Batt.
   The Honble. Mrs. ARTHUR SOMERSET.
     Lynch House, Winchester

Hon. Secretaries 7th, 8th, 9th, 11th, 12th & 13th Batts.
   Mrs. TOM MORRIS
   Mrs. WALTER STEWART
   Miss NOWELL SALMON,
     71, Eccleston Square, S.W.

Committee:

Brigadier-Gen. THE EARL OF LUCAN
Brigadier-Gen. HUGH DRUMMOND, C.M.G.
Major HARRY STURGIS
Captain A. C. CAMPBELL

Selborne Lodge, Winchester

18. November 1918.

Madam,

    Now that hostilities with ermany have
ceased, the Prisoners of War are to be
immediately released, and we have therefore
stopped sending parcels to those in our care,
as they are no longer needed.

    We hope that you will before very long
have your Son back with you again, and that he
will soon be none the worse for the hardships
he has had to endure as a Prisoner of War.

    We cannot express to you our sympathy with
all that you and he have had to go through
during his imprisonment, and have been only too
glad to do the little for him that we have been
able.

        Yours faithfully,

N. Burnett-Stuart

       Hon. Secretary & Treasurer.

A notification letter to the mother of Maurice Griffiths.

few of Maurice's colleagues thought about organising an escape, but these battle-weary soldiers opted to accept their fate. Unlike their many friends like David Rhys Davies they, at least, were still alive so for the remaining months of the War, Maurice and his compatriots were Prisoners of War at No. 1 Camp in Cottbus in Brandenburg, to the south-east of Berlin. To be well away from the main theatre of War and the muddy, bloody trenches

Llancarfan CC – July 1935.

was something of a relief for Maurice – as he wrote home in one letter, censored by German authorities – 'I am quite alright and feeling quite happy and satisfied. Also this is a decent camp and there is a nice church. I am going to a service tonight.'

Following the Armistice in November 1918, and his release from the camp, Maurice returned home. There was bunting strewn across the streets of Llancarfan, as well as Union flags hanging from windows, but this was no joyous return for the young man, as he tried to resume life without his closest and dearest friends. For a while, he was completely lost, and wandered aimlessly around the fields and village. "You do not understand what has happened," he would say to friends and relations who tried to lend a helping hand. One day, he stumbled, completely by accident, across another group of young boys, playing an informal game of cricket amongst themselves. For a while, he stood and watched, and remembered those joyous and innocent years before the War when he and his friends had so enjoyed their summer days.

Indeed, watching cricket duly became Maurice's solace and comfort.

Besides following the fortunes of the Llancarfan side as they resumed their activities, Maurice took a keen interest in Glamorgan's elevation into the first-class world in 1921. He ventured by bus and train to Cardiff, and found that watching the county play at the Arms Park – even in defeat – was very therapeutic. He duly took membership of the county club, and became so avid a supporter that visits by train to watch games in Swansea soon followed and during the 1930s he was overjoyed when Glamorgan played, albeit twice, at The Broadshoard ground in Cowbridge. Maurice also ventured across by Campbell's Steamer from Cardiff's Pier Head to Weston-super-Mare for Somerset's annual cricket festival. He stayed, usually for the week, at the Beaufort Hall Hotel in Madeira Cove, and revelled in watching some keenly fought games, especially when Glamorgan were the visitors.

These memories, and other cricketing tales, were duly told to his nephew Campbell, who for a while during the mid-1940s lived with Maurice at Llancarfan following the death of his own father. During this time, he heard about life in the trenches – "You don't go through hell and remain the same person" – as well as more cheery anecdotes about the likes of Glamorgan's legendary spinner Johnnie Clay – "they would knock him about, but he would get them in the end!"

Indeed, it was young Campbell who received a telephone call from Maurice in late August 1948 when Glamorgan won the County Championship for the first time in their history. Maurice had listened to progress on the radio and when the team under the leadership of Wilf Wooller – who had himself been a POW during the Second World War – defeated Hampshire at Bournemouth, it was to his nephew that he spoke to share the glad tidings. He knew how the hardship of internment and the gravities of war can change someone's physique and mental approach, so it was probably with a feeling of empathy that he shared the success of Wilf and his team. But, how Maurice wished that his good friends were still by his side to share in the triumph over the big sides from England, just like they had when Llancarfan had beaten Cowbridge.

23

PLAY RESUMES

On Boxing Day 1918 ten thousand spectators gathered at the Arms Park to watch a New Zealand team defeat Cardiff 8-6, whilst at St. Helen's a Kiwi services team defeated Swansea 3-0. A crowd of over 3,000 were also present at Ninian Park on Boxing Day as Cardiff City defeated Newport County 3-0 to gain solace for their defeat on Christmas Day by the same opponents. A programme of athletic sports and whippet races also took place on December 26th at the Cardiff Stadium, whilst similar events took place in aid of Prisoner of War funds at Aberdare Park.

An aerial view of Cardiff Arms Park during the early 1920s showing the cricket and rugby grounds adjacent to the River Taff.

Arthur Webb, wearing his Hampshire cap.

It was not good news, however, for all sporting families across south Wales as on Christmas Day, in a military hospital in Cardiff, Reginald Steele Wakeford, a talented rugby player and cricketer, died at the age of 25. The stockbroker's clerk from Meadow View House, Penarth had represented the resort town before serving from 1915 with the Glamorgan Yeomanry before joining the Lancashire Fusiliers. Early in 1918 he switched his allegiances again to the Royal Flying Corps and after successfully training as an observer, he flew many sorties over enemy lines from April onwards. But shortly before Armistice Day, he contracted pneumonia, and despite medical attention in France and transfer by the Red Cross back to south Wales, he died from this lingering illness.

With the rifle range being in the process of being dismantled and removed from the outfield at the St.Helen's ground, Swansea RFC was able to organise a series of trials from mid-January onwards. Shortly afterwards, Briton Ferry Steelworks CC held their AGM, and besides appointing captains for a 1st and 2nd XI for 1919, they agreed to offer professional terms again to Arthur Webb as well as to Eddie Bates, who switched his allegiances from the Town club. A fixture secretary was also appointed, and as other leading clubs followed suit, a draft programme of games was drawn up for 1919.

With many of their key figures still awaiting demobilisation, several clubs only agreed a skeleton programme of games, whilst Llanelli opted not to hire any professionals as it was unlikely there would be many games with the crack clubs. Some clubs also found that their facilities were still in use by the military authorities – an example was at Griffithstown in Monmouthshire where the local cricket club used the spacious grounds of Panteg House, adjacent to the steelworks run by Baldwins.

Panteg House had acted as both the headquarters of Panteg CC as well as the home of the works director but, during the War, Baldwins gave the use of the House to the military authorities so that it could be used as a hospital and rehabilitation centre for troops. Nurses were still tending men in 1919 so only a handful of games took place in the grounds of the House with tents used as temporary changing rooms. The military authorities returned the House to Baldwins the following summer, but rather than reverting to being the home of the works director it was taken over by the Panteg

Employees Club and Recreational Institute who subsequently oversaw the operation of the cricket club, besides creating a bowls green on one of the House's lawns.

Several clubs, such as Crickhowell, had created an emergency committee to look after, and where possible, preserve their ground during the hostilities. Indeed, the club's minutes record – in a quite patriotic way – how the Crickhowell CC committee believed they had 'a duty to tend our facilities so that the returning heroes can resume playing once the War comes to an end.' In addition, the emergency committee oversaw matches between the club's members who were available – and wanted to practise – in 1915 and 1916.

Abergavenny CC had followed suit and also organised practice games amongst their members whilst, in June 1916, they organised a match at the ground in Pen-y-Pound against members of the Abertillery club, with proceeds from the contest going towards the Alexandra Rose Fund and other War charities. The game proved to be both a low-scoring encounter – a local newspaper commented on how players were out of practice – as well as being the only wartime fixture staged by the Abergavenny club.

Usk CC - 1920. What stories these men could have told.

In 1919 they were also able to boast having a first-class cricketer in their ranks, following the selection of Dr. William Tresawna, their long-serving batsman, in H.K. Foster's XI for the match against the Australian Imperial Forces at Hereford. The good doctor had been a mainstay in both the club's line-up before the War as well as in the Cornwall side between 1898 and 1913, mixing his duties as Senior Medical Officer at the town's Victoria Hospital with appearing for his native county in the Minor Counties Championship.

Born at Lamellyn, near Probus in April 1880, Tresawna had attended Sidney College Cambridge, before completing his medical training at St. George's Hospital in London and securing a post in a practice in Abergavenny. He had made his Minor County debut in 1898 with the undergraduate first playing for Cornwall against Dorset at Blandford Forum. During this time he played several times against Glamorgan and, following his subsequent move to Abergavenny and his success for the town side, Tresawna was chosen in the South Wales side which met the Indians at the Arms Park in June 1911. Batting at number four, he made scores of 37 and 12 as the Welsh team defeated the tourists by seven wickets, largely through a twelve-wicket haul by pace bowler Stamford Hacker.

During the War, Tresawna served in France as a captain with the Royal Army Medical Corps, being mentioned in despatches, before returning to his wife and family in Abergavenny, and securing the post at Victoria Hospital. Despite having played little cricket for five years, he accepted the offer to play for Foster's XI in their two-day match at Hereford Racecourse against the Australian Imperial Forces in July 1919, and celebrated his only appearance in a first-class game with scores of 55 and 21, much to the delight of several of his friends from Abergavenny who had travelled to Hereford to watch their pal in action.

By this time hostilities had drawn to a close, so Abergavenny's emergency committee had been able to draw up a skeleton fixture list, and attempted to overcome the loss of eighteen club members, several of whom had been quite active with either the club's 1st and 2nd XIs. Indeed, the loss of leading figures and influential players was a massive hurdle to be overcome by many clubs, but all were adamant that life should return back to normal as quickly as possible and in the spring of 1919 officials from clubs – both large and small across south Wales – met up to discuss plans for the coming summer.

The following announcement posted in the local newspapers on March 20th by Whitchurch CC was typical of the situation which many of the smaller, and suburban clubs found themselves in – 'the Club will resume play during the coming season. Most of its members joined the Army and many made the great sacrifice including Capt. J.L. Williams, Capt. W.J. Richards, Capt. Percy Richards and Lieut. Evans.'

Not everyone, though, was looking to be swiftly demobilised, getting back to their normal jobs and playing sport. For Hubert Prichard, who had played for Glamorgan in 1899 and 1900, his main concern in 1919 was to ensure that all of the prisoners of war and other so-called 'aliens' in his charge at a detention camp in Scotland were safely repatriated back to Germany and other parts of Eastern Europe. Prichard, who lived at Pwll-y-wrach House near Cowbridge, had previously served with the Glamorgan Yeomanry before being promoted to the rank of Captain in the 3rd Battalion the East Yorkshire Regiment. He subsequently became a Commandant of the POW camp, and was later awarded the CBE for his efforts.

Howell Moore-Gwyn, the Sandhurst-educated amateur who had also played for Glamorgan between 1903 and 1912, was keen to continue his military career which had already seen the gentleman from Duffryn House near Clydach win the Military Cross in June 1915, the *Croix de guerre* in May 1917 and the DSO in 1918, all whilst serving with the 4th Battalion of the Rifle Brigade. He had first joined the Brigade in August 1906 and mixed his military duties with time playing as an amateur for the Welsh county and playing club cricket for Neath.

In 1914 he travelled out to France with the British Expeditionary Force and duly fought in France and Belgium. After being promoted to the rank of Major, Moore-Gwyn spent time with the Mediterranean Expedition Force between July 1917 and May 1918, before returning to the Continent for

The Cardiff CC team of 1920 with Norman Riches (sitting, third left).

the final throes of the Great War, and remained on French soil until August 1919. He subsequently became a Staff Officer at Sandhurst and played for the Greenjackets, before spending time with the King's African Rifles and serving in India, where he also played in domestic cricket, appearing for the Punjab Governor's XI in 1929-30. During this period, he also won the Army racquets doubles championship on eight occasions, besides playing for the MCC and I Zingari during holidays back in the UK.

Many families however, were still in mourning in 1919 as those maimed and gassed during the hostilities failed to recover from their wounds. An example was Walter Lloyd Jenkins of Radyr who had served as a Private in the Fourth Battalion of the Yorkshire Regiment. He was the son of John Lloyd Jenkins, an accountant who worked in Cardiff and had prospered during the late Victorian and Edwardian era as the trade at the town's docks boomed.

John and his wife Matilda had six children and after living in the inner suburbs of Canton and Roath, they moved with their young family to Brynhyfryd, an impressive property in Windsor Road in Radyr. Walter had been a regular member of Radyr CC between 1907 and 1910, and together with his brothers and sisters had thoroughly enjoyed life in the popular suburb to the north-west of Cardiff. But like so many other families, their tranquil existence was cruelly transformed by events of the War. Walter was badly wounded whilst serving with the Princess of Wales' Own Regiment on the Western Front. He returned home for treatment but sadly never recovered and died in Bath War Hospital on St. David's Day, 1919.

As far as the 1919 cricket season was concerned in south Wales, it began on Saturday, May 3rd with Cardiff having an away fixture with Barry – Norman Riches was still not yet back in Cardiff because of his work with the Army Medical Corps so Henry Symonds and James Horspool opened the batting – but the city club were dismissed for just 39 as Barry recorded a facile victory. Elsewhere, Gowerton defeated Pontarddulais whilst the following weekend Ralph Evans of Whitchurch struck the first hundred of the post-War era as he made an unbeaten 101 against Ystrad Mynach. Rain affected several other matches, but at Ebbw Vale, the town's cricketers were able to dodge the showers as they defeated Abertillery.

A match also took place at St. David's College in Lampeter against the University College of Wales, Aberystwyth for whom one of the bowlers claimed an unusual hat-trick, dismissing all three Lampeter men leg before. As the colleges and schools in Wales had been open during the War, they had been able to play the occasional game during the hostilities, although at a time of fuel shortages, travel was a limiting factor, and most schools and colleges had to resort to practice games, or matches between houses.

The Bridgend CC team, plus a four-legged friend, in 1922.

However, the historic annual encounter between Christ College Brecon and Llandovery College was able to resume at the ground of the former on June 29th, 1918.

The return home and the chance to play recreationally again prompted the formation of new teams. One of the best examples of a club to be born out of the horrors of the First World War was in Ynystawe, a small village in the Lower Swansea Valley. When the men of the village returned home, someone had the bright idea of organising a game of cricket to take their minds off the carnage they had seen.

In the early summer of 1919, the first game took place between The Married and The Single on a field at Ynys Farm. Further games took place in subsequent weeks and even though the wicket was quite rough, all concerned so enjoyed themselves that the following year, a formal club was formed. During the year, Swansea Valley industrialist W.J. Percy Player – the owner of the Gurnos Tinplate Works in Clydach – also gave the village a park as a war memorial. Player was a generous benefactor so, with his encouragement, the park became the cricket club's home with Player also helping to fund the erection of a pavilion in 1927.

Pontypridd was another valley settlement where a War Memorial plus decent recreational areas were created during the 1920s. Cricket had been first played in the industrial town in 1858, and like many other clubs in the industrial communities, its origin was the result of the influx of English-born migrants. A formal club was established in 1870 and from 1873 they played at Ynysangharad Farm, owned by Gordon Lenox, the resident director of Brown Lenox, the town's largest ironworks. Lenox oversaw the laying of a decent wicket as well as giving the cricket club a series of funds to buy equipment and kit. His efforts were successful and in 1897 the Pontypridd club entered the newly-formed Glamorgan Cricket League.

The farmland home of Pontypridd C.C. was transformed after the Great War, when the Brown Lenox family offered their land to allow the creation of a War Memorial for the town in memory of the hundreds of servicemen from the area who had given their lives for King and Country. Public subscriptions and grants from the Miners Welfare Fund duly helped to finance the conversion of the farmland into a spacious park and public recreation ground, together with improved facilities and a pavilion for Pontypridd CC. The War Memorial was opened on August Bank Holiday Monday 1923, and it duly proved to be a popular attraction, with Glamorgan taking county matches to the ground during the late 1920s.

One of the Pontypridd club's leading batsmen, Norman Stallworthy, might even have played in these games had it not been for his duties with the Glamorgan Constabulary. Born near Reading in 1891, Norman had

A view from the late 1920s of Ynysangharad Park in Pontypridd with the cricket ground, scoreboard and sightscreen to the right.

secured a position as a Police Sergeant in the Rhondda having served with distinction during the War in the Mounted Military Police in France, Belgium and Italy, besides being mentioned in despatches for his conspicuous conduct in action during forays against German troops.

When cricket resumed in 1919, he became one of the leading batsmen with the Pontypridd club, often batting alongside his brother Dudley. In 1922, Norman was chosen for the Glamorgan Club and Ground side in 1922, and appeared in several one-day games. But securing time off for three or four days to play in a county game was a completely different matter and, with much personal sadness, he had to decline several offers to play for the Welsh county. Nevertheless, Norman continued to play some fine innings, including an unbeaten 164 in just two hours against Treorchy and an extraordinary feat at Barry Island

Norman Stallworthy (left) walking out to bat for Pontypridd with his brother, Dudley.

in 1928 which saw him strike a massive six with the ball sailing high out of the seaside venue and onto the beach across the road from the ground.

Like many cricket clubs and sporting organisations across England and Wales, the pavilion at the Arms Park had been requisitioned by the military authorities. At first, the spacious wood-floored three-story building had been used as a temporary base for displaced families, fleeing France, Belgian and Russia. Several families had arrived by boat at Cardiff Docks, whilst others arrived by train, and had been housed in the Arms Park pavilion before moving to camps elsewhere.

As the fighting intensified, the Red Cross staff at the Arms Park were joined by nurses, other medics and other volunteers as injured servicemen were brought to the Welsh capital. There were still some injured soldiers convalescing in the pavilion complex in 1919 when the members of Cardiff CC resumed their nightly nets at the ground from Thursday April 24th. The pavilion was also still in use by the medical teams and out of bounds to the cricketers when the first competitive match took place on May 17th, 1919 when the opponents were the Glamorgan Police.

Given the hardship and tragedy which had affected almost every family for the past few years, nobody minded having to make do with temporary facilities in a large marquee, adjacent to the rugby ground, and there were huge sighs of relief that life was starting to get back to normal as they donned their whites once again. For the spectators who turned up at the Cardiff ground, another tangible sign that it was nearly 'business as usual' was the sight of Norman Riches walking out to open the batting for the Cardiff club and, as happened so many times before the War, the opener was in fine fettle as he top-scored with 48 as the city club eased to victory. The dentist was in the runs again the following weekend at St. Helen's as he made an assured half-century when Cardiff defeated Swansea by six wickets. Both sides were well below full strength, but it gave Riches and other leading members of the Cardiff club a chance to meet up again with the likes of Billy Bancroft and other Glamorgan players from the pre-War period.

Inevitably, the discussions amongst these leading players touched on when Glamorgan could start up again. The County Championship had resumed, albeit in a truncated way with a series of two-day matches, and Tom Whittington was appointed as the club's captain for 1919. But with many of the amateurs still on military service, it was never going to be possible for Glamorgan to arrange many fixtures.

During 1919, a number of interesting matches did take place, including a game at Knighton between the Gentlemen of Radnorshire and the Pickwick Club from Birmingham, plus a match at Stradey Park between a Llanelli XI and a New Zealand Services XI from Larkhill Camp. The highlight of the latter contest was a century by Dr. Gwyn Thomas who was guesting for the West Wales club. In August the Glamorgan Nomads made their annual tour of the West Country.

Riches remained in outstanding form with the bat, making 80 against Newport plus centuries against Ebbw Vale and Maesteg and, in mid-August, together with Tom Whittington he was named in the Minor Counties side which met the MCC at Lord's. Before the match, the Minor Counties committee met and agreed, with demobilisation likely to be completed by the New Year, that the Championship competition should resume in 1920. The Glamorgan officials returned home looking forward to drafting a fixture list for the following summer, and the first inter-county match since the end of hostilities began at Abergavenny on August 13th, 1919 when an all-amateur side from Monmouthshire entertained the Gentlemen of Carmarthenshire. The latter duly won the two-day affair by an innings.

With the hostilities over, some of the troops remaining on the Continent also took part in inter-service games, with the members of the 11th Battalion Welsh Regiment, known as the Cardiff Pals, enjoying success in games in Turkey, largely against the 23rd Regiment as well as the 25th Punjabis who were also stationed in the area. They used a wicket which had been prepared on a flat area of land at the camp at Bostanjili, although as Capt D.M.Stewart, the leader of the regimental side reported in a letter to the *Western Mail* in October 15th, 'with the grassless soil light and crumbling, and with matting unobtainable, one took one's life in one's hands when facing deliveries which either shot along the ground or whizzed unpleasantly close to one's head.'

Over the winter months a full compliment of fixtures were secured by the Glamorgan officials and on May 24th, 1920, the new programme of games began at The Oval with the Welsh county's cricketers meeting Surrey 2nd XI. To the delight of the Welsh contingent, Glamorgan won by four wickets but at 188-5, and a further 172 runs needed, a Welsh defeat had looked inevitable. But the Neath pairing of Tom Whittington and John Walter Jones had other ideas as they shared a match-winning stand, as Glamorgan reached their target in the 75th over without the loss of a further wicket.

The stirring win was symptomatic of the feel-good factor which was permeating Welsh sport, and society in general, with the Football League having been expanded to include teams from Aberdare, Cardiff, Merthyr, Newport and Swansea. Glamorgan added to this win with a series of further excellent victories, including innings wins over both Monmouthshire at Briton Ferry, as well as in the return match with Surrey 2nd XI at the Arms Park. In addition Devon were beaten by 37 runs at Neath, Wiltshire by eight wickets at Cardiff, and both Carmarthenshire and the MCC went down by ten wickets in the cricket week held at the St.Helen's ground during August

With Glamorgan doing well on the cricket field during 1920, there was excited chatter across Wales about their bid for first-class status. The club's finances were now in a much healthier state and with several exhibition games also having been arranged to further boost the coffers, the club's committee agreed to resurrect their campaign for first-class status. They were overjoyed by the response of the local

Tom Whittington walks out to bat for Glamorgan at Cardiff Arms Park in 1921.

business community, especially steel magnate Sir Sidney Byass who gave them a £1,000 loan over a ten-year period.

Off the field, the Secretary Tom Whittington was told that Glamorgan needed to secure home and away fixtures with a minimum of eight existing first-class teams so he approached the officials of clubs in the County championship to secure sufficient fixtures to support their application for first-class status. Somerset quickly agreed, followed by Gloucestershire, Worcestershire, Derbyshire, Leicestershire, Northamptonshire and Hampshire, although in a couple of cases Whittington was forced to agree that the Welsh county would guarantee a sum of £200 towards the fixture. The enthusiastic secretary duly reported back to the committee in November 1920 that he had secured the support of seven first-class counties. Jubilant at the news, the committee told him to 'obtain the eighth at any cost whatsoever.'

As it turned out strong persuasion was not needed, as both Sussex and Lancashire readily agreed to Whittington's approach, and early in 1921 the news that everyone had been waiting for came through, as the MCC endorsed Glamorgan's application. Messages of good luck were soon flooding the club's small offices in High Street, and there were tears in the eyes of JTD Llewelyn – the 'grand old man' of Glamorgan cricket – and Sam

The jubilant crowd swarm onto the outfield at the Arms Park following Glamorgan's victory over Sussex in their inaugural County Championship match in May 1921.

Brain, their wicket-keeper from the pre-War years, as a series of celebratory speeches were made at the club's AGM.

It proved to be a fairytale start for Glamorgan as a first-class county, as under the captaincy of Norman Riches, they defeated a full-strength Sussex side in their inaugural County Championship match at the Arms Park in May 1921. The visitors included several notable players including Maurice Tate, batsmen Ted Bowley, England all-rounder Vallance Jupp and the Gilligan brothers – Arthur and Alfred – but despite these big names, the Glamorgan side, with a collection of talented amateurs and well-travelled professionals, won the game by 24 runs.

Many of the crowd surged onto the field to congratulate Riches and his men, before the two teams gathered on the balcony of the Cardiff pavilion, with both captains making impromptu speeches. Arthur Gilligan graciously congratulated the Welsh side, saying how they "had given us a magnificent game, and we do not mind being beaten in the slightest. We have been down until today, but today we might have won. We did not – Glamorgan did, and I congratulate them very much."

As events at the Arms Park drew to a close and the cheers had subsided, people made their way home or back to work, several of those who had been watching - and some of those getting changed in the pavilion - spared a few moments to remember those who had shared their dream of first-class status for Glamorgan. Uppermost in their thoughts were those who had died for King and Country during the Great War and who were not alive to share in the joy of Glamorgan's victory over Sussex.

ROLL OF HONOUR

The following are featured in *Front Foot to Front Line*:

Cricketers

Clubs

ST DAVID'S PRESS

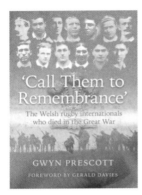

'CALL THEM TO REMEMBRANCE'
THE WELSH RUGBY INTERNATIONALS WHO DIED IN THE GREAT WAR

This book is [an] acknowledgment of the sacrifice made by 13 Welshmen.... Theirs was a sacrifice which needs to be told....Gwyn Prescott, with meticulous and sympathetic attention to detail, tells the story. This narrative is an essential record'. **Gerald Davies**

'These humbling stories describe thirteen individual journeys which began on muddy yet familiar Welsh playing fields but ended in the unimaginable brutality of the battles of the First World War.'

www.gwladrugby.com

'Call them to remembrance', which includes 120 illustrations and maps, tells the stories of thirteen Welsh heroes who shared the common bond of having worn the famous red jersey of the Welsh international rugby team.

978-1-902719-37-5   170pp   £14.99   PB

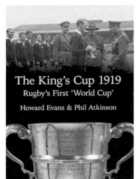

THE KING'S CUP 1919
RUGBY'S FIRST WORLD CUP

'An intriguing retelling of a significant but largely forgotten chapter of rugby union history, superbly illustrated.' **Huw Richards**

'Howard is an authority on rugby's history and meticulous in his research' **Andy Howell, Western Mail**

The world of rugby celebrated the 8th Rugby World Cup in 2015, but a tournament held in 1919, The King's Cup, can rightly claim to be rugby's first competitive 'World Cup'.

Meticulously compiled by Howard Evans and Phil Atkinson, *The King's Cup 1919* is the first book to tell the full story of rugby's first 'World Cup' and is essential reading for all rugby enthusiasts and military historians.

978-1-902719-44-3   192pp   £14.99   PB

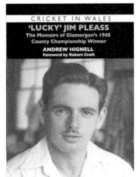

CRICKET IN WALES
'LUCKY' JIM PLEASS
THE MEMOIRS OF GLAMORGAN'S 1948 COUNTY CHAMPIONSHIP WINNER

'I can but only admire Jim's contributions during Glamorgan's Championship-winning summer of 1948 or his efforts with the bat against the 1951 South Africans at Swansea...[without him] I can only wonder at how different the course of Glamorgan's cricketing history might have been'.

Robert Croft, from his Foreword

In 2014 Jim Pleass was the longest surviving member of Glamorgan's County Championship winning team of 1948, the first time the Welsh team won the highest honour in county cricket.

Jim was a very lucky man, as the book explains his narrow escape from certain death when he stormed the Normandy beaches on D day in 1944. If it wasn't for the over-exuberance of a driver on another landing craft, Jim would never have graced the cricket field wearing the daffodil of Glamorgan County Cricket Club.

978-1-902719-36-8   128pp   £14.99   PB